To C...

H.... ...!

Beatrix

About the Author

Marea Stenmark has her own public relations consultancy
in Sydney's Double Bay — Marea Stenmark Communications —
where she is a communicator through the written and spoken
word. She is a gifted speaker and has presented her
workshop, 'The Creative Communicator', internationally as well
as in many parts of Australia. In the 1991 Australia Day
Honours List, she was awarded the Medal of the Order of
Australia. Apart from the fact that she is an aunt many times
over, Marea's warm love of family makes her the natural author
for this lively and entertaining book. Amongst her greatest
pleasures are theatre, music, writing and travel. She loves a good
hard game of tennis and, as a Sydneysider living at Elizabeth Bay,
is never very far away from the sun and the sea.

DEDICATION

'All of us should stand up for what we believe in and should influence others to do the same. And what should we believe in? Well, just an Australian community which is fair, healthy, happy, industrious. Where children can grow up in safety, with hope and opportunity ... and fun.'

— His Excellency, Rear Admiral Sir David Martin,
KCMG AO, the late Governor of New South Wales.

IT IS WITH GREAT PLEASURE that I dedicate this book to Sir David Martin. A true friend in every sense of the word, and a catalyst in bringing this book to fruition.

HERE'S TO AUNTS!

MAREA STENMARK

Angus&Robertson
An imprint of HarperCollins*Publishers*

PUBLISHER'S NOTE

The various terms 'Aunt', 'Aunty' and 'Auntie'
are used within this book, according to the
preference of individual writers.

AN ANGUS & ROBERTSON BOOK
An imprint of HarperCollinsPublishers

First published in Australia in 1992 by
CollinsAngus&Robertson Publishers Pty Limited (ACN 009 913 517)
A division of HarperCollinsPublishers (Australia) Pty Limited
25-31 Ryde Road, Pymble NSW 2073, Australia

HarperCollinsPublishers (New Zealand) Limited
31 View Road, Glenfield, Auckland 10, New Zealand

HarperCollinsPublishers Limited
77-85 Fulham Palace Road, London W6 8JB, United Kingdom

Copyright © Marea Stenmark 1992
    © Individual contributions by the contributors 1992

National Library of Australia
Cataloguing-in-Publication data:

Stenmark, Marea.
    Here's to aunts!
    ISBN 0 207 17831 3.
    1. Aunts - Australia - Anecdotes. 2. Celebrities - Australia -
    Family relationships - Anecdotes. I. Title.
306.87

Printed in Australia by Alken Press

5   4   3   2   1
96 95 94 93 92

CONTENTS

Foreword by Lady Martin   7

Introduction   11

Part One   AUNTS, FAMOUS AND INFAMOUS   15

Chapter 1   Aunts Are Important 16
Chapter 2   Ever-So-English Maiden Aunts 25
Chapter 3   Outstanding Australian Maiden Aunts 34
Chapter 4   Country Aunts 42
Chapter 5   Theatrical Aunts 61
Chapter 6   Aunts In The Movies ... by Bill Collins 69

Part Two   A CELEBRATION OF AUNTS   81

Not A Bit Like A Saturday   Marea Stenmark 83
Aunty Win And Her Precious Lamb   Gordon Chater 95
Auntie Maude   Colleen McCullough 99
Aunt Lily's Ginger Wine   Len Evans 105
Only One Auntie Lottie   Jeanne Little 107
Aunties All Over   Gwen Plumb 112
My Aunt, Baroness Gardner Of Parkes   Beatrice Gray 117
Move Over, Dame Edna   Phillip Adams 125
Making Dreams Come True   Di Morrissey 127
Like A Fine Wine   Richard Morecroft 132
Give Me An Aunt In The Country   Margot Anthony 134
Throw The Ball To Me   Ian Chappell 143
I'm Just Dottie!   June Salter 145
Sweets And Rosary Beads   Gary O'Callaghan 147
Glamour And Fun   Hazel Hawke 149
Small In Stature, Large In Style   Suzie Counsell 152

Nice New Blazers And Starched Linen   Ken Cowley 155
Barnstorming — Thanks To My Aunt   Nancy Bird Walton 161
Nature Will Take Its Course   Ken Done 163
Scottish Kilns, Spanish Hydrangeas   Jill Perryman 165
The Last Of The Great Aristocrats   Colin Stanley-Hill 167
Aunt Aggie Of Lord Howe Island   Rosemary Sinclair 175
More Than Aunts   Henri Szeps 179
Quality Times   Carmen Duncan 181
Always A Dashing Hero   Simon Townsend 183
Italian Connection   Carla Zampatti 185
Aunts, Aunts And More Aunts   Kathryn Greiner 188
You've Got To Laugh   Anthony Warlow 190
My Aunt 'Nuttie'   Judy White 192
My Aunt Carol Coombe   Michael White 196
Great Aunts, All   Michael Kirby 198
Aunts Remembered And Adored   Diana Fisher 202
Total Devotion   Fred Daly 205
Aunt Molly   Nan Witcomb 207

Part Three THE JOY OF AUNTHOOD 209

There Were Twenty Little Steps   Marea Stenmark 210
Hugs And Kisses   Margaret Fletcher 224
An Ample Aunt   Su Cruickshank 226
An Aunt's Story   Wendy Fatin 229
My Life As An Aunt   Paula Duncan 231

Acknowledgements 238

FOREWORD

BY LADY MARTIN

I WAS DELIGHTED WHEN Marea Stenmark asked if I would write the Foreword to this, her third 'family book'. *Mum's The Word* and *Dad's The Answer* have both been outstanding successes and they are now joined on the bookshelf by this delightful, pleasure-giving sequel about very special members of the extended family — aunts.

To me, aunts come in three models:

Real	the sisters of one's parents
Inherited	married to real uncles
Honorary	very close family friends

These three models are quite distinct.

Take, for instance, Harry Graham's aunt, whom he wrote about in *Ruthless Rhymes For Heartless Homes* (1899):

> I had written to Aunt Maud
>
> Who was on a trip abroad
>
> When I heard she'd died of cramp
>
> Just too late to save the stamp.

Most of us have experienced an Aunt Maud. She's there to be interested in and frightened of — 'Pay attention to Aunt Maud.' 'Have you written to Aunt Maud recently?' 'Please offer to take Aunt Maud to the station (or airport, or collect her from the bus terminal).' 'Be polite to Aunt Maud and don't upset her.'

Aunt Maud was very definitely an Inherited model.

Lady Martin.

The Honorary aunts were kind, attentive and loving visitors to the household. They, unlike the Inherited ones, were always welcomed into the bosom of the family, and treated to little family secrets and the latest district gossip. In later life, the 'Aunt' title was dropped and they became friends. To be an Honorary aunt these days is unusual because, as our society becomes more casual, first names are passed around like cocktail canapés and the dignity of being 'Mr' or 'Mrs' or 'Miss' is sadly no longer of importance.

On the other hand, I seem to be an Honorary aunt to animals. People are constantly inviting the cockatoo, pooch or siamese cat to talk to, shake hands with or kiss 'Aunty Susie'.

I now come to the Real models. They are not essential to the family, but if you have one you will understand her intrinsic value. Grandmothers are wonderfully warm, sweet smelling and cuddly creatures who spoil the young and listen to their problems. The double generation gap allows them rare priviliges. But an aunt is really an 'auxiliary mother'. Usually she is of comparable age with a parent, but she can be an ally and a go-between.

I had a brace of paternal Real aunts. During the week I would visit them in the old homestead (we all lived in the country and our house was a mile away from the traditional family home) and they were always either in the flower room or in the preserving room. In the former they would be surrounded on the one hand by discarded spent specimens and on the other by freshly cut blooms in buckets of water, brandishing secateurs, ho-humming. In the latter, like Mrs Tiggy Winkle and Mrs Tiptoes, they would wash, peel, chop and slice for hours on end, preparing preserves not just for the family's future intake but to give as gifts to neighbours near and far.

On Sunday it was a very different scene. More peaceful and still, and everyone spoke gently as we partook of afternoon tea. It was a day I always dreaded for, just as we were due to depart, one aunt would take me aside and compare the length of my fingernails with last week's chart. If they were shorter (i.e. bitten!) I was threatened with amputation, probably with the secateurs.

When they weren't in the flower room or the preserving room or partaking of afternoon tea, this buxom pair were rarely separated from their voluminous knitting bags.

Always wearing sensible clothes and brown lace-up shoes, and sporting identical short tight neat perms, they were a delight to me in my later life. They were generous to a 'T', always arriving bearing practical gifts of strawberries, cooked chickens and, of course, home-made jams and fruit cakes — presents always welcome to a struggling young married niece.

My favourite maternal Real aunt was like an older sister to me. While my mother was busy running the property during my father's absence due to the war, this aunt became an invaluable sibling to not only me, but also to my brothers. She would meet me at the station, take me to the orthodontist (we wore bands on our teeth at my boarding school), treat me to the pictures or fill me up with malted milkshakes and caramel waffles at our favourite feeding hole in the city. It was she who told me a little about the birds and the bees, and it was she who, while watching my mother dress me for my very first formal dance, suggested: 'Really, dear, I do think a little rouge and lipstick would not go astray.'

This charming book has entered our lives just when we need it most. Today's children are finding life's pressures quite threatening, and with both parents so often working to meet the cost of everyday requirements, the family unit is in danger of cracking. It's becoming rare for all the family to have time to even sit down to a meal together! The stabilising influence of the aunt may make all the difference to children's lives.

Marea Stenmark's collection of stories will calm us down, and help us to regain solidarity and household spirit. I wish her the very best of luck, and I congratulate her on the very find example she has set for us all. I know *Here's To Aunts!* will be a huge success, and a joy to all who read it.

Lady Martin
Sydney

Lady Martin, today continues the fine community work of her husband, the late Sir David Martin, former Governor of New South Wales.

INTRODUCTION

*I*T IS A QUARTER PAST the last stroke of midnight on the first day of January. Auld Lang Syne has been played and sung, our icy champagne has been sipped, the fireworks on Sydney Harbour have subsided and the early morning is bright and clear. Music lingers and a few voices carry on the still air. It isn't noisy, instead the mood is reflective. Reflective of the year which has just passed and the year which is newly born. Sydney, with its extraordinary endowments of beauty, looks and feels serene.

One of my New Year resolutions — I always make a few — is to write this book, and although the year is but half-an-hour old I have commenced.

The late Governor of New South Wales, Sir David Martin, before his death in 1990, supported my idea for *Here's To Aunts!* with a twinkle in his eye and sound advice: 'Good girl — better get cracking'! So, with his words ringing in my ears, I can't help but pause for a moment to recall how he wrote the Foreword and launched my last book, *Dad's The Answer*. Such an *esprit de corps* existed between us, as he supported the project in every possible way. He was a wonderful man, a great example to others; sadly, the world has lost a very special person.

So, why a book about aunts? Well, I suppose there are two main reasons. The first is that I am an ardent aunt, many times over. I have twenty nieces and nephews; whose ages range from eighteen to forty, and I'm a great-aunt seventeen times, so far — and most of my nieces and nephews haven't even got their act into gear yet! I know the joy and happiness the role of aunt gives me and, I certainly hope, them. An aunt is a wonderful thing to be. I realise many people consider that an aunt pales into insignificance when compared with a mother, however, the two roles are completely different and, as far as I am concerned, that of aunt is infinitely more enjoyable! The second reason for the book is that I was flicking through the dictionary and the definition of 'aunt' leapt up at me: 'the sister of one's father or mother or the wife of one's uncle'. Is she nothing in her own right? And, 'a term of address used by children to a female friend of the family' — a habit which, when used indiscriminately, I have always found confusing.

Surely an aunt is much, much more. A vital, extended-family member, a worthwhile friend as well as a pivotal part of the family network.

An aunt is many, many things. A human being, a woman, a counsellor, a philosopher, a teacher, a hostess, a listener, a talker. Of course, if she's perceptive and resourceful too, then that's even better. And if she's fun as well, then that's the ultimate. In the 1990s, she probably has a full-time working position as well. A busy person is the aunt.

Aunts come in various categories. They may be noteworthy, notorious, outgoing, outrageous, adaptable, artistic, wise, wonderful, musical or mystical — or any combination of these qualities.

The love of an aunt for her nieces and nephews is very strong — blood is certainly thicker than water. But, not to be forgotten, either, are those sole siblings who can never be related aunts but often become, very successfully, 'adopted aunts'. They, too, provide an extra dimension which otherwise would be lacking.

An aunt has certain intuitive powers — the heart frequently sees better than the eye — and, simply by observation, often prevents a catastrophe arising. Or, at least, is the first person to step in and help when one does occur!

Many an aunt has reared children when mothers have been ill or

PART ONE

AUNTS,
FAMOUS AND INFAMOUS

Chapter 1

AUNTS ARE IMPORTANT

*T*HROUGHOUT THE GENERATIONS aunts, as important members of the family structure, have played a substantial role. And played it very well. There is something about being connected with others with whom we share the same forebears and heritage, the same blood, which enriches our lives and gives us a feeling of solidarity. Aunts are important for this reason and for many others, as well.

Many aunts fill the function of *in loco parentis* with distinction, always being there to be talked to and confided in. They offer a lighter emotional bond and a more detached attitude than do parents — possibly because they're in the happy position of being able to give the children back! Only aunts can 'tell you off' and get away with it. I wish I had a dollar for every time a niece or nephew has confided something to me and immediately followed it up with, 'Don't you tell Mum'! Aunts are the buffer zone in the generation gap between children and their parents, and vice versa.

I am happy to say that more good aunts are recorded than bad. In fact, I'd with Mrs Ewing when back in 1885 she wrote in *The Story Of A Short Life* that:

> There are few people whose youth has not owned the influence of at least one such dear good soul. It may be a good habit, the first interest in some life-loved pursuit or favourite author, some counsel enforced by narratives of real life: it may be only the periodical return of gifts and

kindness, and the store of family histories that no one else
can tell: but we all owe something to such an aunt, the fairy
godmothers of real life.

When Mrs Ewing wrote those words a century ago it was probably true of the majority of aunts. Of course, then, as now, all were
not paragons of virtue.

Tatie Danielle, for example, the aunt in the French comedy film
of the same name, is frequently publicised as being 'a monumental
dragon', 'as much a sweet little old lady as the Titanic was iceberg
proof' and, worse, 'a sly irresistible portrait of mildewed malice'.

Then in Eleanor H. Porter's book *Pollyanna*, first published in
1927, there's Miss Polly Harrington, the formidable aunt who
started out wanting nothing to do with her nieces and nephews:

Just because I happen to have a sister who was silly enough
to marry and bring unnecessary children into a world that
was already quite full enough, I can't see how I should
particularly want to have the care of them myself.

An even more formidable aunt is presented by Oscar Wilde in
The Importance Of Being Earnest, in the form of Aunt Augusta. As her
nephew Algernon declares, when the doorbell rings: 'Ah! that must
be Aunt Augusta. Only relatives, or creditors, ever ring in that
Wagnerian manner.'

Lots of expressions over the years have included the word
'aunt', most of them not too complimentary: 'my fat aunt!', express-
ing disbelief; 'my sainted aunt!', a sign of surprise; and, of course,
'Aunty ABC' (the Australian Broadcasting Corporation), which can
imply an old fuddy-duddy — stolid, unbending and conservative,
with no hint of adventure, colour or excitement. (I'd prefer to
believe that what is meant by 'Aunty ABC' is a solid, reliable presence, a protector, always there to be relied upon ... but I'm not
entirely convinced!)

Remember Aunty Jack? It's twenty years now since she burst
onto ABC-TV screens uttering such beguiling lines as: 'Hello, me
little luvlies ... it's yer old Aunty Jack 'ere ... an' remember, if yer
don't chune in nex' week I'll jump fru yer radio sets and rip yer

17

bloody arms orf!' Who could resist her! The program has been compared to *Monty Python* in its satire, but Australian goonishness differs from the English variety and the subjects of *Aunty Jack* sketches were peculiarly Australian — albeit a satirical representation, a grab bag of things coarse and aggressive in the Australian character. Aunty Jack herself was part panto dame, part Dickensian horror figure, with an Australian accent. A rather large lady, she rode a motor bike, wore a long velvet dress and lace bib, together with a boxing glove, and uttered mouthfuls of threats. She was an inspired blend of incongruities with her heaving bosom, pince-nez and moustache. Grahame Bond, who played Aunty Jack, declared at the time: 'She is a thug, a lovable bastard, a purist. You could say she epitomises the average Australian pretentious Ock.'

Another aunt, of similar ilk, is portrayed in Brandon Thomas's 1892 farce *Charley's Aunt*, in which a male student at Oxford University impersonates an aunt from Brazil with hilarious outcome.

Centuries ago the word 'aunt' was applied to any old woman. In Shakespeare's *A Midsummer Night's Dream*, Puck speaks of: 'The wisest aunt, telling the saddest tale'.

I'm sure there would not be a person who hasn't either secretly admired or openly applauded Auntie Mame, immortalised by author and nephew Patrick Dennis in his 1958 book *Around The World With Auntie Mame*:

> My Auntie Mame is a most unusual woman. She raised me from the time I was orphaned at ten. Not because anyone wanted her to — far from it — or because she herself had any desire to take on a lonely only child during her heyday in 1929. It was simply that she was my only living relative. We were stuck with each other and we had to make the best of it.
>
> But raise me she did in her own helter-skelter fashion, to the horror of my trustee, Mr. Dwight Babcock of the Knicker-bocker Trust Company, to the horror of the masters at St. Boniface Academy in Apathy, Massachusetts (where Mr. Babcock finally put me after Auntie Mame's forays

into progressive education), and sometimes even to the horror of me.

We lived in many places together, Auntie Mame and I. We lived in a duplex in Beekman Place during the twenties when Auntie Mame was still Miss Dennis, still rich, and still in her Japanese phase. We lived in a carriage house in Murray Hill during the Depression before Auntie Mame found love and marriage and even more riches as Mrs. Beauregard Jackson Pickett Burnside. For a while we lived on a plantation in Georgia with Uncle Beau. Then, when Auntie Mame became the ninth-richest widow in New York, we lived in a big town house in Washington Square. We also lived in various other places around the world until I grew up and got married. After that, Auntie Mame's address — whenever she stayed still long enough to have one — was the St. Regis Hotel ...

But as unorthodox and eccentric — her detractors have even used such adjectives as depraved and lunatic — as Auntie Mame's methods of child care may have been, I don't think that any of the unusual things she did ever hurt me.

Mame made and broke every rule she felt like and had a motto for every occasion. I still chuckle when I recall 'life is a banquet and most poor sons of bitches are starving themselves to death'. And 'keep a little brandy handy' has helped many of us over the years, medicinally, if for no other reason! She used to churn out these words of wisdom to her very young nephew — who she continued to call 'Patrick, my little love' until he was very much a man!

Then there was the intriguing Aunt Augusta in Graham Greene's *Travels With My Aunt*, published in 1969. What an extraordinary character she was! Greene, acknowledged as one of the finest English novelists of his generation, and nephew of Robert Louis Stevenson, tells us:

> One of the few marks of age which I noticed in my aunt was her readiness to abandon one anecdote while it was yet

unfinished for another. Her conversation was rather like an American magazine where you have to pursue a story, skipping from page twenty to page ninety-eight and turning over all kinds of subjects in between ...

'The question of names,' my aunt said, 'is an interesting one. Your own Christian name is safe and colourless. It is better than being given a name like Ernest, which has to be lived up to. I once knew a girl called Comfort and her life was a very sad one. Unhappy men were constantly attracted to her simply by reason of her name, when all the time, poor dear, it was really she who needed the comfort from them. She fell unhappily in love with a man called Courage, who was desperately afraid of mice, but in the end she married a man called Payne and killed herself in what Americans call a comfort station. I would have thought it a funny story if I hadn't known her.'

More than fifty books flowed from Graham Greene's pen — novels, plays, short story collections, essays, travel items and three compelling volumes of autobiography. All this from a man who claimed he wrote by putting down words then pushing them round! He had a traceable lineage back to the Norman Conquest. A sense of family, immediate and collateral, shaped his life. His writings return constantly to his childhood. And so it is with *Travels With My Aunt*. Having not seen his septagenarian aunt for some fifty years, and re-meeting at what he supposes to be his mother's funeral, posed many problems and lots of questions for a nervous nephew, especially as his aunt had a precarious profession:

'The business I was in,' my aunt said, 'was peripatetic. We moved around — a fortnight's season in Venice, the same in Milan, Florence and Rome, then back to Venice. It was known as *la quindicina*.'

'You were in a theatre company?' I asked.

'The description will serve,' my aunt said with that recurring ambiguity of hers. 'You must remember I was very young in those days.'

Chapter 2

EVER-SO-ENGLISH MAIDEN AUNTS

A LAS AND ALACK, THE DAY, or at least the heyday, of the maiden aunt is over. There are still unmarried aunts, of course, but they are more like bachelor aunts today, and there are few who would regard being an aunt as a vocation.

In the eighteenth century the maiden aunt played an important role in family life. By the nineteenth century she positively flourished, performing countless social services. Still active in the Edwardian era, she survived the breakthrough of women into industry and later the professions, emerging as a splendid example and an undeniable force in the shaping of nieces' and nephews' lives.

A considerable number of maiden aunts deserve a lasting memorial because of their relationship to famous men and women. Where would the world of letters be without Charles Lamb's Aunt Hetty, who provided him with the sympathetic understanding he did not receive from his parents; without Alexander Pope's Aunt Eliza, who taught him to read and write; and without Edward Gibbon's cheerful Aunt Kitty, who was 'the true mother of his mind as well as his health' (in fact, we probably owe the existence of *The History Of The Decline And Fall Of The Roman Empire*, written two centuries ago, to the exertions of that particular maiden aunt)?

Some maiden aunts, however, have earned recognition in their own right — and this is not as rare as one might think, because talents are often crowded out in a married woman whereas the maiden aunt has an opportunity to develop hers naturally. Christina Rossetti, Jane Austen and the Brontë sisters are notable examples.

Historians, too, owe a great deal to organised maiden ladies, such as the educator and writer Maria Edgeworth, who formed the valuable function of preserving family letters and journals.

Indeed, many maiden women have played enormous roles not only within their own families but in the world generally.

HISTORY BOOKS TELL US OF the great British inventor and pioneer of the railways, George Stephenson (1781-1848). Apart from several locomotives and the famous 'steam blast', he invented many other useful things including a miner's lamp, a fishing lamp and an alarm clock. With the wealth from his inventions and locomotive factory, he became a philanthropist. His night schools for miners and his libraries, music clubs, recreation rooms and schools for miners' children were as original in his day as were his inventions.

After such success himself it was hardly surprising that George Stephenson was extremely ambitious for his young, and delicate, son Robert, always pushing the child to tasks way beyond his strength. However, the invaluable maiden aunt, Nelly, stepped in. After quickly assessing the situation she defied her brother, kept Robert away from his books whenever she saw they were too much for him, played with him in the fields in summer, filled him with good food and saw that he had a donkey to carry him the ten miles to school and then back again each day. Aunt Nelly saved young Robert from physical exhaustion as well as mental collapse. Thus, the world benefited as Robert Stephenson became almost as famous as his dad.

Robert Stephenson (1803-1859) was chiefly noted for the great bridges and viaducts he built, and for his invention of the tubular bridge. He built railways in Germany, Switzerland, Canada, Egypt and India. Without Aunt Nelly's urgings and understanding, Robert may never have survived infancy and the world would have been deprived of a great talent, especially as he later took up politics and served in the British House Of Commons for over a decade.

IN HER WONDERFULLY INFORMATIVE book *Cordial Relations* Katharine Moore tells of a great-niece of the Anglo-Italian writer Christina Rossetti, who recalls how she and her sister were taken, as children, to see a regular collection of maiden aunts:

> First, there was the poetess in black with a white lace cap, 'a mild religious face' and prominent huge grey eyes. She would sit with folded hands waiting for the kettle to boil. Then there were two much older aunts in big frilled night-caps and flowered bed jackets who lay in beds on opposite sides of the room with a strip of carpet between them.

Only the pleasure of seeing Aunt Christina, who used to say 'Welcome, merry little maidens' and make them eat a large tea and admire her goldfish, and give them sweets made the visit bearable!

Christina Rossetti's works, especially her poem *Goblin Market* published in 1862, have often been described as being as imaginative as Samuel Taylor Coleridge's *The Rime Of The Ancient Mariner* and comparable to Shakespeare for insight.

FANTASY, TOO, ACKNOWLEDGES the importance of aunts. Beatrix Potter's creations Aunt Porcas and Aunt Dorcas represented strength to Pig Robinson.

Then there's Edward Lear's Aunt Jobiska — a lady very partial to standing on her hands — whose nephew was the title character in *The Pobble Who Has No Toes*. Aunt Jobiska had the right word for every occasion and dispensed home-style wisdom in steady doses:

> And she said,— 'It's a fact the whole world knows,
> That Pobbles are happier without their toes.'

Aunt Jobiska was a great favourite with school children, because she believed that too much study taxed the brain!

MISS BRANWELL, WE ARE INFORMED by Katharine Moore in *Cordial Relations*, gave up the comfort of her own home at Penzance on England's Cornish coast to 'behave as an affectionate mother' to her nieces, Charlotte, Emily and Anne Brontë, and nephew, Branwell. In doing so, she left behind a wonderful life where she had been happy, respected and appreciated. As she was over forty when she took on the new role, it would have been difficult for her to adapt to new surroundings and duties, especially as they were so different from those to which she had become accustomed. However, adapt she did, with good grace, coping with Anne who was but a babe and with young Branwell, the only son, who became her darling.

On her death, Branwell said: 'I have now lost the guide and director of all the happy days connected with my childhood'.

A schoolfriend of Charlotte Brontë, Ellen Nussey, described Miss Branwell as:

> ... a small antiquated little lady who wore caps large enough for ½ a doz. of the present fashion and a front of light auburn curls over her forehead. She always dressed in silk and talked a great deal of her younger days, the gaieties of her native town, the soft warm climate and social life, re-called with regret. She took snuff out of a very pretty gold snuff box which she sometimes presented to you with a little laugh as if she enjoyed the slight shock of astonishment visible on your countenance.

Charlotte herself, perhaps the proudest and most independent member of the Brontë family, once wrote to her aunt seeking her guidance and financial assistance in carrying out her plan to spend some time in a foreign school:

> I feel certain, while I am writing, that you will see the propriety of what I say. You always liked to use your money to the best advantage. You are not fond of making shabby purchases; when you do confer a favour, it is often done in style ... I feel an absolute conviction that, if this advantage were allowed us, it would be the making of us for life ... who ever rose in the world without ambition? ... I want us *all* to get on. I know we have talents and I want them to be turned to account. I look to you, Aunt, to help us. I think you will not refuse.

Miss Branwell obliged, so we have her to thank for the literary results which the Brontës certainly 'turned to account'.

influenced by Maria's writings — is known to have expressed the somewhat radical opinion for her times, in a letter to her daughter Princess Victoria: 'I think people really marry far too much'.

THESE EVER-SO-ENGLISH maiden aunts, literary, philanthropic and reforming, all added lustre to their own and to others' lives. Today grandparents, parents, sisters, brothers, nieces and nephews must manage without them. Housekeepers, secretaries, friends, nurses and nannies must do their best as substitutes for them, because we shall never see people like them again. ✳

Chapter 3

OUTSTANDING AUSTRALIAN MAIDEN AUNTS

*A*USTRALIA, TOO, HAS HAD its share of maiden aunts — a vivid gallery of leading lights whose lives reflected a sense of purpose and a love of country rarely found in this century.

Outstanding among these worthy women is author and suffragette Catherine Helen Spence from Adelaide, who never married but raised a number of families of orphaned children, and feminist and social reformer Rose Scott from Singleton in New South Wales, who adopted her sister's baby boy when she died in childbirth.

CATHERINE HELEN SPENCE WAS Australia's first female political candidate and a tireless fighter for female suffrage.

She was born in Scotland in 1825 and arrived in South Australia with her parents in 1839, just three years after the establishment of a British colony there. She was dismayed at what she saw. The lack of elegance, the barrenness and the loneliness so upset her that she sat down on a log and cried. One hundred and fifty years ago South Australia was a far cry from the beautiful garden city it is today.

When Catherine was seventeen years of age, her family fell on hard times and it was she who, working as a governess, supported her parents, brothers and sisters. Later, intermittently, when she felt it necessary, she helped to raise orphaned children.

Women in the Spence family were strong, particularly Catherine's aunts. When her grandfather suffered a stroke and could no longer run his farm he did not turn it over to his eldest son, but to his daughter Margaret, Catherine's aunt, who managed the eight hundred acres profitably for the next thirty years. Catherine remembered her Aunt Margaret as a 'vigorous business-like woman'.

Another aunt, Mary, established a boarding school in Scotland.

Thus it was that Catherine learnt from her aunts that '...women were fit to share in the work of this world, and that to make the world pleasant for men was not their only mission'. Indeed, when Catherine's father died at the age of fifty-seven, her aunts were able to provide her mother and herself with crucial financial assistance.

At twenty, Catherine Spence tired of her occupation as a governess and decided to open a school in South Australia, like her Aunt Mary on the other side of the world.

Fiercely independent, well educated and extremely clever, she was deeply involved with politics and culture for most of her life.

As a regular contributor to the *South Australian Register*, she wrote articles about women and marriage in the early days of the colony, observing that 'women were not so scarce as to be spoiled or so abundant as to be neglected'.

In *Catherine Helen Spence: An Autobiography*, edited by Jeanne F. Young, we learn:

> I account myself well-born, for my father and my mother loved each other. I consider myself well descended, going back for many generations on both sides of intelligent and respectable people. I think I was well brought up, for my father and mother were of one mind regarding the care of the family. I count myself well educated, for the admirable woman at the head of the school which I attended from the age of four and a half till I was thirteen and a half, was a born teacher in advance of her own times.

Catherine Spence demonstrated extraordinary energy as a novelist, critic, accomplished journalist, preacher, lecturer, philanthropist, and social and moral reformer.

Throughout her long life she retained her Scottish accent. She had an engaging speaking manner, formed by relating fairy stories or reciting poems to her small nieces and nephews. She was particularly conscious of her voice and once remarked, 'I am more susceptible to voices than to features or complexions'.

Catherine's *Autobiography* records that she had two offers of marriage but chose to remain single. She may have refused both men because she did not love them:

> I believe that if I had been in love, especially if I had been disappointed in love, my novels would have been stronger and more interesting; but I kept watch over myself, which I felt I needed, for I was both imaginative and affectionate. I did not want to give my heart away. I did not desire a love disappointment, even for the sake of experience.

In *Unbridling The Tongues Of Women*, biographer Susan Magarey quotes Catherine Helen Spence's niece Lucy Morice, who tells of her aunt's extraordinary energy and attitude:

> On one occasion she was going to lecture at Peterborough ... that necessitated catching a train at about 7 a.m., and as she was then living in an outlying suburb meant very early rising, and a long tramride in a horse-drawn car. She would get to the township in the afternoon, be met and entertained by some (perhaps) sympathiser ... attend the meeting, lecture and conduct a demonstration, and probably get to bed about midnight! Leave the next morning by an early train, and on the occasion I have in mind, go on to speak at Port Adelaide in the evening — a marvellous feat of endurance, but for a woman nearing the eighties it was indeed a wonderful triumph of physical and mental strength and courage.

Lucy, who admired her aunt's courage and sympathetic concern for others, also recalled that her mother felt Catherine's 'demands upon my father's purse for her pet schemes or necessitous "cases" were excessive', though she acknowledged that Catherine herself was never even moderately well off.

Another of Catherine Spence's nieces remembered that she was skilful with her hands, and did beautiful broderie anglaise and point lace when she was eighty. Much of her early education had taken place listening to her teacher reading aloud to a class of girls doing needlework.

In October 1905 the city of Adelaide celebrated Catherine Spence's eightieth birthday. At an official party South Australia's chief justice proclaimed her 'the most distinguished woman' Australia had ever had. She responded:

> I am a new woman, and I know it. I mean an awakened woman ... awakened to a sense of capacity and responsibility, not merely to the family and the household, but to the State; to be wise, not for her own selfish interest, but that the world may be glad that she had been born.

No wonder she has been described as the 'grand old woman of Australia'!

In her *Autobiography* Catherine Helen Spence left this lasting testimonial:

> I have lived through a glorious age of progress. Born in 'the wonderful century', I have watched the growth of the movement for the uplifting of the masses, from the Reform Bill of 1832 to the demands for adult suffrage. As a member of a church which allows women to speak in the pulpit, a citizen of a state which gives womanhood a vote for the Assembly, a citizen of a Commonwealth which fully enfranchises me for both Senate and Representatives, and a member of a community which was foremost in conferring university degrees on women, I have benefited from the advancement of the educational and political status of women for which the Victorian era will probably stand unrivalled in the annals of the world's history. I have lived through the period of repressed childhood, and witnessed the dawn of a new era which has made the dwellers in youth's 'golden age' the most important factor in human development. I have watched the growth of Adelaide from the condition of a scattered hamlet to that of one of the finest cities in the southern hemisphere; I have seen the evolution of South

Australia from a province to an important state in a great
Commonwealth. All through my life I have tried to live up
to the best that was in me, and I should like to be remembered as one who never swerved in her efforts to do her
duty alike to herself and her fellow-citizens. Mistakes I have
made, as all are liable to do, but I have done my best.'

Biographer Jeanne Young agreed, celebrating her 'not merely as
a woman pioneer of South Australia alone, but as a pioneer woman
of the world, opening new paths for her sisters to tread'.

Catherine Helen Spence's economic security came from an
aunt's bequest. Her financial independence came from her own efforts and determination to earn her living. She used her pen, energy
and time to further the status of women and people generally, and
all Australian women who speak and expect to be heard today owe
a debt of gratitude to her. She was truly a remarkable Australian
maiden aunt who believed in herself as a 'human being and nothing
is outside my sphere'.

ANOTHER SUPERB AUSTRALIAN MAIDEN aunt was Rose Scott who
was a rebel with many a cause, one of the most influential women of
her time and an Australian pioneer of women's lib.

It was through the writings of William Shakespeare that Rose's
ardent interest in feminism was sparked. With her sisters and
brothers, she was educated privately. Among the entertaining literature her mother read to the young brood was *The Taming Of The
Shrew*. Rose was appalled and highly indignant that Katharina, the
shrew, took off her cap at her husband's bidding and trampled on
it. 'I'd have thrown it in his face,' she announced. She was similarly
nauseated when Katharina obeyed her husband and delivered a
sermon about the duties of wives to their husbands, their 'lord, king
and governor'. Furiously, Rose stormed from the room, declaring
she would not listen to any more. Later, she wrote:

Afterwards, I paced the garden with clenched hands and
fury in my heart. The craven witch, to give in in that servile
manner and worse still to turn the tables on her own sex!

From that moment, Rose Scott revolted against all injustice and wrong, particularly the oppression of women, and decided to devote her life to women's interests and social reforms.

Rose Scott was born on the 8th of October 1847 at 'Glendon' on the Hunter River in northern New South Wales. She was one of eight children — five daughters and three sons. The family was part of the Hunter Valley 'squattocracy'.

When her father died in 1879, Rose and her mother moved to Sydney. The rest of the family had all married. Mother and daughter were financially secure. Rose had a private income of her own through an inheritance from a relative. She was on friendly terms with her cousins, the Merewethers, and they visited each other frequently. She also often visited her sister Millie at Singleton and her Aunt Rose, after whom she was named, at Newcastle.

Rose and her cousin David Scott Mitchell were very close friends. In fact, he was her mentor, and she played a large part in inducing him to bequeath his magnificent collection of historic records and other data about Australia along with a large sum of money for the establishment of a library in Sydney — the Mitchell Library, named after him, is today housed within the State Library of New South Wales.

Soon after moving to Sydney, Rose and her mother purchased a beautiful two-storey cottage, 'Lynton', in Jersey Road, Woollahra (which later became one of the best known residences in Sydney). About this time one of her sisters died in childbirth and Rose adopted the baby boy, taking on her new role with flair. She threw herself whole-heartedly into her auntly duties and refused all offers of marriage, saying that 'life is too short to waste on the admiration of one man' and 'women think they marry men to have someone to lean on — but it's the men who lean on us'. She also once declared that 'the true place of women in society is not beside man but just in front of him', and on other occasions described marriage as 'friend-ship under difficulties' and love as 'the highest friendship'. Rose was a beauty with a flawless complexion, and a taste for fashionable clothes and eye-catching hats, and it was said she did not marry because she could not choose one man from many suitors.

If ever there was a woman with a social conscience, it was Rose. As an aunt she became vitally interested in the protection of children. She was responsible for the banning of children under thirteen from working in factories and of children under sixteen from working more than forty-eight hours a week. She also advocated a new law which regulated the conditions under which children were allowed to be adopted. Another innovation for which she fought was the payment of support benefits by the fathers of children born illegitimately.

As well as her battles for the welfare of children, Rose Scott campaigned on feminist issues. She was horrified that women and girls often toiled in shops and factories from eight in the morning till nine at night on week days and till eleven in the evening on Saturdays, and campaigned vigorously for shorter hours. She organised meetings, bombarded MPs with petitions and badgered clergymen into joining her crusade.

Having taken up a cause, Rose Scott never gave up the fight until she won. Early in her public career she persuaded a politician to bring up the matter of the legal age of consent for girls in the New South Wales House of Representatives. Rose believed the age should be raised from fourteen years to twenty-one. There was little support for the issue, but Rose persisted and after nearly twenty years she had some satisfaction in seeing *The Girls' Protection Act*, which raised the age of consent to sixteen, passed in 1910.

Another of Rose's battles was to obtain the right to vote for women of New South Wales. Governments came to power and governments toppled, and all the time her Women's Suffrage League calmly and sensibly kept up the fight for the vote. Rose knew that victory was inevitable. In 1894 she saw women get the vote in South Australia, and five years later in Western Australia. Her own triumph in New South Wales came in 1902 when the government approved the *Women's Suffrage Act*, adding 300,000 voters to the electoral roll. That same year the new Federal Constitution gave the vote to both men and women. Tasmania gave

18 May 2006

286 2669

4AR.

Dear Board Member

with compliments

Please find enclosed the March MIP.

Please bring this with you to the north board
meeting on 25 May 2006

Kind regards
Jane Dogboe
020 7245 2298

CITYWEST HOMES

21 Grosvenor Place
London SW1X 7EA

Tel: 020 7245 2000
Fax: 020 7245 2001
www.cwh.org.uk

OPENING THE DOOR TO BETTER HOMES

CityWest Homes Limited A local authority controlled company of the City of Westminster.

INVESTOR IN PEOPLE

women the vote in 1903, followed by Queensland and finally Victoria in 1909.

Rose Scott was not content to rest on her laurels simply because women had achieved the vote. Now she was concerned to ensure they knew how to use it! In *Silk And Calico*, Betty Searle reminds us of Rose Scott's now famous words:

> What is the Australian woman going to do with her vote? ...
> Who is to guide woman? Certainly not man ... Woman must
> be guided by her own conscience and her wonderful percep-
> tive powers ... We must in fact think for ourselves.

Rose Scott died on the 20th of April 1925, at the age of seventy-seven. Throughout her long life she showed that much can be achieved by a private citizen inspired by zeal for helping humanity. And she achieved it all with a soft face and stylish bonnets. 'What a mother she would have made,' summed up one obituary. 'Yet, as matters were, she mothered all the world ... she was above all a great Australian.' And she was undoubtedly a wonderful aunt.

CATHERINE HELEN SPENCE AND ROSE SCOTT are but two outstanding Australian maiden aunts who gave so much to this country. Many others have also made great contributions, publicly or privately, and are worthy of our admiration and heartfelt thanks. ✳

Chapter 4

COUNTRY AUNTS

*'W*HAT YOU NEED IS A GOOD dose of country air.' How many city youngsters have heard those or similar words? As children, my brothers and sister and I were often packed off to the country for a few weeks and on our return we knew we had benefited from our stay there. There is something special about the atmosphere in the country — and it's not just the fresh country air, but the people too.

Somehow people in the country have a way of bringing one back to basics. They remind us to 'take the time to touch the morning', to laugh, to think, to do. Families seem to be more relaxed. There is not the urgency of running to clockwork.

To me, country people are the salt of the earth — dependable, practical, hospitable and so resourceful. Their values are genuine.

On the whole, country women firmly believe husbands and wives must first and foremost be friends, because theirs are generally not only partnerships of marriage, but of work too. Indeed, the total circle of life revolves around their marriages.

Country women always seem to be strong characters, who make wonderful aunts. They are a breed apart — secure in themselves and very friendly.

I was recently invited by Sandra and Peter O'Brien to spend a few days on their beautiful property of three thousand hectares, called 'Hatton', sixteen kilometres from Warren in the central west

Sandra and Peter O'Brien's property, 'Hatton' near Warren.

of New South Wales. I had never been there before, but soon learned that it is some five hundred and twenty-five kilometres from Sydney and has a total population of just four thousand, half of whom live in the town.

Europeans first visited the Warren area in 1818, and settlement began in the 1840s. It is prime agricultural land, and the early economy was based on grazing sheep and cattle. The district played an important role in the development of the medium wool merino sheep industry in Australia. Today, the economy is based on irrigated and dry land cropping, together with cotton farming and the traditional wool and cattle industries.

Descendants of a number of the early settlers still live in the district, some after six generations. Among the old rural families are names such as Egan, Perry, McAlary, McKay, O'Brien, Irving, Wild, Hunt, McCalman, Firth and Falkiner.

But back to aunts — country, pastoral or rural. During my visit women arrived for lunch at Hatton, laden with photographs of their aunts from the family vaults. Some of the lunch guests had travelled one hundred and thirty kilometres to be there — nothing to a country woman! They stayed for hours regaling me with stories of their aunts, all great country women who had lived up to good old-fashioned values such as the need for perseverance, the wisdom of economy and the virtue of patience — extolled in *The Country Woman* journal more than half a century ago.

Although we're more than half a century down the track now, the same appreciation of life is still found among country folk.

BARBARA McKAY REMEMBERS HER Aunt Anastasia, usually known as 'Aunt Statia', as a perfectionist who even used to polish the brass taps in the garden! On one occasion when she upended her dinner plate, sending the contents in all directions, she picked it up, declaring: 'If I can't eat off my own floor, then I can't eat at all!'

SALLY FALKINER, IN HER TWENTIES, is one of the younger aunts of the Warren district today. She is also the new girl to the area, indeed to Australia. When she married husband George and stepped into the huge role of mistress of famous 'Haddon Rig' in the mid-1980s, her biggest hurdle, in her own words, was 'being the boss's wife' — not surprisingly, because in anybody's language Haddon Rig is large. The property is about 24,000 hectares in area and has a staff of more than twenty.

After years of working as personal assistant to the chairman of an advertising and film company in England, Sally initially considered Warren to be 'the back of beyond' and Australia to be 'a cultural desert'. It's a different story today. Sally loves country life and has made many true friends.

Sally is an aunt to seven children and has one aunt of her own. She laments that less concentration is placed on the role of aunt today than was the case in generations past.

BARBARA ANDERSON FONDLY remembers her rural aunts:

> My early years were spent with my parents, Luke and Kathleen McAlary, on our property, 'Castlebar'. My sisters [Jackie Ballhausen and Doone McKay] and I enjoyed taking an active part in the running of the property.

I remember studying our correspondence lessons, and riding our ponies five miles through the paddocks to the old homestead, 'Milawa', where my grandmother lived with our three aunts and several uncles. There we would meet the mailman, post our lessons and collect a new set for the following week.

We girls saw a lot of our aunts — they played an important part in our lives. Agnes Philomena McAlary (Mena), Mary Bertha McAlary (Molly) and Eulalie Eileen Hobbs (Lalie). I remember them as welcoming and friendly. They were extremely independent and proud women. Mena and Mollie never married, but Lalie wed her beau of twenty years later in life.

These women were all born on the family property,

Agnes Philomena McAlary (Mena).

Mary Bertha McAlary (Mollie).

educated by governesses during their early years and later on sent to Loreto Convent in Sydney. They were part of a large family of seven sons and three daughters. 'Milawa' was really a small settlement in those days, with fourteen to sixteen people living in the main house, about fourteen men in cottages and up to fifty people on the property during shearing. So it was a world of its own for these women. They lived there ten months of the year, and then ventured to the city for a couple of months during summer.

All the McAlary aunts were musical — they had lovely solo voices and played several instruments. I recall visiting them, sitting at a huge table for dinner and then all gathering around the piano. Mollie could play any request from jazz to Beethoven, and the rest of us would sing and act.

Mena was to me the most colourful of my aunts; she was rather 'theatrical'. She had a good sense of humour, was

Eulalie Eileen Hobbs, née McAlary (Lalie).

extremely proud of her family, and stuck firmly to her beliefs and traditions. She adored hats, and it was said that at
district hospital board meetings (she was a long-time board
member) she had never worn the same one twice. She
would arrive in town and step down from a large truck,
stylish hat poised on her head, but many times would forget
to remove her dust coat and gardening shoes! Short in stature, with black hair and large brown eyes, she wore an air of
importance and commanded respect.

Mena was my godmother, so she was special to me. I
enjoyed spending time with her — she was fun, entertaining
and generous. She gave me my first riding outfit, complete
with boots and gloves. On my twenty-first birthday she presented me with a fairytale evening dress that I will always
remember. We all recall her taking us out on Sundays from
boarding school. We would dine at the best restaurants and

she would ask the waiters to give her nieces special attention! In some ways Mena's forthrightness embarrassed me, but in many ways I admired her.

Mena lived for some years on her parents' property, Milawa, after she left school, but then moved to live on her own part of the settlement, which she called 'Wangaratta'. She managed her land with casual labour and oversaw every detail herself.

The fact that Mena's father gave his daughters so much independence and so many good opportunities for decision-making, at a very young age, gave Mena a confidence that her contemporaries did not have.

Mena died suddenly in her rose garden in 1978. She was a unique character, and we still miss her.

SANDRA STUART BECAME SANDRA O'BRIEN when she married Peter, son of a large family with many older members including women of worth who were respected and admired. At first Sandra was 'killed with kindness', which she initially found to be overwhelming, but twenty years on she is breathing her own country air:

Marrying into a family well aware of its own history, both in this country and before some of its members migrated here from the Emerald Isle, was a daunting experience for me, a city-bred girl with my own 'liberated' philosophies!

Not the least of my intimidators were the three O'Brien aunts. First was Aunty Margaret, a strong and direct personality with a sharp mind, all contained in an erect but frail looking frame. She discoursed sitting upright on the edge of her chair, and ate and drank with the appetite of a bird. Then there was Aunty Winifred (Aunty Win), a gently rounded, smartly dressed lady who, though always warm and chatty, nevertheless strongly translated to me, the newcomer, that there are right and wrong ways of just 'being'. Lastly, there was Aunty Kathleen, known for some reason as 'Aunty Pud'! She was a stooped little lady, clad in dark colours, head always adorned with a hat or beret. An aura of eccentricity wafted from her, but lurking beneath it was a phenomenal memory for every detail of life's happenings as they occurred to all members of the large O'Brien family. Aunty Pud always greeted people warmly and concluded every greeting with the words, 'Say a prayer for my Special Intention'. Numerous of her nieces and nephews, feeling themselves wayward creatures by her standards, thought they indeed must be the special intention!

Aunty Margaret and Aunty Pud never married, but cheerfully accepted what seemed to be the lot of many country daughters of their period — they devoted their lives to their mother, who in their case lived to be ninety-nine. Aunty Winifred took a long time to say 'Yes', but eventually married at the age of forty-five. The Christian attitudes (with an Irish stamp) of all three were exemplary.

I remember the day Aunty Margaret and Aunty Pud came to 'inspect' me, the new relative, a long awaited someone dwelling in what is the old family homestead. I had been up ladders with paint brushes, titivated and fussed, and had generally given the large dark house a facelift, as much as my husband and I could afford at the time. I thought my efforts were remarkable and that no one could do else but notice the difference between the 'before' and 'after', and so I launched the aunts into the grand tour. They immediately went into the halls of reminiscence — of happy days long ago. 'Do you remember the old chair that was here?' 'This is where Danny slept!' 'That's where Mother kept the tea!' And so on. My work went unnoticed and I guess the deflation I felt taught me one of the many great lessons I have learned from the O'Brien family — that the lives of young people should be as happy as possible because people carry the joys of youth through the years. These aunts always delighted in the memories aroused by their old family home.

HELEN O'BRIEN, COUSIN-IN-LAW of Sandra and Peter, takes up the tale of these three aunts from a distinctly different angle:

> My first born arrived with great excitement from family on both sides, all anxious for an introduction — especially the three doting and loving O'Brien aunts.
>
> This particular day my mother was visiting me in hospital and we were discussing who my son looked like. The aunts arrived and we chatted only briefly. Before their departure we walked to the nursery to view this small bundle in his crib. One by one, each aunt went to the window, stepped, glanced briefly and commented, 'Typical O'Brien'. My mother, in close proximity, commented that the baby was really just like his mother.
>
> But the aunts' decision was fixed and final, and they left the hospital.

PHILOMENA SIMMONS (NÉE O'BRIEN) is an aunt *extraordinaire* — with seventy-three nieces and nephews at the last count! She is one of eleven children herself and has eleven children of her own. And so the family line continues.

This slim, smiling, multi-blessed aunt revealed:

> I rejoice in many things: new shoots of grass after a dry time; sun on my back; good health; and in my many nieces and nephews — seventy-three rejoicings! So many good friends. So many young people doing extraordinary and amazing and ordinary and kind and clever things of whom I proudly say, 'That's my niece' or 'That's my nephew'. They are, without exception, exceptionally beautiful people — not a dud among the lot!
>
> It's wonderful having so many young people believing I am a very worthy person because of my close relationship with their parent. And in their intelligence and patience I see a reflection of my parents: how couldn't I love them? When I open the door to a tall slim young lady, with raven curling hair to her waist, the deepset eyes of a French aristocrat and

the bearing of a beautiful Portuguese princess, who says, 'Aunty Phil ...', I rejoice.

I thank God often for my children; I thank Him also for peopling the Earth with the rest of the magnificent young men and women around, so many with whom I can claim the relationship of 'aunt'.

PAM RUSS, WHO WROTE *The Road To Nevertire*, a book giving a vivid and poetic background of country life, recalls:

My earliest memories of my aunts are that they were all elderly, tall and straight, and some a little severe. Their homes were always immaculate, dark, and almost all had an aspidistra or two growing in the front room. My brother and I were told to stand and sit up straight without wriggling or scratching when visiting aunts, to speak only when spoken to, and, above all, to be polite. I had a large number of aunts on both sides of my family and was very much in awe of most of them.

There were, however, two notable exceptions, Aunty Maude and Aunty Bess. Aunty Maude, my mother's youngest sister, was unmarried and lived in Sydney. When I went to boarding school at only ten years of age I spent most of my free time with her and she became a second mother to me. Aunty Bess, a sister of my father, I remember very fondly. My paternal grandmother was very musical and Aunty Bess must have been so, too, because it was she who gave me my very first piano tuition and helped to instill a love of good music which I have to this day. And I think that she, along with my father, was very 'good' with words and it was from them that I developed any small talent I may have in that direction. It was not until I seriously began to consider publishing a book of poetry that I thought about this in any depth and came to the realisation that I had been 'playing with words' for as long as I could remember, and memories of Aunty Bess sprang to mind at that time.

SUE BEACH TELLS OF HER sister-in-law, who is also her aunt, and only seven years older than she is:

> My family had a mothercraft nurse — a wonderful woman who had very strict and firm ideas! As a small child I remember being placed on a 'potty' and not being able or allowed to move until the job was done! My aunt — sick to the back teeth of waiting for me — whipped me off, sat down and did the job herself, then put me back on the pot and called out to the nurse, 'We can go and play now, she's done it'!

ANNETTE IRVING FROM 'OLD BUNDILLA' had a web of aunts. As she explained, 'Aunts are the mothers of cousins and cousins are only a step removed from one's brothers and sisters in the family web'. A very close relationship.

Annette nostalgically recalls how her Aunty Lu (Lucy) was given a washing machine for her birthday in 1948. It was a secret. Uncle Dick put the machine in the laundry overnight so Aunty Lu knew nothing about it. He took her there next morning after the other presents had been opened. Overwhelmed, she burst into tears. As a little girl of seven or eight, Annette couldn't understand why there was such joy and excitement over a washing machine!

Aunty Jean was Annette's godmother. She was also her father's first love, but she'd married his cousin George instead. She could well have been Annette's mother had her Uncle George not cut her father out! It can and does become very complicated in the country. Anyway, Aunty Jean and Uncle George had one daughter, Merle, who in turn gave birth to Sigrid Thornton, so all was not lost!

Aunty Jean had a broad, cosmopolitan approach to life. Well educated and cultured, she influenced Annette's reading and familiarised her with Sydney and city life, taking her to theatres and pantomimes, going to the Art Gallery, walking over the Harbour Bridge, going up the Pylon, visiting the Museum and the Technological Museum, admiring the Botanical Gardens, eating at Cahill's restaurants... Wonderful entertainment for a little ten-year-old girl

'Infant aunt'.

'Schoolgirl aunt'.

'Travelling aunt'.

from the country whose mother had died. Annette recalls being 'pop-eyed' at the nudity of male statues — the Archibald Fountain and the like — and Aunty Jean managing to convey the narrowness of this reaction and encouraging 'a more discerning appreciation of art and sculpture'.

Aunty Jean lived in Melbourne in her later years, until her death. Annette's brother arranged for their father to be flown there to give the eulogy at the funeral service of this aunt — his first great love.

Then there was Aunty Marge, Annette's great-aunt, her maternal grandmother's youngest sister. This aunt did much to help school boarders at weekends, providing clothing, coping with their homesickness and smoothing out difficulties in their new environment. She would tell Annette, 'Take life by the yard and it's hard, take it by the inch and it's a cinch' — a philosophy her niece has always regarded as worthwhile. Another of Aunty Marge's favourite adages, especially about mistakes, was 'Let it go down the drain'. Very country.

Aunt Annie, another great-aunt, was but a child of fifteen when she came overland from the Riverina by buggy and horse-wagon to the 'Eurobla' property at Warren in 1881. She had no children of her own but was so devoted to her nieces — Annette's mother and Aunty Lu — that she left them her property when she died. Aunt Annie was born in Victoria and grew up in the Riverina area, near Darlington Point. She went to school at Oxley Plains, a one-teacher

'Bridal aunt'.

'Teenage aunt'.

school nearby. She was a strong, intense personality and a great rider of a beautiful mare named Lochreive. She was always a wonderful cook, especially of sponge and fruit cakes, not to mention gigantic omelettes which we relished!

A famous saying from her pioneering days was, 'If a thing will do, make it do'!

LORRAINE GREEN, ANOTHER CAPABLE and energetic country woman, lovingly describes her Aunty Edna, a widow who has been a tireless worker for the CWA and Red Cross and now regularly enjoys the companionship which the VIEW Club offers:

> Edna Lyle Budd married Robert William Elder and came to Nevertire to settle on a property which they called 'Alandoone'. In 1939 their home was burned down and they lost absolutely everything they owned. With their two children they moved into an open shed and a tent to live

until their present home was built. Being wartime years, not many materials were available, but the end product was like a mansion to them. It still stands majestically on the plain, now surrounded by a beautiful garden.

During the 1940s and the 1950s there were terrible droughts and, while my uncle was on the roads with most of his stock for months at a time, Aunty Edna would battle on her own to keep alive the horses and cattle left behind and to school the children, a daughter and a son.

I will never forget this aunt of mine as she was always like a mother to me. Between 1945 and 1952 I was far away from home, attending Dubbo Central School and Dubbo High School, but I was able to go to Nevertire most Saturdays for a few hours. I would catch a train at 9 a.m. and arrive at 11:30 a.m., and there would be Aunty Edna waiting to take me to her place for a hot lunch with all the trimmings. Then we'd have to be back at the railway station by 3 p.m. for the return trip. I would be loaded up with treats such as fruit and cakes, because we students were always hungry! I went on to do my nursing training and continued to visit my aunt on my days off, whenever possible, receiving the same care.

One of my fondest and most amusing memories is when we, as nurses, did night duty and were never warm enough as in those days of strict dress regulation you were allowed to wear only a cape over your uniform for warmth ... so my aunt went through her husband's 'Long Johns' and gave me several pairs to hand around to my friends to wear on the cold wintery nights. I can tell you, thirty-five years later, that Uncle Ben's Long Johns are still a talking point at the Dubbo Base Hospital's nurses' reunions.

LORRAINE ALSO PAID TRIBUTE to Eileen Lorraine Anderson, who was not related to her but was an 'institution' in the Warren district. She was 'aunty' to hundreds, a woman with special warmth, an

Eileen 'Auntie' Anderson.

approachable and wise human being. She was well ahead of her time and known to all as 'Aunty A':

Aunty A arrived in Warren as a city bride, having married the local chemist. In due course she had two children, a son and a daughter. Following the death of her husband, when she was thirty-nine, she experienced some hard times, continuing with the business and schooling the children — who were educated at private boarding schools. Her son went on to study pharmacy, then came home to take over the business in 1952.

Aunty A's chosen career was to spread happiness and companionship amongst people from all walks of life. Everyone was made welcome in her home at any hour of the day, and she always had hot meals ready in case someone was hungry.

She was gifted with being able to entertain people of

different social backgrounds in the one room without anyone feeling uncomfortable. Throughout her lifetime there would not have been one jackaroo from the nearby sheep studs who did not feel her kindness at some time. When these fellows came to town they all congregated at her home, where she would feed them, then they would go off to play their Union football game on Saturday afternoons, returning for a hot shower. If any of them over-indulged after the match, Aunty A would not allow them to drive home but would bed them down on her balcony. Many parents were ever grateful to her for seeing to their sons' care — many of these lads came from other States as well as from elsewhere in New South Wales.

Her home was a great haven to all the nursing staff at the local hospital, and some of her nearest and dearest friends came from there. If any of them were feeling down they knew they only had to pay Aunty A a visit to be cheered up.

Aunty A was well known around the town for her matchmaking abilities. She would study her visitors over a period of time and then make sure they were invited to her home again and again until she was sure Cupid could carry on without her help. Many married couples still laugh about her wedding presents to them — always a bassinet!

I am quite sure no one who knew this fine lady will ever forget her. When she died in her eighties, in 1983, Warren lost one of its greatest, most lovable aunts.

AUNTY A OBVIOUSLY TOUCHED many hearts. Another tribute to her was made by Bruce Gemmell, who recalls:

There were so many happy and memorable visits that I, and later we as a family, made to Aunty's home behind the shop. Eileen really was 'aunty' to very many people. I think it could be safely stated that there would not be a town in New South Wales that did not have at least one inhabitant who knew who Aunty A was and where she lived. Her home was a 'home away from home' for literally hundreds of people.

On one particular Saturday night in March 1959 I paid a visit to Eileen's home. Walking to the door I could hear the piano belting out a tune, much singing and laughter — with obviously plenty of liquid refreshment being consumed. My knock at the door was answered by Aunty herself: 'Come in, Ducks, get yourself a drink, sit down where you can. Tonight we are celebrating a Haddon Rig book-keepers' convention!' It so happened, there were three former Haddon Rig book-keepers present, plus the book-keeper of the time. A great night was had by all!

THESE COUNTRY OR RURAL or pastoral aunts, and others like them, have played roles of great variety and importance in shaping our heritage — and Australia's history. ✳

Chapter 5

THEATRICAL AUNTS

*F*OR EVERY MRS WORTHINGTON who has heard the words 'Don't put your daughter on the stage', there have been at least two aunts pleading the opposite! They are the 'theatrical aunts' — aunts who have a love of theatre running through their veins.

Some of these aunts may never have braved the stage themselves, but they've been determined that their favourite niece or nephew must indulge in their unrequited love. Others may have possessed true talent and thoroughly exercised it, and wanted to see the family name upheld — ideally in lights! Regardless of the motive, there is no doubting the influence of theatrical aunts.

ENID BLYTON, ACKNOWLEDGED for generations as one of the world's greatest children's storytellers, was very nearly lost to the world of letters simply because she looked like her Aunt May! From Barbara Stoney, in *Enid Blyton — A Biography*, we learn:

> From earliest childhood Enid had been schooled in the belief that she would eventually become a musician. She had always been told how much she resembled her Aunt May, both in looks and temperament, and knew that her father was convinced she possessed a similar musical talent.

But, having endured months of piano practice and tuition, Enid at the age of eighteen realised music was not her forte and that her talents lay in creating and writing poems and stories. These gifts came to her easily and gave her far greater satisfaction, and she knew full well she would never be able to express herself in the same way musically. And so we, her readers, over many decades, have thrilled to *Five Go To Smugglers' Top*, Noddy and Big Ears (prior to banning days!) and countless other Blyton gems.

THE ILLUSTRIOUS ACTOR AND director Sir John Gielgud, whose plays, films and interviews have entertained and informed us for many years, confides in his autobiographical book *Early Stages* that his love of theatre owes much to his family background — and not least to the influence of his famous thespian aunt, Ellen Terry.

Christmas, when the family came together, was always one of Sir John's favourite times of the year:

> On Christmas Day my various Terry relatives used to come to lunch or tea, and then my stage-struck heart would beat and I was in a state of unmitigated rapture. First, Grandmother, stout and jolly, with a special armchair at table and special pickings from the turkey (the Terry appetite was as unfailing as the Terry charm). Then my mother's three sisters, Janet, Lucy and Mable. Next to appear would be Marion, making a superb entrance with her gracious smile and beautiful sweeping carriage. After lunch we would hear someone else arriving with a jolly laugh and jingling of coins, and Fred's head and shoulders would loom up over the screen, with Julia behind him in lovely clothes, her arms laden with beautiful and expensive presents.
>
> All of a sudden there would be a hush in the room. An old lady had come in and was finding her way from one group to another, settling at last in a low chair. It was Ellen Terry, bowed and mysterious, under the shadow of a big black straw hat, covered in scarves and shawls, with a large bag holding two or three pairs of spectacles, like a godmother in a fairy tale. She wore a black and grey gown, very cleverly draped on her slim body, too long in front (as she always wore her stage dresses), and bunched up over one

arm with wonderful instinctive grace. When her hat and shawls had been taken from her, there were coral combs in her short grey hair and coral beads round her neck. With her lovely turned-up nose and wide mouth, and that husky voice — a 'veiled voice' somebody called it once — and her enchanting smile, no wonder everyone adored her. We children, of course, found her far the most thrilling and lovable of all our exciting aunts and uncles. Even though she was vague and we felt she was not quite sure where she was or who we were, her magic was irresistible.

What a thrilling effect Aunt Ellen must have had on the young John Gielgud. How lucky he was to have been so influenced by her.

THE VERSATILE AND VERY clever Joyce Grenfell, whose wonderful one-woman shows made us double-up with laughter as well as shed a tear, felt the same way as does Sir John Gielgud about the celebration of Christmas. This event was always spent with her mother's sister, Aunt Nancy, at 'Clivedon' — Aunt Nancy being none other than Nancy Astor, the first woman to sit in the British House Of Commons. In her beautiful autobiographical book *Joyce Grenfell In Pleasant Places*, she describes in great detail the pleasures of those huge family Christmas gatherings:

> The feast itself was always, from as far back as my memory goes, spent staying at Cliveden with Aunt Nancy and Uncle Waldorf Astor and their five children. My ambivalent feelings about the place exercised me a good deal. I was torn between wishing we could have our own family Christmas at home — decorating our own tree, putting up our own holly and mistletoe — and the greedy certainty that at the big house there would be lots more people, presents, festivity and foods. As the day drew nearer I settled for greed and hoped there wouldn't be a family row and that pleasures would be plentiful.

According to Joyce, the great thing about Christmas at Cliveden was the way the pattern was adhered to. No matter what was happening, either within the family or in the world at large, one could count on the day's festive agenda remaining the same:

> In the front hall we saw the giant Christmas tree was where we expected it to be, at the foot of the oak staircase. The banisters were festooned with garlands of box, yew, bay, ivy, holly and other evergreens that, as well as the humea, gave off a subtle aromatic scent. Only once were we allowed to help decorate the tree. The job was usually done by a gardener on a step-ladder, with the housekeeper handing him the tinsel and coloured balls. I always made sure that certain favourite decorations were still there; the glass birds in little tin cages were regulars I looked for.

What memories for an aunt to bequeath, what reception from her niece! And the tree was only the beginning:

> After tea Aunt Nancy went to her present-room, a small dark panelled study next to her boudoir used for storage. No child was allowed to go there, particularly at Christmas-time, but, once when I was about sixteen and was sent in there to fetch something for her, I saw it was like a little shop. Piles of sweaters of all colours and sizes, men's, boys', women's and girls'; silk stockings, silk scarves, chiffon squares and boxes of linen handkerchiefs, from the Irish Linen Stores, initialled for everyone in the party. There were evening bags, men's ties, golf-balls in boxes, little packs of tees, diaries, toys, games, books and candy. Lots of candy. There was never a more generous present-giver than Aunt Nancy, but she was always careful about her candy store; most of it came from American friends, and she didn't let it out of her keeping except in very occasional bestowals of a caramel here and a sour-ball there. She also had a great many boxes of chewing-gum and was never without a supply in her pocket. Presents from the store were given to everyone in the house, family, friends, staff and visiting staff — in those days ladies' maids and valets always accompanied their employers. Aunt Nancy's private secretary

helped by doing much of the present buying, and all the
wrapping up in layers of best quality tissue-paper tied with
inch-wide red satin ribbon. Aunt Nancy wrote the tags ... In
that house it was the custom to give on a scale unknown to
most people, even from the same background. If the giving
had been limited only to those who already had, it would
have been indefensible, but my aunt and uncle were sharers
on the grand scale with all and sundry, and their imaginative generosity, undiscovered for the most part, was their
special gift. And not only at Christmas.

Nancy Astor certainly had a profound effect on Joyce Grenfell's
life. We are told with great honesty and simplicity in *Joyce Grenfell
Requests The Pleasure*:

I owe Aunt Nancy a very great deal. Her imaginative
generosity to me as a child, as a girl, and to Reggie and
myself as a young married couple was unending. She gave
me new clothes and I shared a coming-out dance with her
daughter Wissie; she gave us our wedding reception and
half our first house in St Leonard's Terrace. I was always on
the receiving end of her generosity and not only on birthdays and at Christmas.

Joyce confesses, however, to her ambivalence about staying with
her aunt at Cliveden:

Half of me loved the big scale of it and the luxury; half
resented the tension I sensed between my mother and Aunt
Nancy. The rows that happened there were a strain and for
years my feelings about the place were coloured by dread.

Obviously, she was torn between her affections for her charming, attractive and witty aunt and her feelings of criticism which
continued throughout her life:

I thought her interfering and narrow. She was. But occasionally she was right and she was always a fascinating
character. She thought me headstrong and self-willed. I was.
We came to love each other in the end. As a child I was
scared of her sharp tongue. She had an uncanny knack of

knowing just where to put the salt in the wound. She teased me for being fat, crying too easily and for my cowardice about riding. I was thin-skinned about myself, easily wounded and I resented Aunt Nancy's criticism of my mother, although secretly, I knew some of it was justified. But I was fiercely loyal and I also dreaded the rows and the tears and the unhappy atmosphere generated by my powerful aunt. Now I can see her side of the picture and sympathise with her despair over my mother's repeated escapades. She rescued her time and time again and showed much understanding in the last year of my mother's life, when she was living alone in New York, lonely and unwell. Aunt Nancy opened up Little Orchard, the house she had built for my mother, where she was happy for so long, and took her back there to be cared for among her many friends until she died in 1955.

It's impossible to forget generosity and caring of this nature.

Joyce Grenfell also recalled that after Nancy Astor's death she received a three-inch-thick file with her name stencilled on the cover. It contained her own letters to her aunt over a period of thirty-five years:

In almost every one of my letters to her I am thanking her for something. We continued to argue on paper and, from 1939, largely about my job in the theatre. She had a puritanical attitude to the theatre and thought it wicked and, although I think she would have denied this, I believe it lay behind her endless nagging at me to 'get off the stage'.

The box also contained a very special letter that her aunt had written after Joyce's Broadway debut:

I must write to you once more to tell you how delighted I am to think of your great success. I have passed round the notices and I might say someone has kept them, but that doesn't matter. The thing is that it (the first night) is over and you are a success.

Joyce Grenfell truly treasured that letter from her aunt.

ANDREW LLOYD WEBBER — composer and creator of such hits as *Jesus Christ Superstar*, *Evita*, *Cats* and *The Phantom Of The Opera* — is one of the most successful theatrical hit-makers in the world today. As a small child he was helped in developing his talents by his Aunt Vi, the retired actress Viola Johnstone.

In the biography *Fanfare*, Jonathan Mantle reveals Aunt Vi's influence in transferring her nephew's classically trained musical talents to the popular stage.

> Rodgers and Hammerstein's *Oklahoma!*, *The King and I* and *South Pacific* all successfully crossed the Atlantic to England in the early and mid-1950s. Andrew, who would eventually cross the Atlantic the other way and sweep away the old Broadway musical tradition, was taken by Aunt Vi to see numerous West End musical shows. The young boy and his aunt formed a close and lasting attachment; so close that, when Jean [Andrew's mother] suggested that his enjoyment of the real-life theatre was jeopardising his academic career, Viola suggested that he build a toy one of his own.
>
> This was the brick auditorium and turntable-revolving stage that now stood on the table in the Lloyd Webbers' flat. Andrew's management of it was autocratic; he built and owned the theatre, wrote and played much of the music, wrote and typed the programmes and invited the audience. He also hired and fired the staff; Julian, three years younger, was a willing unpaid hand who was allowed to operate the lead soldiers that passed for actors and castigated mercilessly for any mistakes. The Andrew Lloyd Webber Toy Theatre Company, perhaps not surprisingly given its origins in the frustrated psyche of its young proprietor, was not an equal opportunity employer.
>
> The early productions more or less directly reflected the shows he managed to see with Aunt Vi. *The Importance Of Being Earnest* was an early effort: complete with backstage as well as onstage banter, it reflected Aunt Vi's ability to get herself and her stagestruck young nephew through the

stage-door and into the looking-glass world of actors and impresarios. At a time when the West End stage musical was rediscovering its identity in a way it had not done since the salad days of Noel Coward, Ivor Novello and Gilbert and Sullivan, and Rodgers and Hammerstein were giving way to Lionel Bart's cockney epics *Fings Ain't Wot They Used t' Be* and *Oliver!*, it was no coincidence that the sounds of music hall piano and a kind of patrician South Kensington cockney began to reverberate around the revolving stage of the toy theatre at 10 Harrington Court.

Not surprisingly, the audiences watching these performances were tiny, often comprising only Andrew's mother, father and aunt! But the toy theatre was a complete imaginary cast — and it was Andrew's brainchild, at the suggestion of his aunt. Who knows, if his Aunt Vi had not trodden the boards herself, then Andrew Lloyd Webber's genius may not have been discovered as early as it was and his success may never have been so great.

THEATRICAL AUNTS, THOSE GREAT inspirers, have indeed swayed and directed the lives of many a niece or nephew. ✳

Chapter 6

AUNTS IN THE MOVIES

BY BILL COLLINS

Bill Collins.

*There is no better person in the world to tell us about these favourite
and famous aunts in the movies than film buff extraordinaire, 'Mr Movies'
himself, Bill Collins. His must surely be one of the best known faces
television has ever produced. His infectious smile, his jackets of different
hues and, of course, his wonderful descriptions of movies that whet the
appetite for what is to come — all are trademarks unparalleled. Add to
that his extraordinary knowledge of the silver screen, which he passes on
through his newspaper columns, videos and television and radio programs,
and we have 'the total package'! So with verve, warmth and humour
Bill Collins presents, in his inimitable style, his favourite aunts...*

*M*Y FAVOURITE AUNTS? AUNTIE Lil must come first. Without Auntie Lil in my life, I might not be writing for this book now, or presenting movies about wonderful aunts on television.

Auntie Lil was an usherette at our local picture theatre when I was growing up, and I would unequivocally count her as the single most powerful influence on my subsequent career. Through Auntie Lil and her always-available seat in the stalls, I discovered the magic of movies and many unforgettable movie aunts.

There are so many of them I hardly know where to start, but here are just a few that remain indelibly printed on my memory of movies past — and for that matter, movies present, because great movies never die. These films, and these aunts, are as fresh today as when they first enchanted me.

In George Cukor's 1935 production of Charles Dickens' *David Copperfield*, Edna May Oliver is unforgettable as Aunt Betsy Trotwood. Edna May Oliver was truly a Dickensian woman, as she

Freddie Bartholomew as David, Lennox Pawle as Mr Dick and Edna May Oliver as Aunt Betsy Trotwood in 'David Copperfield' (MGM/UA).

Clara Blandwick as Auntie Em, Judy Garland as Dorothy, holding Toto, Margaret Hamilton as Miss Gulch and Charley Grapewin as Uncle Henry in the 'Wizard Of Oz' (MGM/UA).

proved again in *A Tale Of Two Cities*, and always played marvellous spinsters and aunts.

And who can forget Auntie Em? When Judy Garland, as Dorothy, returned from her trip to Oz in *The Wizard Of Oz*, Auntie Em was waiting with open arms. As played by Clara Blandwick, she was living proof that there was indeed 'no place like home'.

Judy's frequent co-star and lifelong friend Mickey Rooney also had a very special movie aunt — Sara Haden as schoolteacher Aunt Milly, who appeared in all but two of the Andy Hardy series, even returning in *Andy Hardy Comes Home* in the 1950s. During my screenings of the series on television, I even had viewers write asking for patterns for her dresses, or at the very least pictures of them!

Of course, no list of movie aunts would be complete without Rosalind Russell as Auntie Mame — the aunt we'd all like to have, even if we wouldn't exactly want her living with us! When author Patrick Dennis wrote his novel, he had Rosalind Russell in mind, and in the 1958 film version she is magnificently, outrageously

Rosalind Russell as Auntie Mame in the original screen production (Warner Bros).

Lucille Ball as Auntie Mame in the musical film entitled simply 'Mame' (Warner Bros).

gowned by Australian Orry-Kelly, the Kiama boy who became one of the greatest of all costume designers in the Golden Years of Hollywood. Auntie Mame has also been played on stage by such notable performers as Beatrice Lillie, Greer Garson, Constance Bennett and Sylvia Sydney.

In the movie musical version, called simply *Mame*, in 1973, Lucille Ball made her last big-screen appearance in the title role, following in the footsteps of Angela Lansbury, who had taken New York by storm in the original Broadway production. Ann Miller was also terrific as Mame on Broadway.

I am sure everybody knows that *Gone With The Wind* is my favourite movie of all time — and it features one of my favourite movie aunts, Aunt Pittypat, played by Laura Hope Crews. I have even been with my wife Joan to a restaurant called Aunt Pittypat's, near the Peachtree Plaza Hotel in Atlanta, Georgia, the city that figures so vitally in *Gone With The Wind*.

Not all movie aunts are filled with the milk of human kindness, of course, and I am thinking here of Jean Adair and Josephine Hull, repeating their Broadway success as the two lethal old ladies in the

Laura Hope Crews as Aunt Pittypat in 'Gone With The Wind', with Olivia de Havilland as her niece Melanie (MGM/UA).

celluloid version of *Arsenic And Old Lace* in 1942. And yet, murderous though they may be, they are oddly lovable. In early 1991, two of Australia's great ladies of the theatre, June Bronhill and Gwen Plumb, played the deadly old dears in a stage revival.

Most of us think of Margaret Rutherford, that great eccentric of British films and theatre, as Agatha Christie's Miss Marple, but in 1954, several years before she became Miss Marple, she starred in a charming little British film called *Aunt Clara*. Adapted by noted comedian Kenneth Horne from a novel by Noel Streatfield, and directed by Anthony Kimmins, *Aunt Clara* also stars such great British players as A. E. Matthews, Ronald Shiner, Fay Compton and Raymond Huntley — who could all give Margaret Rutherford a run for her money in the eccentricity stakes.

Another great British aunt is Maggie Smith, Oscar-nominated for her portrayal of Aunt Augusta in *Travels With My Aunt*, a 1972 film version of Graham Greene's novel, directed by George Cukor.

Josephine Hull and Jean Adair as Cary Grant's aunts in 'Arsenic And Old Lace', with Edward Everett Horton (MGM/UA).

Margaret Rutherford in the title role of 'Aunt Clara', with Anthony Christoforou as Albert, Jack Emblow as Sidney and Barbara Archer as their girlfriend Jessie (London Films).

Maggie Smith as Aunt Augusta in 'Travels With My Aunt' (MGM).

Greer Garson as Aunt March in the made-for-television movie 'Little Women' (Universal).

There was a lot of Auntie Mame in Aunt Augusta, as she led her straitlaced nephew, played by Alec McCowen, on a whirlwind tour of Europe.

Like Margaret Rutherford and Miss Marple, the lovely Greer Garson is always associated with the character of Mrs Miniver, but I also remember with great affection her performance as Aunt March

77

Jack Benny as Babbs (posing as Charley's Aunt) and Kay Francis as the real aunt Donna
Lucia, in the 1941 movie 'Charley's Aunt' (Twentieth Century-Fox).

in *Little Women*, a stunning 1978 made-for-television movie in which
Greer made her television movie debut, in company with such fine
young talent as Susan Dey of *LA Law*, Meredith Baxter Birney of
Family Ties and Eve Plumb of *The Brady Bunch*. Add to this list
Robert Young and Dorothy McGuire, and you have a version of
Louisa May Alcott's novel which can hold its head high. But Greer
is still the best reason for seeing it.

Finally, one of the most famous aunts in the history of show
business — an aunt who wasn't an aunt! I refer, of course, to
Charley's Aunt, the indefatigable Victorian farce by Brandon Thomas
that has been a staple of amateur (and professional) theatre groups
for more years than most of us can remember. She's the 'invented'
aunt from Brazil (where the nuts come from!), and has been imper-
sonated on the screen by Arthur Askey, Ray Bolger and, most
memorably, by Jack Benny in Archie Mayo's 1941 production, in

Cecelia Parker as Marian, Lewis Stone as Judge Hardy, Sara Haden as Aunt Milly, Fay Holden as Emily Hardy and Mickey Rooney as Andy Hardy in 'The Courtship Of Andy Hardy'.

which the real aunt is played by the lovely Kay Francis.

So there you are. Wonderful movie aunts, all of them — and really only a mere handful among the many who should be included. But they are all special to me, and I know they are special to many, many other people. I thank them all for the hours of pleasure they have given me — and I thank Auntie Lil for bringing them into my life. ✳

PART TWO

A CELEBRATION OF AUNTS

Not A Bit Like A Saturday

A Personal Recollection By
MAREA STENMARK

*I*F THERE WAS ONE THING MY aunt did better than anyone else, it was make the best cup of tea. It was a ritual. First she would select the cups, a variety of sizes, shapes and colours for different members of the family. My father, Ossie, liked his strong and dark in the biggest cup possible. Next came my mother, Marcella, who favoured a small pastel-coloured cup in the finest bone china. She claimed the colour altered the flavour. My eldest brother Jim had his own large special cup too, and my brother Tony's was different again. My sister Anne would be given the daintiest of cups, even though she always had several refills, and the ceremony would be completed by my aunt's pronouncement, 'and that's Ree's ... with the spoon'! I estimate, conservatively, she would have used that expression over one thousand times.

Whilst Mum would insist on using our full names, our aunt would always abbreviate them. So, as long as I can remember, she called me 'Ree' rather than Marea.

We were a family of four children and I was the youngest member. Two boys and two girls, nicely balanced. Finally, I joined the land of the living. Jim had married and his first child had arrived by the time I was a teenager. Consequently, I have spent most of my life as an aunt and am still enjoying the challenges which continue to come along in great variety. Of course, there are times...!

Marea Stenmark.

As far back as I can recall I had an aunt, not many aunts, just one — my mother's only sister, younger by a few years. She was an important link in the family structure: gentle, kind, musical and always interested in and enthused by everything we, her nieces and nephews, did — especially our theatrical activities. When rehearsals were held at our home she would listen unashamedly as we sang round the piano and would be the first to tell us if she considered our harmony to be less than perfect.

Her name was Eileen and in the early stages we called her Aunty, then Aunt. As teenagers she became Eileen, next came Eile Pile, then Fair Isle (yes, she was a good knitter) and finally, companionably, Eile. She was an elevating influence and the least critical person I have known, always quite content to be surrounded by her sister's children and their friends. She, together with Mum and Dad, represented emotional security to us. She came to every family frolic, and there were many over the years. She was forever singing around the house, dusting to 'Sally', washing up to 'Chu Chin Chow' and humming to 'Our Miss Gibbs' as she put on the kettle. So much so, our friends would liken their visits to comic opera.

There were countless trips to the theatre — *Annie Get Your Gun*, Gilbert and Sullivan — morning, noon and night. I particularly remember a visit to the old Theatre Royal to see *The Two Mrs Carrols*, and a special treat to see Elisabeth Bergner because she was Swedish and we were patriotic of our father's background! Later on, Anne and I introduced Eile to all the 'little theatres' of Sydney. She enjoyed them immensely, declaring the most avant-garde to be 'full of interest'. However, she always disliked plays with only one set, considering them to be dreary: 'all in the same place,' she'd declare, with a wrinkle of her nose.

Thanks to our Irish grandmother, Myra Atkinson, née Dillon, Eileen was incredibly superstitious and full of fables which she swore she didn't believe — but I have my doubts! When she first told me some of these extraordinary stories I exclaimed, 'Eile, you're dreadfully superstitious', but she simply replied, 'No Ree,

Eileen Atkinson.

it's just what I heard', which is exactly what Grandma used to say to her, only in a beautiful soft brogue, which came out, 'Noo Aileen, it's just what I haird'! If you rose on Saturday morning and told Eile that you'd had a vivid dream she would quickly admonish, 'Friday night's tale on a Saturday told is bound to come true no matter how old'. So all the pleasure of telling a good gory dream was spoiled just in case she might be right! I'm afraid I am superstitious, too, and absolutely refuse to walk under a ladder or whistle in the dressing room or say the last line of a play before opening night! However, I do ignore 'Never sweep out after dark'.

As children, Anne and I would always show Eile our new clothes. Knowing how she would hate to upset anyone, I'd deliberately ask her whose outfit she preferred. Undeterred, she would reply, 'Yours suits your colouring best, Anne's suits hers best'. As a youngster I would sometimes 'play up' and test this obliging lady to the limit. She would caution me with a long look and a shake of the head, saying, 'You're rude and you don't know it', to which I would reply — absolutely proving her point — 'I do so know it'! She was a gentle soul, in many ways like a child. Even when we were children we seemed to take her hand rather than she take ours.

Mum and Eileen were great friends as well as sisters. They were reputed to look very much alike and went to lots of places together. Sometimes people would stop them in the street if they were on their own, mistaking one of them for the other. They devised what we children called a 'Do Mrs Plan', which meant they would smile and nod to anyone who looked in their direction and mumble 'Do Mrs'. That, of course, was an abbreviation of 'How do you do, Mrs whatever-name-they-had-forgotten'. My brother Tony and I still say 'Do Mrs' when we haven't a clue of the name of any woman to whom we are speaking. I don't know what sign we had back then for unknown men!

Eileen once told me that as a child she used to stroke her hair with the palm of her hand one hundred times daily to maintain its shine. It paid off because she and Mum both looked so pretty with their dark shiny hair as they sang and harmonised duets at Sydney soirées or around the piano at home. As sometimes happens with musical sisters, their voices blended magnificently, and over many decades they brought enormous joy to great numbers of people. When they were young women they both gave recitals at the Conservatorium Of Music in Sydney, and all through our childhood and into our teens, and even later, we would listen to the best renditions of 'Perfect Day', 'Oft In The Stilly Night' and the inevitable 'Heigh Ho, Come To The Fair', with Mum not only harmonising but providing the musical accompaniment, while Eile stood, straight and serene, at her side. As immature youngsters we tended to laugh at them and send them up. But as we got a little older and, hopefully, developed a modicum of maturity, we realised what incredible musicians they were and why anyone who knew about music considered them to be quite sensational.

I remember, as just a little girl, winning the junior school singing competition with a rendition of 'Who Was Dorothy Perkins?'. When I got to the line about 'give her name to a rose', nothing could go wrong: Mum, who tutored me, had made certain of that during the practice sessions by literally putting her finger into my mouth so that the vowel 'o' would come out as '*roese*' instead of 'rowse'. I had the best 'o' vowel in the world because of Mum's finger!

Eile was a dreadful card player, while Mum and Dad both came from a strong 'solo' school — they always counted their trumps and knew precisely what card was in which person's hand. Not so Eile. She never counted how many trumps had gone and, therefore, always botched up the system. She would take an embarrassingly long time to sort her hand, still longer to make up her mind which card she would play next, then she would look at Dad and say in a small voice — I'm not sure whether hopelessly or defiantly — 'I think I'll do *that*'. Dad would stare straight ahead endeavouring to be polite, but even from right across the other side of the room I could hear his teeth gnash! As children we used to hear the three of them playing cribbage: 'Fifteen two, fifteen four, fifteen six — and a pair's eight!' I still don't understand the importance of these words but they still ring in my ears.

Dad was terribly fond of Eileen even though he used to speak of her in jest. I remember a letter I received from him, when I was living overseas, in which he described events at home: 'Eileen continues to state the obvious, then repeat herself, then explain it'. If Eileen realised that we, lovingly, made fun of her, she took no notice whatsoever and just went on being herself. She was always the first to 'sniff out' a southerly. In the midst of almost anything Eileen's nose would give a most delicate twitch followed by a gentle sniff before she would utter, 'A southerly' — and, sure enough, a few minutes later the air would be cooler. It was surprising really, because she wasn't from the land; it was just something she instinctively knew. One night, when she sniffed and Anne said, 'Don't tell me we're going to have another southerly', Eileen fixed her with the same straight glance for which she was known and said, 'No, Anne, I think the chops are burning'. Yes, she was always good humoured and always expected everyone else to be so, too.

I remember Mum and Eileen taking up smoking when they were both well into their fifties. For the life of me I can't think why they did it, because they were ladies after all, but smoke they did and continued this habit almost until the time they died. Knowing that it would offend their mother, they never smoked in front of her. But Grandma Atkinson wasn't anybody's fool and she said one night in a very sophisticated tone of voice: 'How much do cigarettes cost, Eileen?' There was a pause before Eile replied with a shrug of her shoulders as she made for the door, 'Oh, different prices, Mother'. Anne and I still say 'different prices, Mother' to each other when we don't want to divulge the price of something. Many of our friends have borrowed that quote! It reminded me that, as children, whenever we asked Eile a question she didn't want to or couldn't answer, quick as a flash she would reply, 'Ask your Mother', and change the subject.

Mind you, Eile got her own back one night when Grandma was walking purposefully out of the kitchen and Eileen asked her where she was going? Obviously heading for the bathroom, Grandma didn't even bother to turn around as she delivered over her left shoulder, 'Some place, Eileen'!

I often used to ponder over Grandma's comments. As an elderly lady she would watch me as a teenager racing round the house, setting off for tennis matches, hurrying to rehearsals, getting ready for a Ball, and she would beam and say, "'Tis a wonderful thing to be young', but, musingly, she'd follow this remark up with, 'What a pity youth is wasted on youth'. Obviously, she was of the opinion that if the joys of youth — beauty, health, vitality — could be given to older mortals who were not so spry and alert, they would do more good, would be handled with more wisdom. I wonder. I guess we'll never find out whether she was right or otherwise!

I never knew Eileen to write a letter. In fact, rarely did she even sign her name. All the time I was living overseas or was away, I would receive these wonderful letters from Mum in her own flourishing writing and down the bottom in the far right-hand corner would be one word in a different coloured pen, and certainly a different hand, namely 'Eileen'. But I knew she followed every single thing I did, and that I was never very far from her thoughts, so the fact that she didn't write a letter meant nothing.

Last thing at night, in summer, Eileen would spray the room for Grandma so she wouldn't be bothered by mosquitoes. Outside, Anne and I couldn't wait for her to raise her voice and say, 'Close your eyes, Mother'. As soon as we heard these words the concert was over, so to speak, and whenever I spray a room to this day, even if I am on my own, I feel the need to say right out loud, to some unsuspecting mosquito, 'Close your eyes, Mother'.

Eileen was softly and well spoken. She didn't use rough language — I don't think she even knew any rough words. The most she could handle when she was really annoyed was 'Bust it'! One night she said 'damn' in quite a loud voice and when I looked at her in utter astonishment she added without missing a beat, 'the river, blast the rock and blow the fire to blazes', attempting to explain to a stupid child that what she was saying made perfect sense if used in context. The worst word she ever said was 'strewth', still very politely, and Anne and I were thrilled with her.

Apart from leaving us a windfall of wonderful Irish expressions, she disliked sloppy speech and would be horrified at children being 'bought up' ('there's an "r" in that word', I can hear her say) or the 'goverment' ('where is the "n"?'). And she would rue the pronunciation, if you'll forgive the pun, of 'Febuary'. She simply would not recognise 'rekkernise' and would be aghast at 'also, too'. If she were to hear me speak today with a constant upward inflection, I know she would ask me to repeat my question. But I do share with her a dislike of not being addressed by name.

It was Eileen who inculcated in me the need for distinct and sharp consonants in both speech and singing. She would musically illustrate the difference between the 'd's' and the 't's', and our 'n's' positively *zinged*! It was an invaluable lesson and made all the difference in the world to our diction generally and, of course, to our stage work. Even today, as I mentally correct everyone who ignores consonants, I can see vividly in my mind's eye the expression on Eileen's face. If anyone asked her if she had a clear 'pitcher' of something, I know she would think they meant a transparent container! She would turn in her grave to hear people today, even on radio and television, referring to 'Austraia' — in fact, she might even be tempted to exclaim, 'where the "l" is the "l"'! Today, when I hear 'rider' and 'writer', 'file' and 'fail', 'mistake' and 'mystique', 'warder' and 'water', and 'winner' and 'winter' pronounced indistinguishably, I'm convinced she has a point. Why do we hear 'munts' instead of 'months', and when was the last time we were given a 't' in 'innernational'? I must stop. I'm making her sound like a tartar rather than someone who simply loved the Queen's English and wanted us all to pronounce it correctly.

Just as Eileen's speech was never sloppy, nor was her dress. She was always in 'a good frock' ready to receive, with lipstick carefully applied, a touch of rouge (before blusher made an appearance), hair well brushed and a smile on her face. She and Mum were always dressed to go out, each claiming 'all I have to do is put my hat on'. If that remark were true, then it took them a very long time to do so because Dad was always saying, through clenched teeth, 'Set,

Chick? ... waiting in the car'!

Eileen was never formidable. On the contrary, she was always approachable, keen to have a chat and an excellent listener. She never told me what to do but would simply ask at the end of my spiel, 'What are you going to do, Ree?' — and somehow, because I'd talked the problem out, I'd found the answer. A wise woman.

She was the quintessential peace-maker, gentle, calm and serene. She had the smallest sneeze I have ever heard — it was an apology for a sneeze — like its owner, it too was gentle, calm and serene.

Another lovable characteristic I remember of Eile is that she always spoke beautifully of each of us to the other. She would say to me, 'You know, Ree, Anne is a marvellous girl, she's so intelligent, so appealing and so thoughtful', and elaborate on Anne's virtues in sheer admiration. When our two brothers married, she would speak of their wives just as charitably: 'There's no doubt about Tess, Ree, she's a wonderful person, wonderful housekeeper, has a wonderful sense of humour, a wonderful temperament', 'Pat is a beautiful creature, Ree, so full of good humour, always good natured and so pretty'. Then I would ask, 'And what do you say to them about me, Eile?' Unabashed, she replied, 'Ree can have a thing done whilst another person is still thinking about it'. Years later I put it to her again, 'Eile, is there any advance on "Ree can have a thing done whilst another person is still thinking about it"?' She insisted with a warm smile, 'It's true, Ree, and you know it'.

One of Eile's idiosyncracies was that every time 'visitors' were coming (as opposed to people who 'dropped in' constantly) she would remove the existing toilet roll — which she always referred to as 'toilet tissue' — and replace it with a new one. Years later, when she moved house and we were helping her to pack, I counted no fewer than forty-eight half used toilet rolls which fell out of a plastic bag to greet us.

She was very much a creature of habit, slow to change, liking certain things to happen on certain days. When they didn't occur exactly as planned, she would shake her head and sigh, 'Ah, Ree, it's not a bit like a Saturday'!

Not only did all our family love Eileen, but our friends did, too. The good humour and goodwill and the loving attitude she extended to others certainly came back to her twofold. Recently an old family friend was musing about our growing up days and said, 'I often think of Miss Atkinson'. I looked up in surprise. To everyone else she was Aunty or Aunty Eile, but to him she was 'Miss Atkinson', and he couldn't help adding: 'and she was one of the nicest people I have ever met'.

Yes, she was an extremely nice person — a lovely aunt who would pick up a cloth and clean my silver because she knew it was a job I loathed. She was a friend who not only made a wonderful cup of tea, but the best dark brown gravy with no lumps in it. And she would put heaps of butter on my toast. Her first routine question after every function we attended was, 'Many there?', not that it made any difference if our answer were three or three hundred — she just wanted us to know that she was involved and interested.

In the later years of her life, when necessity demanded that she be placed in a nursing home, she was cared for most beautifully by the nuns in the Home Of Compassion at Wagga Wagga in New South Wales. There I would visit her and she would go through my long list of friends — many friendships spanning several decades. Taking up the threads again she would question: 'Who else, Ree? How is Margaret? Didn't she marry a pharmacist? They had several children, didn't they? Was it four girls? I thought so. Do they still live on the south coast? And who do the children look like, Ree? Are they fair or dark?' And on she would go, always interested, always caring, wanting to know as much or as little as we cared to tell her.

Towards the end, after suffering a slight cerebral spasm, she walked very slowly with the aid of a frame. I would accompany her down a long corridor on the way to the car for a drive. Each time I asked a question she would stop walking to answer me. At first I was utterly charming and gentle as I encouraged her, 'Come on, Eile, keep walking'. Then, when it seemed an interminable time later and we had progressed only minimally, I would ask her something else. Again, she would stop walking and provide the answer. On the third occasion, when it was becoming quite apparent that our afternoon drive was disappearing because we had still not left the hospital corridor, I exclaimed in utter exasperation, 'Come on, Eile — walk, *and* talk'. A beautiful smile came over her face as she calmly replied — stopping, of course, to do so — 'You haven't changed one little bit, Ree'. If only we had another chance to be more considerate and sensitive — two attributes I was certainly taught but on occasions have overlooked. The beauty of Eile, though, was that she loved you unconditionally.

Eileen was not the wittiest aunt in the world, and she was not the most eccentric. Nor was she the cleverest and perhaps she wasn't even the most interesting, but she was the one and only aunt we had and we loved her accordingly. I continue to miss her and whenever I hear any of her songs a lump comes to my throat immediately. I remember her kindness, I remember her goodness, I remember her caring attitude; and I remember the fact that she loved to be with us and all our friends and associates. I do not remember one nasty thing. Of course, she wasn't without faults. She was often inflexible and infuriating, stubborn as a mule and quite unable to be hurried if she didn't want to be, but she had such a softness and sweetness to her that one couldn't remain infuriated for long. She even smelled sweetly — I can savour her fragrance now as I write.

In 1991, after my Investiture at Government House, some wonderful friends gave me a memorable party in a private function room at a Sydney hotel. It was a rare day, and an event I'll never forget. In due course, speeches — warm, clever, genuine speeches — were made by equally warm, clever and genuine friends. Good times were recalled, with Eileen's name being mentioned on several occasions. Remarks like 'she graced the home', 'she was always pleased to see you' and 'what a calm, gracious person she was' filtered through the conversation. She left us all a legacy of serenity and truth. Yes, aunts do have a lasting effect.

As the expression goes, 'she was always there for us'. I just hope, especially in latter years, that we were there for her.

Eileen Atkinson died peacefully, as she had lived, on the nineteenth day of April 1983 at the age of eighty-two. Through our tears we all agreed, it wasn't a bit like a Tuesday. ✳

AUNTY WIN AND HER PRECIOUS LAMB

BY GORDON CHATER

English-born but Australian-claimed, Gordon Chater has entertained and made Australians laugh — despite the importance of being earnest — for decades. He had a close affinity with his aunt, who aided and abetted him on his way to stardom.

M Y FATHER HAD A LOT OF brothers and sisters. The men of the family, including the in-laws, were relatively successful; all in 'respectable' professions like The Church, The Armed Services, The Stock Exchange or Medicine — and they had children programmed to follow in their respectable footsteps: *except me*. From age five, when Mother took me to Drury Lane because she couldn't get a sitter, I announced my intention of a life upon the stage. My father, his brothers and my cousins all felt their respectability had been violated: the whole family was alarmed — with one exception, Aunty Winifred, married to my father's brother, the Surgeon Rear-Admiral (who clicked his teeth and said 'Little Boys Should Be Seen and Not Heard').

Once Aunty Win had heard of my aspirations I believe she thought of me as an ally: secretly she had always wanted to be an actress. She spoke with booming clarity and even if she walked from the dining table to the sideboard it was as if she were making a grand entrance. The hips revolved slightly — the toes were turned out — the floor knew it was being stepped on.

She was a devoted wife and mother, and I became a second son — a special son — and to the day she died in 1972, when I was fifty, she called me, boomingly, in public and private, 'My Precious Lamb'. Of course I loved her. She understood about the theatre. I

Gordon Chater.

could hardly wait to be asked to stay with her and Uncle Harold in their home at Southsea, next to Portsmouth.

Before retirement they had been stationed in China and the house was full of mementoes. I especially remember a series of different sized china Buddhas because they, along with Aunty Win, were my first audience as I gave my impression of Arthur Prince and Elsie, whom Aunty Win had taken me to see headlining at the Southsea Hippodrome. I was six.

Time passed. Uncle Harold died and cousin Gerald (their son and my favourite cousin) was killed in the last moments of World War II. But no matter where I was, Aunty Win always wrote to 'My Precious Lamb' — and when I had compromised with the family and was studying medicine at Cambridge she would write: 'You *will* end up in the theatre. I know. And I shall come to your first nights. Train your voice reading the bible *loud* and *clear* — don't believe any of it, just *read* it!' (She was an atheist as well as a paragon of rectitude and compassion.)

I came to Australia in 1946. Aunty Win and I kept up our friendship by letter. Things were not easy for her on a small Admiralty pension but she never moaned — just lived simply and did crosswords. After my father died and my mother moved into a 'Separate Tables' hotel on the coast of England, Aunty Win was almost the only member of the remaining family to visit her, at great cost to herself, and effort — the bus trip from Petersfield, in Hampshire where she now lived, was long and a strain on the pension fund. She wrote to me constantly about my mother, whose memory was becoming a little bizarre: one letter said 'Eva [my mother] says she cannot understand why you are in Malta'. I had been worried that the lifelong weekly letters from my mother had ceased. Then my mother died, and there was a bundle of letters in her room returned to her, addressed to me in Elizabeth Bay, New South Wales, Malta.

To try to return a modicum of Aunty Win's kindness to me I shouted her a trip with me to New York in the 1950s, on the *Queen Elizabeth*, and when we parted I arranged for her to visit her relatives in Montreal. She was up in years now, but still booming, still a leading lady. Flowing evening gowns from the twenties at dinner every night on the ship, dangle-down earrings as big as chandeliers — 'Take my arm, My Precious Lamb, and watch the heads turn as you escort me down the main staircase to dinner'. On arrival at Pier 90, thirty years ago, regulation demanded the opening of every case for customs. Aunty Win got out of that with a dramatic feigned heart attack — a tremendously successful performance which not only got us passed through customs quickly but found us the elusive cab. Once in that she was booming again, 'Oh, My Precious Lamb, this is so *exciting!*'

We were staying at the now sadly missed New Weston Hotel. Having registered, we got in the elevator when, as the doors closed, Aunty Win espied the black elevator operator. She boomed: 'Stop the lift! I have never been in the same room with a nigger!' — shades of all the coolies at her beck and call on the China station.

In those days funds travellers could take out of England were limited, but my travel agent said I could pay the hotel bill by English cheque — so it was to our advantage to eat in the hotel. 'Much too expensive!' boomed Aunty Win, 'Let's find somewhere cheaper.' To please her I showed her Schraffts and the Automat. 'Too common!' she said, so I told her: 'Darling Aunty Win, you choose — anywhere you like.' Finally she saw a place that she thought economical and acceptable and we ate there. It was only the then very expensive and exclusive Sardis East!

I took her to Radio City Music Hall, and when the lovers kissed in the movie her voice boomed loud enough to be heard on the

Avenue Of The Americas — '*Disgusting*'!

When finally the moment came for me to say *au revoir* to her on the train for Montreal at Grand Central I settled her in her 'roomette' and went in search of the conductor — a charming sixtyish, white-haired, fatherly black man. I gave him twenty dollars and asked him to look after Aunty Win. Five minutes later as we sat talking, a little sad at parting, the conductor put his head round the door. 'Evethin' OK?' 'Fine, thank you,' and he left. Aunty Win grabbed me: '*He's* not looking after me? He's a nigger* — he'll rape me!' I couldn't resist, 'Wishful thinking, darling!' Later she wrote that his 'exquisite manners and concern for my welfare have completely altered my attitude towards niggers*'.

I never saw her again. She wrote. Then her friends wrote. I became aware that her paltry fixed pension was inadequate and, as tactfully and as often as work permitted me, I sent her cheques: 'Just had a windfall — thought you might like to have a dinner on me'. She was a very proud elderly boomer now!

And then in 1972 a solicitor's letter came to me in Australia: 'You are one of two beneficiaries in Mrs Winifred Chater's will.' I wrote back thanking him for his letter but declining any cameo or watercolour or trinket she might have left me — I have spent the last twenty years divesting myself of Things. I had underestimated her: she had managed, on my behalf, to save and leave me nineteen thousand pounds! *

* Publisher's Note: Whilst the term 'nigger' is both antiquated and considered offensive today, it accurately reflects attitudes of the time.

AUNTIE MAUDE

BY COLLEEN McCULLOUGH

Colleen McCullough, Australian author of international acclaim, was educated in Sydney. Since her marriage, she has lived on Norfolk Island where the peace and natural beauty of her surroundings provide her with the perfect lifestyle for writing bestsellers. One after another!

I COME FROM AN ALMOST exclusively male family, so aunts were in very short supply — short to the point of non-existence. Except, that is, for Auntie Maude. When one is a child — especially forty-five to fifty years ago — one does not question relationships. To me, Auntie Maude simply belonged to Uncle Spence; he was the blood relation, she was not. Further than that I never thought to go until after I was well and truly grown.

Uncle Spence was the eldest of Mother's enormous number of brothers, and undoubtedly the family Black Sheep. A diminutive, beautifully built man of the very dark kind both inside and out, his jet black hair was slicked back like patent leather on either side of a centre parting; he had wickedly gleaming narrow black eyes, and a sinister glitter of gold in his smile from the fillings in his teeth. It is hard to remember his lineaments, but I don't remember his being at all handsome; that he must have been very attractive to women I now understand. By temperament he was a genuine devil. Hopelessly addicted to alcohol, he had a short fuse at the best of times, and when he erupted it was always with extreme violence. By occupation he had been a professional boxer and then a professional bartender; the last did not help his drinking problem.

As a toddler, I loathed Uncle Spence. This attitude of mine seems to have stemmed from the time when he lay mortally ill in hospital and I had listened to macabre women's talk of tubes and syringes and bags and blood, but upon his recovery he didn't help me to overcome my antipathy. Instead he selected me as the chief victim for his practical jokes. Once he chased me everywhere with a sheaf of burning paper, threatening to set me alight; once he brandished a huge pair of scissors and threatened to cut off my toes; once he thrust a giant lolly down my throat and nearly choked me. Perhaps tiny children sense evil where none exists, but I always believed he would do what he said he was going to do because I thought him evil. His last practical joke (we moved after this back to the country) was his worst. He found me proudly wearing a new cardigan my mother had knitted me out of bright red wool. It had the cutest buttons — little red padlocks. Uncle Spence inspected them closely, then took a tiny key from his fob pocket and laboriously locked me into my new red cardigan.

'Ha, ha, you'll never get out of it!' he cried, swallowing the key with slow relish before my very eyes.

Hours later I was found hiding in the coke shed, crying my eyes out, convinced that I was forever locked into my cardigan. Of course everyone thought it a huge joke. But I didn't.

Only the prospect of Auntie Maude made the thought of Uncle Spence bearable; as much as I loathed him did I adore her. But being a noticing sort of child, it never failed to puzzle me why whenever Uncle Spence and Auntie Maude were expected, my mother and grandmother fell into a frenzied orgy of cleaning and dusting, of positioning the antimacassars and the ornaments, of making sure the best tea-things were taken out, of making and icing delicious little cakes. For no one else did they do this; only for Auntie Maude. As I was an inquisitive child as well as a noticing one, I early realised that neither my mother nor my grandmother *liked* Auntie Maude. I couldn't understand it! But there they would be before her visit, muttering about her under their breath as they rushed around making the dust fly, their tones disapproving, all their exclamations ones of horror and disgust at her advent.

The pieces fell into place after I was grown up and had ceased to live at home. Auntie Maude was not my Uncle Spence's wife!

Auntie Maude was my Uncle Spence's mistress! *They lived in sin!* A worse crime by far than murder or rape, especially because it was Uncle Spence who was the bludger, not Auntie Maude — he lived with and off her, not the other way around. *And she was older than he was!* If anything had been needed to reinforce my conviction that being a man's mistress was far more intriguing and glamorous than being his wife, the family's reaction to Auntie Maude was it. For benefit of Auntie Maude our house got cleaned backwards, frontwards and sideways; for benefit of Auntie Maude the best china and glassware came out of otherwise permanent storage; for benefit of Auntie Maude yummy cakes were made and the conversation over the teacups was arch, bright, feverish, gushing, artificial.

Auntie Maude was Jewish, a fact she made no secret of or apology for; she was the only Jewish person I ever knew as a child, and made me wish fervently that I was Jewish too. She was so wonderful, you see. Not tall (she was even shorter than Uncle Spence), she was very fat and very jolly. Such humour! Such liveliness! Such exquisite manners! Such good taste! She dressed superbly, down to the colour of her gloves and the selection of brooch or earrings. I remember the Victory outfit she wore to celebrate the end of the War, all in red, white and blue; her shoes were white kid with navy toes and heels and laces made from broad scarlet ribbons, her skirt was navy, her blouse white silk, her jacket scarlet. And her hat was a white felt creation shaped like a soldier's slouch hat, with a navy puggaree around the base of its crown and two stiff scarlet feathers; her gloves were navy kid, as was her bag. And it had all been put together with that indefinable touch which knows no impediments of figure or face — a sense of *style*. Even when she became a very old lady she kept her sense of style, she still looked like a million dollars.

Auntie Maude's voice was deep, melodious, and her accent completely pear-shaped — fraightfulleh-fraightfulleh, you'd say. But more than these vocal joys, Auntie Maude could sing. And did sing. In our austere, repressed, undemonstrative world where everyone's chief dread was to be noticed, the very fact that Auntie

Colleen McCullough.

Maude would sing the moment you asked was a minor miracle; here was a person who didn't give a damn about that dreadful solecism, 'making an exhibition of yourself'. Her singing was one of the great treats of my young life. As for her trips to California on the *Monterey* or the *Mariposa* — I drank up her descriptions of them. She was my exemplar, as I yearned even then to be noticed, and was already showing all sorts of unpalatable tendencies towards what my family considered exhibitionism — I spoke out of turn, I had opinions, I was not humble or self-effacing. In fact, I was a darned sight more like Auntie Maude than any member of my family! It would be interesting to know how much of my later indifference to the fact that I was fat could be laid at Auntie Maude's door; quite a lot, I suspect. Auntie Maude was not only my sole exposure to Jewishness, she was also the only fat person I knew save for myself.

Memory is elusive. Not one of the many conversations she had with us when she visited can I conjure up, yet my mind insists that she was highly intelligent and educated, witty, well-read and utterly charming. Extremely wealthy (she owned a good deal of property in inner Sydney), she lived in an old three-storeyed terrace house and was never without three or four mongrel dogs of various sizes — always males, and always referred to as 'The Boys'. When she visited us The Boys came with her, much to the irritation of my mother and grandmother, who regarded dogs as dirty smelly creatures which rounded up stock and lived in kennel runs. Had Auntie Maude been Uncle Spence's wife rather than his mistress, I am sure The Boys would never have been permitted to enter our house; as it was, they bounced inside with the same zest and innocence as Auntie Maude did.

But as the years slipped away and all of us became older, Uncle Spence's mental and moral disintegration intensified. He beat Auntie Maude mercilessly — something he had always done from time to time, but now was a regular manifestation of his continuous cups. After a particularly bad drubbing, Auntie Maude would come out to see my mother and grandmother, wearing dark glasses to hide her black eyes, and sit there weeping bitterly. Not so much complaining as seeking support and consolation. My family being kind-hearted (if mortified by this unorthodox liaison), comfort was always given her. Looking back, I can only marvel at the degree of what must have been her loneliness and lack of friends. To be a man's mistress instead of his wife in those times was a status precluding much respectable company, and her own family lived far away in Melbourne.

In 1963, I left Australia. Like so much else and so many other people, Auntie Maude faded into the blurred pattern of an epoch quite finished for me. I heard about her only when something of major import happened. Like the death of Uncle Spence, so tough and durable that he managed to live into his eighties. And after he died, though the beatings were over and the undeniable strain of living with him had vanished, Auntie Maude ceased to sing, to be jolly, to get about. Now it was my mother and grandmother who visited her in her home; whatever he was, Uncle Spence had mattered enormously to Auntie Maude.

Auntie Maude is dead now. Whatever chances she might have had to ensure immortality passed her by; her only children were The Boys. But in this small tribute of mine, gone though she may be, perhaps I can ensure her a measure of remembrance. *Ave atque vale*, Auntie Maude. I love you still. And I thank you. ✳

AUNT LILY'S GINGER WINE

BY LEN EVANS

*Bon vivant, wit, author, restaurateur, wine buff and popular host,
Len Evans had a soul mate in his Aunt Lily.*

*I*T WASN'T THAT AUNT LILY drank too much. Some, more
Rabelaisian, members of the family felt she didn't drink enough.
It wasn't that she drank often. But when she did drink she did it
with all the protocol and fastidiousness of the true connoisseur.
And what she mostly drank then was her own wine. Ginger wine.

Aunt Lily, you see, did not own a chateau in Bordeaux, a strip of
great Burgundian vineyard or even a patch of the increasing vineyards of Old England. Yet she was a winemaker, and she tended to
her craft with great care. And she made her wine from fresh ginger.

Aunt Lily, though married, behaved as a spinster as far as our
family was concerned. On a visit to us she would be immaculately
well-dressed yet would take no place in the foreground, the battle-
field of family play. Rather, she would hover and occasionally
snipe. Yet when one visited her, she dominated; dominated with
kindness and every courtesy and consideration, no matter how
restricting. One behaved as one should. The rewards, it has to be
said, were considerable — magnificent chocolate eclairs, incredible
meringues, deep-mixed fruit cake to fill up with, and delicious milk
coffee. And, at a comparatively young age, a thimble glass of her
ginger wine, fiery yet soft, sweet yet biting. It was offered with all
due pomp and circumstance, and was not hurried over. Indeed, I
can remember long chats with the wine in the glass before us,

Len Evans.

sinking as slowly as the sea.

Not that Aunt Lily was a prude. I can remember when I was only four or five, inadvertently passing wind with loud sound effects, probably for the first time 'in company'. I blushed and muttered my apologies. 'Don't worry, dear,' said Aunt Lily, 'even the Queen does that sometimes.'

Years later, in fact over a half a century later, I went to see Aunt Lily for a moment, just to see how she was after the death of her devoted, background husband. She had followed my career, read my books, knew of the activities of the wine companies in which I was involved. 'Would you like a glass of wine?' she asked. I nodded and wondered what had been saved for such an occasion, the oenological equivalent of the fatted calf.

Aunt Lily returned with the identical Victorian glasses of my youth, topped with a pale yellow fluid with just a hint of green. I sniffed and sipped and my boyhood rushed at me.

'Yours?' I enquired.

'Of course, dear,' she replied. ✳

ONLY ONE AUNTIE LOTTIE

BY JEANNE LITTLE

Jeanne Little is small by name and frame but large by repute, no dispute! Entertainer, television personality and author, she and her husband — Sydney interior designer Barry Little — place great emphasis on the importance of family life. Jeanne's sense of fun comes to the fore as she describes her aunt's escapades. Madcap aunt, madcap niece!

S HE HAD MET HIM ON the boat coming to Australia and married him at sea. He was an uncouth little man with a weird Scottish accent nobody could understand, except Auntie Lottie — who was a sex maniac, Mumma maintained, and probably didn't have much need for conversation anyway. Uncle Murray was a painter and decorator but he was out of work most of the time because his wallpaper paste was always lumpy and his paint peeled off the walls in sheets. Also, he had very short arms, which must have been a disadvantage in his particular trade.

Although Mumma didn't like Uncle Murray, she felt sorry for Auntie Lottie so she gave them one of her houses to live in, telling them they could pay the rent when they could afford it. Of course, Uncle Murray never paid a cent because he was a Communist and maintained that all the wealth in the world should be equally distributed, a view Auntie Lottie shared, for although she had no political convictions of her own she believed everything her husband said — even when he told her he could have led the Party if he hadn't had the mumps when a child.

Mumma accepted the situation, but being determined to find Uncle Murray work she didn't rest until she secured him a permanent job painting the Sydney Harbour Bridge. When Uncle Murray told her he was terrified of heights she shrugged and advised him,

'Close your eyes and hang on'! She was sick of keeping him and Aunt Lottie, and perhaps felt it would do everyone a favour if he did fall off.

When he was in his sixties, Uncle Murray read that cooking in aluminium saucepans gave you cancer. He had Auntie Lottie throw all her pots and pans away and buy new enamel ones. It must have been too late, though. Ironically, a few months later he died of stomach cancer. He had been such a charmless little runt of a man that Auntie Lottie found she couldn't squeeze out a single tear and at the funeral she amazed the family by talking and laughing gaily all through the service. Instead of mourning she distracted herself by having an affair with her best friend's husband, which caused a delicious scandal while it ran its course.

Occasionally I was allowed to spend a few days of my school holidays visiting Auntie Lottie. I loved staying with her because living in the 'slums' was fascinating. Barefooted children played cricket and hopscotch in the street or tottered about on stilts made from old jam tins. Vendors trundled by with barrows of skinned rabbits, or clothes props, or blocks of ice for the funny little iceboxes the people had in their kitchens. Mumma used to carry her provisions home in a sugarbag slung over her shoulder, but here a man brought everything from fresh fruit and vegetables to groceries on the back of a truck.

Auntie Lottie did not remain a widow for long. There were a few more clandestine affairs with married men that came to nothing, then one night she met a charming old gentleman at bingo and really fell in love for the first time. Her new husband, Desmond, was quite well off — he had a nice house in a respectable suburb, and a car — and Auntie Lottie quickly became a Capitalist, declaring, 'Why should we have to pay taxes to help support all the good-for-nothings!'

Uncle Desmond was as much in love with Auntie Lottie as she was with him. He treated her like a piece of delicate china and showered her with gifts. For years she had envied Mumma her talent as a tailoress so, of course, the first thing she had Uncle Des

Auntie Lottie in her heyday.

buy for her was a fantastic sewing-machine that did a hundred different stitches. She took a crash course in dressmaking and, with a toss of her head, told Mumma there was 'nothing to it'!

'I hope it's better than her knitting' was Mumma's only comment. Auntie Lottie had always been the family knitter but her sweaters were usually so full of dropped stitches they went into holes as soon as they were worn, and she once knitted a glove with three fingers and a thumb. The first garment she made on her new sewing-machine was a jacket she cut from an old tartan overcoat. Not one check matched and, because she had forgotten to stiffen them, the lapels curled up like celery stalks in iced water. Worse

109

still, there was a buttonhole under each armpit. 'Very good to let the perspiration out,' Mumma observed drily. Another dress she made must have had the sleeves set in backwards as she couldn't raise her arms; so when she was travelling on the bus and it stopped, she had to grab hold of the nearest person to save herself from falling over. Auntie Lottie was a scream and we loved her for all her faults, but a sewer she would never be!

Perhaps the funniest thing that happened to Auntie Lottie in all her hilarious existence was at our wedding. Instead of the traditional wedding breakfast, Barry and I had a champagne party with groups of people coming and going all afternoon and the relatives supposedly leaving in the first group. But as it happened, it was one of the worst heatwaves ever and even all the wowsers consumed enormous quantities of champagne. We were frightened some of the old aunts and uncles would hurt themselves as they started to do the highland fling in the cramped Paddington terrace where Barry and I were to live. My cousin Keith offered to take them to his club for something substantial to eat, so they were herded into his van in which seats lined either side. Auntie Lottie was the last in, with the big door closing behind her. The van trundled along around several corners when the jolt of the door slamming awakened some of the sleeping passengers.

'Auntie Lottie's missing!' one of them cried. Panic struck. They poked each other until the passengers closest to the cabin banged on the window. 'Auntie Lottie's missing!' they all laughed in their silly inebriated states. Of course Keith kept driving, laughing to his wife beside him, 'All the oldies are drunk!'

After much yelling and banging he finally stopped, went round and opened the door. Old aunts and uncles poured out saying Aunt Lottie must have slipped out somewhere.

Keith quickly retraced his tracks and two blocks back, there, lying in the gutter, was Auntie Lottie, still sound asleep. They worked out that the latch hadn't quite clicked on the big van door. It must have silently slid open going around a bend, with Auntie Lottie tumbling out and rolling into the gutter, while the van continued along with the door slamming shut when it turned another corner.

The whole party picked her up and took her to St Vincent's casualty where the nurses couldn't believe such a noisy crowd had accompanied an old battered lady, but after checking all her bones she was sent home with scratches and a few elastoplasts, the bruises to follow.

It was all so dramatic that the whole van full couldn't stop laughing and returned to Barry's and my wedding which was now full of caftan-clad interior decorators, mad, outrageous friends and people we had thought ... well ... just maybe wouldn't mix well together. One guest was so sloshed that he ate my wedding bouquet. More champagne was purchased from the local pub.

Auntie Lottie made our wedding famous. I must have told this story on television a few times, and our family and friends probably related it to half of Sydney.

The next day, still worried about Auntie Lottie, I telephoned to see how she was.

'She's out at the clearance sales,' my uncle said, 'even though she looks as if she's been bashed up!' *

AUNTIES ALL OVER

BY GWEN PLUMB

*A grand 'old trouper', Gwen Plumb is well known to audiences for her
auntly role in 'Arsenic And Old Lace'. Gwen is a performer par excellence,
her shining career having embraced television, film, radio and live theatre.
Her aunts brought loving involvement to her life and have left her with
many happy memories.*

*M*Y AUNTS ON MY FATHER'S side were rather grand. Mahala
Elizabeth Ellen married (for the third time) an executive of
the Stutz luxury car firm and travelled the world, popping into
various Government Houses. I saw her only infrequently, staying at
the top hotels in Sydney. In England there was Hannah Violet
Grace, married to a Major Rawdon Campbell whose brother Sir
Harold was Equerry to King George VI, and Adelaide Victoria
Louise who married Major Newman.

Mother's side was a different cup of tea — Billy compared to
Twinings. My Welsh grandfather, Edward Lloyd Thomas, was the
captain of a sailing ship called the *Merioneth*, but he jumped ship at
Newcastle in New South Wales to go looking for gold. He found a
five-foot gutsy bush nurse named Mary Ann Abrahams and married her instead. So, in due course along came my mother Ann and
aunts Nell, Ruth, Gwen, Elsie, Jean and Rose, all different as chalk
to cheddar, but all acknowledged to be the belles of Newcastle.

Well, all except Aunty Ruth, who grew to be plain, plump, had a
slight cast in one eye and was the one I loved most. She was kind,
cuddly and hospitable, though poor as a church mouse. Her first
rented house, I remember, was a fifteen-foot frontage, two-storey
terrace in the Sydney suburb of Paddington, yet there was always a
bed to share with my cousins Molly and Nancy, always tea in the

Gwen Plumb's Aunty Ruth.

pot and something to eat. Poor Aunty Ruth, how her mouth would droop when the larder was really low.

They moved later into various flats at Bondi, so I was in Heaven spending (uninvited) weekends on the beach. Molly was rather like her mother, timid. Nancy had a touch of class, always looking wonderful when she was dressed for the evening to go to a Ball with some gentleman. That streak of gentility and pride was noticeable in my mother. I remember staying in a country boarding house with her; she generally ate very little, especially at breakfast when it was just tea and toast, but on this occasion our hosts kept piling her plate with fried eggs which she wrapped in her handkerchief to dispose of later, rather than disappoint them.

Aunty Rose was beautiful, elegantly mannered, dignified to the last day, which was just seventeen days from her one-hundredth birthday. She had been looking forward to the Queen's telegram, but then got so weak she begged the doctor to let her die. She went

Family group, circa 1900. At the back are John Plumb and his wife Martha. In front of them are Mahala (May), with her hand on Hannah's shoulder, and Charles with his sister Adelaide. The two old ladies are Mahala Caplin (left) and Elizabeth Plumb (right), sister and widow respectively of Robert Plumb (1809—1881), John's father.

Aunty Nell on her ninety-seventh birthday.

Gwen Plumb, about seven years old.

Mahala (May) Rawlins, née Plumb.

quite blind at about eighty, but used to *listen* to the TV — especially if I was on — sitting straight in her chair, bathed, hair done and dressed carefully.

We Plumb kids had wonderful holidays with her. She was married to Jim McIntyre, the headmaster of Barrington Tops School in northern New South Wales. There were apple trees and corn paddocks for nibbles and a rowboat on the river. My sister Peggy and I would give concerts on the verandah by the headlights of Father's old Crossley and people would walk, ride, come by buggy and boat from miles around for a bit of entertainment and Aunty Rose's great country suppers.

But then, I infested every aunty's home.

Aunty Jean Tanner lived at Springwood, in the lower Blue

Gwen Plumb in the play 'Arsenic And Old Lace'.

Mountains, and I would be put on the train in the care of some strange lady, with a basket of clothes and a five-shilling postal note for lollies and lemonade. Cousin Paulie and I would go down to the gully to cook potatoes in a fire, swim and yell and have a lovely time.

Aunty Elsie married another Tanner boy and lived at Parramatta where cousin Desmond played the Hammond organ at the Roxy cinema. He was a musical genius, that boy — could play anything — but we preferred exploring the bush and taking picnics down by the dam.

Talking of picnics, when all the aunts and cousins went for a picnic, we occupied the whole park — oh, the noise! Then the tablecloths were laid out, and what tucker! Everyone vied for the best spread and the *pièce de résistance* was always flummery. ✱

MY AUNT, BARONESS GARDNER OF PARKES

BY BEATRICE GRAY

Beatrice Gray was born and educated in Sydney. She is a barrister, part-time lecturer in law at Sydney University and has served as an alderman on Woollahra Council. Beatrice comes from a large and loving family and is an aunt twelve times over.

*M*Y AUNT, BARONESS GARDNER of Parkes, is today a life peer of the British House Of Lords. A dentist by profession, she married a fellow Australian dentist and they have three daughters. She and my uncle reside in Knightsbridge, London, fifty paces from Harrods in a home originally built for thay store's manager.

As the first and only Australian to have achieved a life peerage in the House Of Lords she has enormous curiosity value that belies her human qualities. To me, she remains Aunt Trixie, my younger brother's godmother and my father's favourite sister-in-law.

Trixie, the second youngest of nine McGirr children, bears a first name which I find difficult to believe is her proper name. Partly because of her merry personality and gusto, it seems more like a 'pet' family name generated by a play on the word 'trick', but since all official announcements are in that name I accept that she was christened 'Trixie Rachel', the latter after her mother.

Whilst Trixie, like her grandfather, was born in Parkes, I do not associate her with the original family home, 'Sunrise'. Rather, I associate her with a house at Cammeray, both appropriately and inappropriately named 'Sunray', which her parents moved to when I was still young. It was a large two-storey Federation home built on an enormous tract of land now occupied by several ugly high-rise complexes. The grounds of Sunray sang of a sunny existence,

117

having a tennis court complete with umpire's chair and grandstand, a cricket pitch, an aviary with pheasants, a goldfish pond and office and staff accommodation. The interior of the house was anything but sunny. Its gloomy rooms, accentuated by dark, highly polished wooden floors, were decorated in the style of the Victorian era with antique furniture and *objets d'art*. The whole of the interior presented a tantalising temptation to young fingers ... especially the elephants' tusks in the front parlour.

Visits to Sunray often led to miserable experiences as the young perversely refused to be banished to the grounds so that Grandma could indulge her pleasure in her adult children. Trixie, living at home as a young adult, was a benign bystander to these encounters and I do not recall her ever being other than good humoured; remarkable in itself since the family tree was so extensive she must rarely have had a period without visitors.

Despite, or perhaps because of, all the visitors to Sunray, Trixie later insisted on living in the heart of London to ensure that any one of us travelling would be sure to visit — at one stage she even provided a separate 'mews' house to facilitate a stay. Eventually the potential family visitors numbered seven married brothers and sisters, and thirty-five nieces and nephews who likewise married and commenced to multiply. Hospitality seemed to come naturally to her so that when she visited Australia it was still Trixie who was hostess and gathered the family together.

For over thirty years Trixie has resided outside Australia, with London as her permanent home. Whilst many would think that was enough to sever her Australian origins, she has tenaciously retained that connection and firmly clings to it. One of her most distinctive personal features is her Australian accent which is not broad, but typical of a convent-educated, professional woman. Apart from re-taining her distinctive accent, she is a sentimental person with a soft manner that belies the tough career politics inevitably presents. It was her sentimentality that chose the title 'Gardner of Parkes', a combination of her married surname and the place of her birth, a country town in western New South Wales, which was itself named

Baroness Gardner of Parkes, prior to her introduction to the House Of Lords.

after Australia's founding father of Federation, Henry Parkes. Despite all her success in England and her long residency overseas, it was to her roots she returned when she reached the pinnacle of her career.

On a visit to Australia for the Bicentenary in 1988, though her time was precious, she returned to Parkes for an official reception. In 1957, on a visit there with my mother, a walk down the main street was a walk through the family tree of a town that was often called 'McGirr Town'. By 1988 the few reminders that remained were the original family home, Sunrise, donated to the Catholic Church but now hidden behind a high wall, and the fountain and memorial to her sister Clarinda who died in childhood, located in Clarinda Park at the end of Welcome Street, a street entirely built by her father. The journey back to Parkes at the height of an Australian summer, to a woman who had emerged from the depths of an English winter, was, to me, a measure of her commitment to renew origins and revive her inspirational sources.

Trixie was the only family member who displayed any interest in food beyond it being a necessity for life. The combined disinterest of the family in food preparation was extraordinary as my grand-parents' home had kitchen staff. Regular features for afternoon tea were apple sandwiches and caraway seed cake served on fine bone china and sparkling clean silver. Plenty of style but definitely not a culinary experience.

When Trixie completed her education she faced the unenviable task of finding a place for herself within a family of high achievers. During her schooling she had been relieved of those stresses because the five sisters had been divided between the two local convent schools of Loreto and Monte Sant' Angelo. In the 1930s and 1940s it was unusual for women to pursue a professional career but within the McGirr family it was unquestionably expected. Grandfather was in the first graduate class of pharmacy students at Sydney University whilst Grandma proudly framed and hung her Master of Arts degree, also from Sydney University. Grandma was proud of her achievements, which included an OBE and a Papal

Honour, and expected no less from her children and grandchildren. She spent many hours describing the life of the university and related in detail the personal idiosyncracies of the female under-graduates from each faculty, gleaned from daily meetings for morning tea at the Women's Union located in a temporary wooden building, Manning House.

The challenge for Trixie must have been daunting because she was at the tail-end of a family in which her siblings had completed tertiary education and married fellow graduates. The family order of merit was: Jack (medicine, married to Joyce, law), Beatrice (arts/law, married to Tom, medicine — my parents), Gwen (medicine, married to Michael, medicine), Patty (social work, married to Bing, engineering), Raymond (arts with University medals in languages, married to Nell, arts), Gregory (Hawkesbury Agricultural College, married to Maureen, pharmacy) and Nona (arts with Honours, married to Peter, law). Whilst the merit list was not complete by the time Aunt Trixie selected her career, it was beginning to show its format. She headed in a totally different direction and chose dentistry, graduating in 1954. It did not prove to be an abiding passion and I've always felt law would have been a more natural choice.

The lifestyle of the family was one in which money was not the motivating factor; it was rarely mentioned. They were wealthy and relieved of the burden of having to match finances with ambitions. This freedom did not mean that Trixie was either self-indulgent or spoilt. Whilst she never wanted for anything, she was to experience first-hand the turning point in the family's life — the death of her father. When Grandfather became ill, Trixie suspended her studies and, as a temporary arrangement, completed a cooking course at East Sydney Technical College. Years later she gained a *Cordon Bleu* diploma.

When Grandfather died in 1949 even I, as a child, was aware that from that time onwards the family home at Sunray died: the shutters were drawn and the house descended into a state of mourning from which it never emerged. Grandma was about sixty-one years old, but she seemed thereafter to lack vigour and to be a woman who had internalised her feelings. The permanent domestic staff was reduced from nine to three. The grounds and rooms remained as they had always been but were permanently under-utilised. Trixie's dog, 'Roy', with his pug nose, seemed to have the grounds all to himself. The large family Christmas gatherings around the gigantic fir tree, complete with Father Christmas (George, the butler/chauffeur), the extravagant gifts and large extended family gatherings were relegated to memories in the photograph album. If I and my siblings knew that the house was sad, how much more acutely must it have been felt by Trixie!

Trixie's visits to my parents' home were quite another thing. They were filled with mystery and high drama, the exact nature of which we, as children, rarely discovered — but in a general way they fell under the headings of 'romance' and 'politics'. Occasionally these dramas assumed Shakespearean proportions, such as the occasion when Trixie renounced a loved one due to different religious beliefs. She was no Mrs Wallis Simpson. Periods of romantic drama were followed by exiles 'to forget' at another family country property, 'Pomeroy' at Oberon, just beyond the Blue Mountains, where a young woman in love could do little else but pine and/or make another batch of scones. Ironically, there, on the main wall of the family dining room, hung a large nineteenth century print entitled 'Absence makes the heart grow fonder'. Through generations Pomeroy, which was later bought by my father, was a place of exile for 'wrong turnings' in romantic encounters and its success rate was predictably abysmal.

Trixie's wedding was in the late 1950s, in the Catholic Cathedral in Paris, to fellow-Australian Kevin Gardner who had graduated with her in the dentistry class of 1954. The marriage was celebrated by the family in Australia with a gathering at my parents' home and the guests included Kevin's parents, Rita and George Gardner. My parents were excited and rejoiced in her happiness. *The Australian Women's Weekly*, the bible of society weddings, recorded a picture of the event, with Trixie looking her loveliest in full bridal regalia and beside her a dashingly handsome stranger decked out in morning suit. Since the wedding occurred at such a distance I do not know if it was accompanied by the traditional drama that surrounds our family weddings.

Trixie's political career commenced long before her first run for the House Of Commons in the British elections of 1970 (as a conservative candidate against Barbara Castle in an unwinnable seat). Politics was in the McGirr blood and as a family they thrived on elections. In the 1920s Grandfather was the Minister for Health and Motherhood and later the Minister for Education, and the youngest brother, by 1949, was the Premier. Unlike Trixie, they were serving in Australian Labor Party governments.

The McGirr's move away from the ALP had commenced before Grandfather's death with Uncle Jack, who tried to win a seat as a Country Party candidate, causing a stir in the press but not within the family. The 1950s ALP split at its national conference in Hobart and the formation of the DLP, an event which had a great impact upon the Catholic community of Victoria, was a significant event in the lives of the McGirrs. They were first and foremost devout Catholics from Irish ancestry and passionately involved with the ALP. The crisis experienced within the Party as a result of that rift was replayed within family debates for years afterwards and, like the split itself, remained without a resolution.

It was not surprising that Trixie in London joined the Conservative Party in 1962. She worked within the party till 1970 when she was defeated in her bid to gain entry to the House Of Commons, but she succeeded in being elected to the Greater London Council which was Labour-controlled. Trixie did not mind occupying the cross-benches, after all she had plenty of training in coming from behind the ranks to achieve her own successes. It was her obvious tenacity and achievements within the GLC that led to her appointment in 1981 by the then Prime Minister, Margaret Thatcher, to the House Of Lords. She, in turn, encouraged her husband to enter politics and by the time of their Bicentenary visit to Australia it was he who was the official guest, as Lord Mayor of Westminster.

My memories of Trixie cannot do her justice because they are, after all, the memories of a child, and like all memories of children, I do not know where the dream world has merged with reality. But they are my recollections and perceptions and I do not feel they are inconsistent with the woman we re-met in Sydney in 1988. ✳

MOVE OVER, DAME EDNA

BY PHILLIP ADAMS

Hailing from Melbourne, Phillip Adams now resides and works in Sydney where his fertile brain is evidenced on ABC Radio National's 'Late Night Live'. He is an outstanding broadcaster and interviewer, wit, film producer and advertising guru, but writing is his favourite medium.

MANY YEARS AGO I NEEDED to interview Mrs Edna Everage (this was long before Gough Whitlam gave her Damehood) and was working on an appropriate set. It needed, of course, to have flights of ducks up the wall and a Trenchikov painting. The wallpaper, the occasional table, the couches, everything had to be just right.

After weeks of trying to get everything together, in one place at one time, I suddenly realised this was wasted effort. Because my aunty lived in the perfect house. Edna's creator Barry Humphries was a bit dubious about this claim, but when we arrived for the filming he was captivated by Aunty's total commitment to his vision. Nothing needed to be removed. There was nothing to add. It was the total suburban statement, the quintessence of Edna's taste in fabric, wallpaper, nick-nacks. My uncle, her husband, also entered into the spirit of things by being a dead-ringer for Sandy Stone. When Aunty went on the *Women's Weekly* World Discovery Tour, 'Sandy' would write to her every day, keeping her up-to-date with what was happening in *Bellbird*.

It isn't often that life so perfectly imitates art. I have long believed that my aunty should be given a classification by the National Trust whilst her home should be preserved under a huge glass dome for future generations, anthropologists and archaeologists. She also makes a wonderful sponge finger. Come to think of it, she could augment her pension by giving guided tours. I've no doubt that my aunty's lounge, particularly her lounge, could become a major tourist attraction. *

Phillip Adams.

MAKING DREAMS COME TRUE

BY DI MORRISSEY

Di Morrissey is a prominent romantic novelist who lives and works in beautiful Byron Bay on the far north coast of New South Wales. Formerly she was a television presenter and entertainment and travel reporter, both in Australia and the United States.

*T*HE FIRST REFERENCE TO my aunts was Nana saying, 'Oh, we have so many aunts in our family tree'. I went away to digest this strange remark. The vision of a tree — I imagined it to be fat and spreading — hung with assorted aunts like globs of fruit from branches bewildered me.

Fat Aunts in spotted dresses and doughy arms, suspended like ripe figs. Skinny Aunts with rimless glasses, beaky noses and thin lips, in tightly buttoned blouses dangling like dried up bunches of grapes. And in this family tree, lurking under shadowy leaves and knotty branches, were those relatives one saw only at large family gatherings, or who were referred to in hushed tones as having 'passed away'. Yet they were allowed to stay in the family tree. Somewhere it grew, sheltering the burgeoning members of our family, past and present.

I longed to see The Family Tree. But the clearest picture I had of it was its peak. I knew, without doubt, that at the top of that tree, perched like the fairy riding the star atop a Christmas tree, would be Aunt Celine.

I probably wouldn't normally have been allowed to associate with her, but there was no getting round the embarrassing fact (to the rest of the family) that she was a True Aunt.

I had lots of other aunties. Family friends and good neighbours we knew too well to call 'Mrs', so 'Auntie' they became. Some took the position of indulgent, caring and interested aunt, giving me small gifts, birthday cards, treats after school, and asking me to 'be a dear' and run messages. Others tolerated or simply ignored me as they sat with my mother over the teapot and talk that was only occasionally worth listening to for some titillating snippet.

So when Aunt Celine invaded our lives, I was scooped up and swept away, so to speak, despite the mumbled protestations from my mother that I might be too much trouble or, later, feeble excuses of pressing homework. In truth, to other adults Aunt Celine was a bit of a worry. I'd heard them describe her as weird, or whacky, but to me she was wonderful. Though I could see, that yes, she was ... different.

She was an aunt by marriage. The third wife of an obscure older uncle whom I recall only in hazy images. But Aunt Celine, once met, was never forgotten. She was beautiful. More beautiful than any doll I'd ever coveted. Although, her 'look' was criticised by the family. The wild abandoned curls, which were never constrained into the currently fashionable regimented hairdos, were described as 'never having seen a comb'. Her clear skin, naturally thick dark brows and eyelashes, and lack of make-up, were considered 'washed out'.

While other aunts wore sensible skirts, twin-sets and boxy plaid wool jackets, Aunt Celine favoured flowing gypsy-style clothes. Skirts of sheer and exotic fabric swirled about ankles, with loose off-the-shoulder blouses (and horrors, no brassiere) and a glittery scarf tied gaily about her head to trail through the curls tumbling down her back.

Aunt Celine was more fun than a kitten or a puppy and definitely more wise than any owl. She said things like 'If you love someone, tell him — don't play games and hard to get'. Or, 'sand makes a great soap'.

She was the first person I heard talk about horoscopes and mysticism, and magic and making dreams come true. When Aunt Celine said, 'You can make anything happen', one believed her. That secret dream, deep in one's heart and soul, didn't seem so

Di Morrissey.

impossible after all when you listened to Aunt Celine tell you to 'follow the steps of the moon'.

On visits to Aunt Celine there were only ever the two of us. Uncle Milton seemed to be perpetually 'away on business', an arrangement that appeared to suit my aunt.

Everything about her life was different. Meals didn't have to be eaten at the table. Some evenings we reclined on the floor — 'like pashas' — on big fat cushions eating with our fingers from a brass tray. The food we ate wasn't the meat and three veg variety. Spicy curries, fruit and nuts and delicious salad concoctions with herbs and sprouts and seeds and more than one kind of lettuce. Tinned beetroot was never seen in Celine's house.

But it was the outings. My first visit to the theatre, the ballet and a concert. She took me to such worlds! But the best place of all, was the world of the imagination. She led you along paths and through doors to enchanted lands. Were her stories real? I cared not. For me, never without a book in my hand, I now found I could close my eyes and create wondrous places and people of my own.

Her favourite place was the beach. We shared the same star sign of Pisces which, she said, was why we were drawn to the sea. She chose beaches that were nearly always deserted. Knotting food in a coloured scarf, which she'd sling across a hip or shoulder, we'd clamber to the furthest headland and picnic in the shelter of the cliff. Then ... roll down sand dunes, over and over, hair and face sand spattered.

I'd chase after her as she ran, swift and barefoot, along the water's edge, arms stretched above her head, laughter and joyous shouts echoing behind her. She splashed through waves, her long wet skirt clinging to her shapely legs. Finally, clothes would be peeled away and she'd skip naked into the ocean like a sea nymph. Hers was the first adult woman's body I'd seen and I worried that I found her so beautiful. I swam in sensible cottontails, hugging budding breasts.

Aunt Celine dived through waves, arching and plunging like a porpoise, and could swim for frightening lengths of time beneath the surface. Emerging from the ocean, she'd sometimes find seaweed to make a crown for her hair — and she'd give me necklaces to wear of round, beadlike chains of seaweed. These brown baubles were full of water and burst in a satisfying shower when popped. Finally she's rub handfuls of coarse wet sand along a brown thigh, over arms and on her face, rinse in the sea, dress and we'd lie on our backs to 'cloud gaze'.

These were times to talk. You could ask Aunt Celine anything, talk about anything, unlike the taboo topics one wouldn't dream of broaching with even a best girlfriend let along a grown up.

When I think of Aunt Celine, her image is incandescent, sparkling with light. How she dazzled me with her spirit of childlike simplicity and joy, her earthy sexuality, wisdom and depth of understanding.

Aunt Celine never had children. And far too soon, her bright white light was extinguished. I was hurt she'd never told me she was ill, and that so swiftly she faded away, leaving me with burning memories.

The family went to the funeral. I did not. I went to the beach and was considered callous by my cousins, strange by their parents. But I danced for Aunt Celine. Along the beach, among the rocks and in the sea. I sang for her, I saw the shape of her head with windswept hair amongst the clouds. And then I wept for her.

I treasure her gifts ... intangible and indelible. Some people take up residence in your soul. And there she stays.

Years later I am to care for a hesitant small girl who stares thoughtfully at me with judgemental eyes. She is to stay with me during a family pilgrimage to places and relatives we both know to be boring. 'You be good. And careful,' the child is advised.

In an aside to her mother, Granny describes me as being — 'a bit too much like her Aunt Celine ... if you know what I mean'.

The girl comes to me and slips her hand in mine and squeezes it. And in her eyes I recognise she knows who I am, and my heart smiles. ✳

LIKE A FINE WINE

BY RICHARD MORECROFT

Richard Morecroft joined the Australian Broadcasting Corporation full time after completing an Arts degree in English and Drama at Adelaide University. Today he is the principal newsreader for ABC-TV in Sydney ... and author of the wildlife book 'Raising Archie'.

*I*F A FINE WINE USUALLY gains strength and character with age, then the same must be said for my unforgettable late Great-Aunt Gladys. Great-Aunt Gladys was irrepressibly energetic and enthusiastic about almost everything. She was English, and when she visited my family in Australia at over eighty years of age she had no sooner arrived than she was doing laps up and down the swimming pool (wearing her rubber bathing hat), and badgering my brother and me to join her on the tennis court where she put up an energetic display. She seemed constantly delighted by the wild Australian countryside and would stride on walks, frequently clapping her hands together and exclaiming, 'Oooh, it's lovely!' Even when the weather seemed (to everyone else) cold and miserable, Great-Aunt Gladys would breathe in and out vigorously, proclaiming with a smile that it was 'Nice and Fresh'!

Richard Morecroft.

She was quite a short woman,

and I remember on one occasion as we were walking along by the beach my brother and I simply linked our arms into hers and lifted her off the ground. Her legs kept pedalling in mid-air and she squealed and laughed as if she were eight rather than eighty.

Great-Aunt Gladys was a wonderfully positive person and, at an advanced age, her energy was an inspiration to the rest of us. In fact, if the truth be known, there were times when she had us quite exhausted ... but I wouldn't want to admit that, now would I? ✻

Richard Morecroft's Great-Aunt Gladys.

GIVE ME AN AUNT IN THE COUNTRY

BY MARGOT ANTHONY

Margot Anthony is well known for the varied community work she achieved with distinction for many years as wife of the leader of the National Party, Doug Anthony. Born in Murwillumbah, New South Wales, country life is in her blood. Her eighteen aunts have given vitality to a strong family unit.

*M*Y MOTHER AND FATHER each had nine siblings. Life for my brothers, sister and me was awash with aunts, uncles and cousins. As my mother's family lived a long way away, in Sydney, these aunts remained shadowy characters whom I rarely saw. The 'Murwillumbah Aunts', however, were as colourful and diverse as the sub-tropical flowers and trees that filled my childhood with riotous vitality.

My father's family was musical and my earliest memories are of 'singsongs' around the piano with Dad and his bright-eyed young sister, my Aunt Dorrie, singing duets of 'nightingales' soft tunes and blighted Victorian love. She married a wheat farmer and moved to Queensland. When I was seven years old I was invited, with my brother, for a holiday. I must have had my birthday while I was there, because I well remember the deep portent of the 'number seven of pestilence and famine'. As there was a mice and caterpillar plague on the farm, this took on ominous significance. I marvelled at Aunt Dorrie's good humour as she disposed of the dead mice and washed caterpillar-stained sheets.

In Murwillumbah, in northern New South Wales, we lived with the drama of extravagant seasons. The high point, literally, was the recurring floods when the rain sluiced down with a roar on the galvanised iron roof. Dad donned his 'flood gear', mackintosh and boots, and made sober forays to the flood gauge on the river bank. The brown water swirled down from the mountains, debris caught and strained at the wooden bridge, and shopkeepers and townspeople feverishly stacked their goods and belongings to a higher level as the floodwaters lapped into the town.

The aftermath of these flood sagas was that when the seas calmed the fish 'came on' and it was then that the skills of Aunty Tot shone beyond all others. She was of stocky Germanic extraction, drawling and gravel voiced, slow and deliberate of movement and unconcerned by household chores as she read a book or pottered in her garden. Her great skill and love was fishing — a skill she shared with her husband, my father's brother Rex.

Aunty Tot and Uncle Rex had a *real* beach house — with sand-covered sprawling verandahs— nestled under the encroaching sand dunes at Fingal. The unmade beds, piles of unwashed dishes and smoking fuel stove made no impact outside under the sun-speckling banksias. On the rough wooden bench tops, piles of flicking, twisting, freshly caught whiting and bream commanded full attention as Aunty Tot and Uncle Rex gutted and filleted with practiced precision. The oil smoked and bubbled in pans on the primus, bowls of batter were whipped and family and friends feasted as Aunty Tot's laconic drawl recaptured 'ones she'd just missed'.

With all these aunts sprinkled around town there were inevitably many cousins. The two who were my closest friends lived 'around the hill' in a house set atop it and with verandahs overlooking the river. Here, Aunty Daph presided over her kingdom of four children, a busy husband, a large garden and a bountiful kitchen with wonderful ease, authority and warmth. Because their house was on the crest of such a steep hill, the front garden became a series of terraces, the lower ones densely planted with brilliant poinsettias and amaranthus. We made secret cubbies, magic worlds far from prying adults, though we always welcomed the buttered pikelets that Aunty Daph would send down at tea-time.

Aunty Daph's house was a veritable Aladdin's cave of books,

Margot Anthony.

bric-a-brac, Balinese artifacts, photographs, paintings and chests full of discarded clothes for dress ups. In her sewing room at the back of the house she ran up clothes for her family, curtains, patchwork bedspreads, gifts for fetes, all with apparent ease.

Her great burden was a chronic skin condition, psoriasis. As each supposed cure was found, she mixed her creams and potions, covered her body, including her scalp, and soaked it off. Despite the persistent and painful condition, she accompanied our uncle on arduous overseas journeys and welcomed and generously entertained house guests and visitors.

Aunty Daph is now almost ninety. Uncle died a few years ago but she has stayed on in her house and now has taken up two new interests, mahjong and embroidery. We've all received lace-edged, embroidered hand-towels for Christmas. She once came to lunch bearing her freshly made *crème caramel* — and three packets of morning coffee biscuits. The *crème caramel* was a gift for me. As for the biscuits, she wanted to use my food processor to grind them as she was making a hundred rum balls for her daughter's birthday party!

Her little blue Mini Minor is a familiar sight around town, usually early in the morning to 'avoid the traffic'. She says her sorties are carefully worked out so that she 'mainly turns left'! The parking policeman turns an indulgent blind eye at minor offences. He says she is 'one of his rare endangered species' and must be protected. She confessed to me a while back that she has decided not to renew her licence. She always thought people were 'silly' when they kept on driving once they were ninety!

Aunt Olive, like her husband, was a chemist, a rather startling fact in a small country town where few women had professional careers. She, too, had four children to care for — as well as helping to run the chemist shop. She was a small, grey-haired, distinguished looking woman with twinkling eyes and a pleasant mezzo-soprano voice. I loved my visits to their shop and her ready, lively interest. My admiration flowed over when she took the part of Iolanthe in the local Gilbert and Sullivan production, wand in hand, 'tripping hither, tripping thither' into her banishment.

Another uncle married a former local beauty queen. She was also a fine pianist. It was in the days when the magazines were full of photos and stories about the young Princess Elizabeth and Princess Margaret, and I imagined that we, too, were welcoming a real queen into our family of kind hearts and now, indeed, coronets.

As well as our genuine aunts, there were also Adopted Aunts.

Ettie and her husband Herbie had no children of their own, and we became their adopted family. Aunt Ettie, strong minded, full bosomed, bore all before her — events, people, cars and houses. Her family was involved in car dealerships so their succession of latest models dazzled and beguiled us as well as everyone else in Murwillumbah.

Aunt Ettie and Uncle Herbie were great picnickers, but not your ordinary bundle of last minute plates and cakes and thermoses. Their picnic basket, with its Nallyware plates and containers rivalled the Rawleigh man's suitcases. As the last cakes and biscuits were snapped into place, so were we children snapped into the dickie seat in the back of the latest shining yellow Pontiac, and spun off to the beach. They were both great swimmers and great teachers of swimming. They also understood child psychology and practised it quite beyond the patience and capabilities of my embattled parents. And they had unlimited imagination. There are photos of my sister and me, like two little bulging toads, quivering at the edge of the swimming pool. The next sequence would have been the magic pennies miraculously twinkling on the bottom of the pool. Ignoring all childish fears of putting our heads under water, we dived in to see how many pennies or sugar-coated caramels we could retrieve while holding our breath. We very soon learned to swim.

Car journeys were usually a nightmare because we all became car sick. Ettie devised mini eisteddfods in the back seat where we each had to sing or recite, a wondrous device for re-focussing the mind and the stomach!

My younger sister became the victim of her three siblings. She was always in trouble and always left out, and therefore created more trouble. I shudder now when I remember how we ostracised her. Aunt Ettie, the arch psychologist swept in. My sister became her 'fairy' — she was given a fairy costume with gauze wings and pretty shoes. She was spirited away to 'fairy' adventures, all by herself, leaving us mere mortals to mow the lawn and polish the brass taps. Ettie saw her shining spirit, polished her sense of identity and sent her soaring. She has never stopped soaring since!

Uncle Herbie was a great story-teller and when we were ready for bed he created new worlds out of the events of the day, using the initials of our names as the principal characters, weaving together imagination and reality, gently guiding us with wisdom and humour. We adored our bedtime!

My parents escaped our tyranny, on one occasion, and sailed off to a mysterious place full of volcanoes and earthquakes and hot springs, called New Zealand, for a much needed holiday. Aunt Ettie and Uncle Herbie came to look after us. We all developed chickenpox but my only memory is of lying in my parents' big bed with dozens of balloons squeaking and rustling, tied to the mosquito net ring. What a nightmare it must have been for them as the spots appeared on all four of us and our parents were two thousand miles away.

While we were still quite young, Aunt Ettie and Uncle Herbie moved to Lismore and it became even more of a treat to be invited over there to stay. The house was cool and dim with dark green wooden slatted blinds shading the verandah, which was called 'the sleepout'. There was a pervading smell of furniture polish and floor wax. The furniture, heavy and ornate, seemed huge and as it was a child-free household, ornaments and precious vases of gilded oriental porcelains were scattered around. Beside the twin beds in the spare room, the bedside lights had tasselled deep green shades and the blankets smelled of camphor. But the ultimate sophistication was a gas stove in the kitchen, a palpable presence as the lurking smell of escaping gas competed with the aroma of freshly ground coffee.

Aunt Ettie's father had served in the First World War, her brother was serving in the Second. The stern photos of them in military uniform always made me feel I should be standing to attention and saluting.

Aunt Ettie was not a Roman Catholic, yet she took a great interest in the welfare of the nuns at the Presentation Convent and frequently drove them, too, on excursions to secluded beaches to 'dip their toes in the water', with modesty! These were the sequestered times before the heady liberation of Vatican II.

In those days such a thing as pregnancy was a matter to be spoken of in hushed tones and, during the latter bulging stages, women were expected to stay out of sight. Aunt Ettie, being such an avid swimmer herself, thought such false modesty and inactivity a nonsense and whisked her pregnant friends off for beach outings.

Both she and Uncle Herbie had many community interests and focussed public awareness to the need for a thirty-three metre swimming pool and a new district hospital in Murwillumbah.

Auntie Muriel, nicknamed Moo, and her husband, Theo, lived in a large, spreading house made from generously cut wide boards on the banks of the river. It was encircled by verandahs and shaded by camphor-laurel and palm trees. In this lovely setting, it was regarded as one of Murwillumbah's great houses, typical of the period when timber was plentiful, children were numerous, and life, though busy, was gracious.

Just as Aunt Ettie radiated a sense of urgency, of bustling expeditions and new worlds, Moo was settledness, though not dull, static suffocation. The house breathed easily, settled as it was in its rambling garden, its wide stairs flanked by concrete pedestals inviting entry. On our way home from Sunday School, my sister and I played 'Statues' on these pedestals, whirling around in our pleated skirts until Moo called 'Stop'! We'd freeze into appropriate positions with Moo deciding who, in immobility, was the more like a statue. After thoughtful appraisal, we were usually, in her opinion, equally frozen so we'd have to whirl again.

The Sunday visits with our mother were something of a ritual. On each side of the front door were panels of stained pink glass. After pressing the door bell, my sister and I would wait, noses flattened against the glass, peering into the rosy coloured hall, for a rosy coloured Moo to fling open the door and her arms with a welcoming, 'Well, here you are!', as if she'd been just sitting and waiting for us to find time to call in.

While she and Mother sat at the oval dining table with their cups of tea, we made a bee-line for the mahjong set, and, on the carpeted floor, made snakes with the smooth ivories up-ended and placed close to each other. One flick, and the domino theory demolished our painstaking work in a twisting, clattering heap.

Moo's kitchen, large and airy with deep windows to the garden, was filled with the latest electrical gadgetry. One was an amazing labour-saving device called a Mixmaster. Not that she'd trust her sponges or pavlovas to that! The huge walk-in pantry, with its shelves of preserves and cavernous bins of flour and sugar, was a magical place. The biscuit jars and cake tins were never empty —

and no wonder. So many of my memories centre around the kitchen, its wondrous electric stove, Moo serenely whisking and sifting while her girls buzzed up new shorts and shirts on the electric sewing-machine in the sewing room next door.

Moo's lively, wiry husband Theo was, to us, the fount of all knowledge. With his encyclopaedic mind and rasping voice he delighted in testing our general knowledge. My brother startled him one day when he gave the correct reply to Uncle Theo's, 'Why are fire engines red?' Disappointed, Uncle Theo testily asked him how he knew. Grahame laconically replied, 'Because you told me last week ... and the week before!'

Uncle Theo was the shire engineer, and became responsible for the first power station at Murwillumbah. His personality was like a powerhouse of ideas and inventions — which he gave full reign to in his kingdom, the workshop behind the laundry downstairs. The woodworking equipment, curls of woodshavings, scatters of sawdust, screw-top jars of nails and screws, pieces of half re-stored furniture, vied with mysterious out-of-bounds cachets of gunpowder and chemicals. Empire Day, the 24th of May, was the climax of his year's alchemy. The families gathered in a spare paddock opposite our house for the annual perilous display of Uncle Theo's latest batch of home-made rockets and firecrackers. Tension and anticipation ran high, with Moo and my mother constantly attempting to corral us from imminent disaster.

Moo's personality was quite the opposite of her husband's irrepressible energy. Her soothing 'Now, now Theo, dear' still rings in my memory as he catapulted from one activity to another. A welcome, sobering diversion was his love of gardening, in particular his enthusiasm for cultivating prize-winning gladioli. Because they were regulated into raised flower-beds, they escaped destruction as I weaved my way on the narrow concrete pathways between them when learning to ride a bicycle.

Moo's rampant quisqualis vine, with its heavy sweet perfume, could not be tamed. It soared and rampaged over the trellis below the kitchen windows and found its way to discreetly envelope the 'two holer' lavatory in the backyard. It provided a haven for snakes and spiders and I always set out for the lavatory (hopefully with a friend!) with the same anticipation I imagine Dr Livingstone felt when leaving for darkest Africa. Further down, at the bottom of the garden, was an enormous weeping willow tree, its branches made for climbing and its trailing foliage inviting cubbies.

As I write this, I realise how lucky we were to have been born at that time, into such a diverse community of family and extended family. My own nieces and nephews are scattered around the world — the mobility of today, and the smaller nuclear family, has pulled down the curtain on a stage that is eerily empty.

I have lived my life with a rich cast of lively, loving, vital women. There was no thought of self-image or striving for individuality or so-called equality. There was no need, they were already whole. They were immersed in the passage of life and embraced all who joined them on the way. ✳

THROW THE BALL TO ME

BY IAN CHAPPELL

Now a television commentator and sporting journalist, Ian Chappell was captain of the Australian Cricket Team from 1970 to 1975, and during that period — of thirty Tests — we did not lose a series. Ian comes from an acclaimed sporting family, but it was a non-sporting aunt who fostered his early interest in cricket!

I WAS FORTUNATE TO HAVE relatives who were helpful and supportive of my attempts to pursue a sporting career.

I was also lucky that most of them had a good sense of humour. My grandmother Peg is a good example. Peg was Vic Richardson's second wife and being married to a person like Vic, who had captained Australia at cricket, she had a good understanding of what touring was like.

When I was selected for my first overseas tour in 1966 there was a function at the South Australian Cricket Association rooms to farewell Neil Hawke and myself as the two SA tourists. Someone made a speech and in it mentioned that it was terrific that I should be making my first tour to South Africa where Vic had made his reputation as an outstanding captain. In conclusion this guy wished us all the best and said, 'Ian, I hope you follow in your grandfather's footsteps'. No sooner had I finished my reply than Peg was at my side. She wished me all the best but warned: 'I don't think you'd better follow in all your grandfather's footsteps. They'll all be grandmothers by now.'

Sadly, by the time I was appointed captain of Australia Vic had died. But Peg sent me a lovely telegram saying, 'Congratulations, there'll be a hot time in heaven tonight'.

Ian Chappell, aged three, demonstrates a promising batting style!

However, not all my relatives understood about sport the way Peg did. At one family gathering (I was about two years old) a couple of my aunts decided to encourage my sporting instincts. Handing me a cricket ball — we only had hard balls around our place as Dad didn't believe in practising with tennis balls — one of my aunts backed up a yard or so, saying, 'Now come on, Ian, throw the ball to me'.

Delighted to have any excuse to play with a ball, I cocked my arm and threw the ball to my aunt. It whistled past her right ear and crashed into the mirror. What Aunty failed to understand was that Dad also didn't believe in teaching his sons to throw underarm.

It was a good thing anyway, because after that I was sent outside to play with the ball which suited me just fine. ✽

I'M JUST DOTTIE!

BY JUNE SALTER

June Salter is a highly respected and perennial star of theatre and television. Her hits include 'Lettice And Lovage', Madam Arcati in 'Blithe Spirit' and — the jewel in the crown — Queen Mary in 'Crown Matrimonial'.

*H*ER NAME WAS DORIS MARGUERITE, but when introduced she would say, 'I'm just Dottie'! She was a courtesy aunt, a special being who was treated with much love.

Till the day she departed this life (at more than four score years and ten) her hair was raven black — I would suggest only she and her hairdresser knew what her natural colour was! She attributed her clear skin to gin (no, she *never* drank, she used it as an astringent). Her make-up was a dusting of white powder, Petroushka rouged cheeks, a slash of black pencilled eyebrows (her own natural brows having been frightened away by a pair of tweezers long ago), a generous application of crimson lipstick, long crimson fingernails, and black false eyelashes ... and she always smelt deliciously of 'April Violet' perfume.

She loved pretty dresses and millinery, both of which she expertly made herself.

Dottie hated anything ugly, hence she would never read or listen to the news. She avoided the 'real' world, only wanting to live in a fairyland. She adored dancing and in the mid-1960s went to Arthur Murray's School Of Dancing to 'brush up' and learn the samba, mambo, tango and cha-cha. At the 'young' age of seventy-five, she graduated with flying colours (equalled by her gowns, which of course she made). She then went on to be a whizz at

June Salter.

square dancing — again with the appropriate wardrobe, this time with miles and miles of roped hemmed petticoats.

Dottie married her childhood sweetheart when she was very young and they were inseparable. Although they had a lot of friends, her whole life revolved around her beloved husband. Every evening before dinner she would dress in a long gown and they would dance on their sun-verandah to her favourite records — a ritual in their own private world. They needed no one else.

Her beloved went to God some years before she did. She was bereft. Whilst she loved her friends and was always bright and gay and sweet, with a great sense of fun, the light of her life had gone out and she waited for the time it would be lit again. She finally got her wish and I have no doubt that Heaven's Angels every night are playing their harps with request after request in the Heavenly Ballroom for this dear lady and her beloved. ✳

SWEETS AND ROSARY BEADS

BY GARY O'CALLAGHAN

*Popular Sydney Radio 2UE personality Gary O'Callaghan was born
in Melbourne but moved to the Harbour city as a young man, beginning
a long love affair with his adopted home. A former Father Of The Year,
Gary appreciates the importance of an extended family. His Aunt Agnes
left him a legacy of humour and goodwill which he has always retained.*

*M*Y FAVOURITE AUNTY, OF three great ladies, had to be my
dad's sister Agnes. As a child I saw a woman with a radiant
smile, the bluest of eyes, and a voice that had a soft huskiness and a
great intensity.

Aunty Agg was a single woman, who in the 1930s and 1940s
devoted her life to the church she loved, and to the Chinese
community in Melbourne — whom she related to like a member of
the family, and who treated her as one of their own.

I used to sit, even as an eight-year-old, and listen wide-eyed as
she told of her 'prison visits' to the inmates at Melbourne's
Pentridge Prison. 'They are all God's children,' she would say, 'and
no one must ever feel they are no longer loved.'

I left my aunty in Melbourne, and with my mum, dad and sister
moved to Sydney when I was ten years old. Each year, until her
death in the 1960s, my birthday would see a parcel arrive with a
note attached by the post office saying that the parcel had been
repacked by them, as the flimsy wrap Aunty Agg had used would
have fallen apart before the journey was over. Each year, for maybe

twenty-five years, the postie at North Sydney would say, 'Your aunty's present has arrived ... happy birthday!' Each year I received a Holy Picture, sweets and Rosary Beads. After twenty-odd years I could have opened my own religious goods shop.

My Aunty Agg was soft in nature, strong in spirit — and, best of all, I could do no wrong! *

Gary O'Callaghan's Aunty Agg.

GLAMOUR AND FUN

BY HAZEL HAWKE

Hazel Hawke grew up in Western Australia. As wife of former Prime Minister Bob Hawke, she set a fine example for all Australians by her steadfastness, vitality and devotion to her family. Already a splendid pianist, she has embarked on a new career as author and radio host.

*I*WAS LUCKY THAT MY MOTHER'S two younger sisters, my aunties Maud and Nell, lived just down the street when I was growing up. They worked in a store so carried an air of glamour for me and my sister Edith. They also 'spoiled' us generously.

They would curl our hair with pins, rags or tongs, and make special treats at Christmas. Two immoveable rituals were that on Saturdays my sister and I would walk the two blocks to their house, each of us carrying a plate of hot dinner for them to have when they got home from the morning's work. The visit was always a pleasure. But better still, each Tuesday evening they would come from work to our house for tea, and always brought a bag of lollies from the store.

Winter Tuesday nights we sat around the wood fire talking and embroidering or playing cards. On summer Tuesday evenings our Dad would drive us to Perth's wonderful Scarborough beach for a swim and to play on the sand after tea. Such tingly-pleasant memories!

Our funny aunt was Mary, Dad's sister. She kept two goats which had arrived on her wedding anniversary so were named Anna and Versary. Aunt Mary had stiff knee joints so she built a ramp and platform, then trained the goats to run up so she could stand alongside to milk them.

Hazel and Bob Hawke.

She and her husband Syd lived in a house he had built from flattened kerosene tins then lined with hessian. Once, when we had spent fifteen hours driving in the old Rugby car to visit them (they lived far north of Perth), she suggested we have a bath and laughingly offered a kettle of water! That was the ration in the dry country, but she made bathing in a kettleful of water in a tin bath seem great fun. The holiday we spent with them was unforgettably adventurous and humorous.

We always felt special to aunties Maud, Nell and Mary. They were so interested in everything Edith and I did, and so enthusiastic at being aunts. ✳

SMALL IN STATURE, LARGE IN STYLE

BY SUZIE COUNSELL

Born and bred in Adelaide, Suzie Counsell is a flamboyant fashion designer and fund raiser for charity. Her fashion collections have been received with great enthusiasm in London and New York. She also writes, with style, for the daily newspapers.

*W*HEN I LOOK BACK UPON my early childhood and think of people who influenced me the most, one particular person stands out — my delightful Aunty Bobbie.

I have never met anyone since who embodies the kind of spirit she possessed. She was the most wonderful woman in so many ways. She never married, was very religious, tiny (only about four feet six inches tall), artistic, funny and dignified, and just so very special. I was in awe of her.

She had the most exciting house at the Adelaide seaside suburb of Glenelg and I loved going there. It was full of exotic things. It was also a little scary. There was a particularly frightening statue of a witch, adorning the mantelpiece over a fireplace, that one was forced to pass on the way to the bathroom — which, incidentally, was down a flight of stairs in a strange sort of basement-like affair. Next to the witch was a wonderful tapestry with the words 'Today is the tomorrow you worried about yesterday and all is well'. It took me a while to work it out, but when I did it became one of my favourite sayings.

Aunty Bobbie came from a wealthy family who owned what was then the very grand Pier Hotel, as well as several shops along the main street at Glenelg. Her job was to merely arrange the

Suzie Counsell.

flowers, a job which she did with marvellous flair. She never actually worked (for money) in her life but was always doing things for charity and the local church.

She was educated at Walford Church Of England Girls School and remained lifelong friends with many of her school chums.

Some of my most vivid memories of Aunty Bobbie were the traditional Sunday afternoon teas when my sister and I would be dressed to the hilt in our very best dresses. My favourite was a white pin-spot voile number with masses of starched petticoats underneath. We would sit perched up on our chairs, complete with matching dolls (also wearing replicas of our 'sticky out' dresses, thanks to our mother), looking longingly at the tea trolley which would be laden with beautiful fine china and wonderful treats, all baked by Aunty Bobbie. Our mother had perfected the art of control by striking terror with just a look, so we wouldn't dare touch anything on the trolley until the nod of approval was given and then only one treat was allowed. Aunty Bobby always knew that we were dying to really dig in and totally stuff ourselves, and always encouraged us to have just one more. She always managed to make sure we were given some of the goodies to take home.

Aunty Bobbie never lost her sense of being a child. She had the most infectious laugh, and I don't think I ever saw her looking sad or saying anything nasty or unkind about anyone.

Because of her involvement in amateur theatre she had the most marvellous trunk full of wonderful costumes with cloaks and beaded shoes, bags and so on.

She was a most accomplished artist and painted beautiful studies of flowers and landscapes. She made delightful plaster figurines and Beatrix Potter characters — all exquisitely hand-painted. She also used to make wonderful little families of snails out of dough.

There was always a surprise for us when we visited. And I remember that there was always a slight feeling of chaos around the place with lots of unfinished bits and pieces and half-wrapped presents, especially around Christmas-time.

At the age of about seventy-five it was nothing for Aunty Bobbie to walk into the city (approximately sixteen kilometres) just for fun, and then walk home again.

She travelled extensively around the world and made friends wherever she went. People just tended to gravitate towards her. She was never lonely.

I wish she were still alive, but even though she has gone in the physical sense her spirit still lives on. ✳

NEW BLAZERS AND STARCHED LINEN

BY KEN COWLEY

Ken Cowley is Chief Executive of Rupert Murdoch's News Limited and Chairman of the Australian Stockman's Hall Of Fame And Outback Heritage Centre. He is a keen horseman and has undertaken the gruelling Endurance Ride from Winton to Longreach in Queensland on five occasions. As a child he stayed for long periods with his aunt, who played an important role in his young life and beyond.

*E*VERY CHRISTMAS AUNT LIL bought each of my brothers and me a new blazer. They were worn for Sunday best and on the occasions we ate meals with Aunt Lil and formidable Uncle John at their house.

Their house! How grand and awe-inspiring it seemed in comparison to the simple, cluttered, make-do noisy atmosphere of the house I shared with my parents and three brothers.

Life was ordered at Aunt Lil's house. There were no children to disturb the neatness of silver framed photographs, the serried ranks of historical novels arranged in size and colour behind the leadlight doors of the good bookcase, the abundance of small china and glass objects displayed on lace doilies.

It was a house where small boys trod with nervous care and spoke in lowered voices. Uncle John, in the manner of a good English eccentric, had a pristine bowling green in the back garden where only two people every played. We dutifully admired Aunt Lil's neat garden beds and wondered if the neighbours in similar homes along the silent street lived in the same splendour as Aunt Lil.

In our street the house overflowed into the front yard, and there were friends to play with in the space and freedom of suburban creeks and paddocks. Dad drove a bus and was strict, but jovial. My mother always had a smile and a hug for small boys and only ever found nice things to say about people.

At Aunt Lil's, emotions were not on public show. Uncle John's dour Yorkshire nature permeated the house. Mealtimes were the hardest. Uncle never went to the table without jacket and tie. Aunt Lil always wore a nice dress, inevitably of a flowery material, with a piece of jewellery pinned to her bodice. We boys in blazers unfurled unaccustomed starched linen serviettes and struggled with the silverware and best china. We were not allowed to speak, unless spoken to, and manners were scrutinised. They seemed dinners of interminable length, before we escaped to the parlour. Here Uncle John, who only addressed possibly a maximum of twenty words to me, sat at the piano and played to us. Yet such playing! He was a concert pianist, though that meant little to four young nephews. He played with a chamber orchestra and gave formal piano recitals which were highly praised and well attended. I wonder now what made a man of some money and position in England give up a promising musical career to bring his bride to the suburbs of Sydney and teach music?

It was a secret fear of mine that I might one day be sent to Uncle John for music lessons. These lessons were conducted in the front room as we boys played quietly, or nervously tiptoed past the closed door where the drone of the metronome was interrupted and drowned out by Uncle banging a stick and shouting: 'No! No! Now, again!' Fortunately, I was not considered a likely candidate for a musical career. Though I did play a brass instrument in a Salvation Army band in later years.

Yet even then, during those musical evenings when Uncle John played to us, I recognised that this man, who could not bring himself or did not allow himself to show a flicker of feelings, poured such passion into his playing. Aunt Lil always sat and listened, her hands neatly clasped in her lap, with a secret smile and loving

Ken Cowley's Great-Aunt Lil and Great-Uncle John.

expression. It was then I first realised that Aunt Lil, unlike us, loved Uncle John. That between them there existed some bond in the privacy of their lives, which we never saw but was evident in Aunt Lil's demeanour towards a man who seemed to us incapable of showing affection.

Uncle also wrote his own music and often, after the final notes of a particular piece escaped the confines of that overstuffed parlour, Aunt Lil would lean forward and gently say to us with great pride, 'That was one of your uncle's pieces'.

I believe some of his music was published and played by other pianists. I remember after Uncle John died there were boxes stacked with his compositions and when Aunt Lil died I regret they were mysteriously disposed of by a relative before I could intervene.

The extent of Aunt Lil's devotion to Uncle John became evident after he died. My mother took me aside and told me that Aunt Lil wasn't coping, that she missed Uncle and was lonely. And as I was her favourite, I was going to stay with her and keep her company.

Being Aunt Lil's favourite seemed a dubious honour. So at eight years of age my bag was packed, the newest blazer donned and Dad had special permission to drive the bus past Aunt Lil's house and drop me off. Keeping Aunt Lil company was not the brief sentence I had expected. It was to be months. I was put in a new school with strange teachers and no friends. And after school I wandered up and down a street where life was lived in hushed voices behind closed doors without children. And Aunt Lil cried herself to sleep each night and I longed for home.

But there were moments of harmony. Watching Aunt Lil preparing dinner while she talked of her childhood in England. Helping in the garden, and times of feeling adult and responsible. But most of the time I was a lonely little boy. Aunt Lil, kind but unaware of the energy and adventurousness of little boys, considered home-made lemonade and dominoes after dinner quite stimulating, while I desperately missed the Huck Finn rambles with my brothers and hard fought cricket matches played with fruit box wickets on a gravel road.

On occasional weekend visits to my family it was torture to leave for the isolation of life with Aunt Lil. Even if I did have my own room.

But my stay lasted for less time than the adults had planned. One afternoon, bored and lonely, I spent time throwing a ball at the side of a brick wall in Aunt Lil's back garden. I imagined I was Donald Bradman — thunk ... catch ... throw ... thunk. I then took the stick I had been using as a bat and began dragging it along the side of the wall. Its reverberations voiced the frustration I could not show. It was the only time Aunt Lil was angry with me. She hurried from the house, snatched the stick, snapped it, and in a raised and furious voice sent me to weed the garden to make better use of my time.

Dinner was eaten in sulky silence. But before bed, Aunt Lil stood before me and in a sad voice explained, 'I really didn't mind you playing with the stick, but your uncle would never have allowed it, so I couldn't either, dear'.

Following on the heels of this, I mustered the courage to stand by my father as he drove the bus to deliver me back to Aunt Lil's following a visit home.

'Dad, I don't want to go back to Aunt Lil's. She cries at night. And I miss my bruvvers.' I was mad at myself that my trembling mouth had let me down and 'brothers' hadn't come out properly. I waited for the no-nonsense refusal. But Dad was silent.

He must have spoken to Aunt Lil, though the matter was never mentioned again. A few days later Aunt Lil came to me and announced in a firm voice that I was to go back home. For good.

With the selfishness of youth I was elated. 'Oh good. You beaut.' And that night Aunt Lil sobbed more sadly and for longer than I had ever heard. But I hugged my pillow. I was going home.

Years later when I was out in the world running a movie theatre, I had a weekly meeting close to Aunt Lil's house. So every Thursday afternoon I had tea with her. Still she was always nicely groomed and well dressed — she never went to the shops without hat and gloves — her hair tied up in a fussily arranged bun. I liked those visits with a lady whose sense of humour I came to know and enjoy. I think she looked forward to them, too. She always baked a custard tart, light and creamy melting, served with great pride.

As she grew older and more frail her stubborn independence gave way and I took over her gardening on my weekly visit. She had been a lady of means, albeit modest, and had refused any outside financial help. But came the day, with tears in her blue eyes, she whispered to me that she was going to have to take the pension, and 'Oh, the shame of it'.

These were the days when you had to appear in person and cash was pushed across a counter by an officious clerk. I didn't like to think of Aunt Lil, in her hat and gloves, best brooch on her coat, standing in line to collect the pension. I wished I had the means to support her, but knew she would not accept that either.

It had taken time to get to know Aunt Lil. A proud, grand lady of old fashioned values and breeding. I was glad I'd been her favourite then, for now I loved her, too. And when she quietly died, I missed her. ✱

Barnstorming, Thanks To My Aunt

By NANCY BIRD WALTON

A veteran of aviation, Nancy Bird Walton was the first pupil of Sir Charles Kingsford Smith and the first woman in Australia to operate an aeroplane commercially. Her book 'My God — It's A Woman' is compelling reading. Through encouragement and financial backing, her great-aunt played a pivotal role in steering Nancy into her famous career.

*I*T WAS MY GREAT-AUNT, Annie Tommas, who suggested to my father that she would give me the two hundred pounds she intended to leave me in her will if he would put up another two hundred pounds to enable me to buy an aeroplane so that I could go barnstorming when I received my commercial licence. In 1935 barnstorming — taking courageous people for joy flights on a pay-as-you-fly basis — was the only way one could make a living from flying and, although the pilots said the cream had been taken off the cake, I was determined to try to make enough to pay for the petrol and gain the experience of landing in paddocks beside shows and race meetings.

In this endeavour I was joined by a woman pilot who had graduated at the same time as me — who was a much better pilot than I was — and was a wonderful person to have as a co-pilot. Her name was Peggy McKillop (later Mrs Colin Kelman) and she came from Orange, west of Sydney.

I felt a tremendous indebtedness to my great-aunt and tried to do everything I could for her in her old age — she lived to a ripe old eighty-eight. As she had no children of her own she took an intense interest in everything I did (I think she lived her life through me).

Champagne everywhere as Great-Aunt Annie Tommas christens Nancy's aeroplane.

I did not admire my aunts on my father's side very much because they were not very nice to my mother. My father was the youngest and the only boy in the family, with five sisters, so of course he was the apple of their eye. I don't suppose any woman would have been good enough for their dear little brother.

My Aunt Una Bird was one of Australia's first business and professional women, the head of the typing pool in the shipping company Gilchrist Watt & Sandersons. Oswald Watt of that company was a great pioneer of aviation, and the coveted gold medal award given each year for the most outstanding aviation achievement in Australia is named in his honour. He was one of the founders of the Australian Flying Corps in World War I.

Another aunt, Ruby, married one of the Redgraves — a relation of Michael of film fame. This uncle was the principal of a primary school in the Sydney suburb of Wahroonga and was also an authority on Australian birds. ✳

NATURE WILL TAKE ITS COURSE

BY KEN DONE

Ken Done, Australia's goodwill ambassador to UNICEF, was born in Sydney. He left school at fourteen to study art and embarked on a career in advertising which spanned twenty years. It was not until 1978 that Ken first exhibited his work as a painter. Since then his reputation has grown not only in Australia but in Europe, Japan and the United States Of America too. His images of Australia — vibrant colour, striking design and an overwhelming vitality — are the hallmarks of his distinctive style.

*W*HEN I WAS A SMALL BOY — and I hasten to add extremely small (in fact, it would be more correct to say 'baby') — I was involved in a situation that became one of those old 'family stories'. It seems that one day my mother and two of her younger sisters decided that I should be taken from Belmore, the Sydney suburb in which we then lived, for my first big day in the city. I guess my mother was in her early twenties and my two aunts were teenagers.

As both of my aunts were great sewers, knitters and crocheters, I am sure I looked like a cross between a tea-cosy and the Easter Bunny.

I guess a great day in town was had by all, and I would have been constantly fed and cuddled by my adoring young aunts. So far so good. However, on the trip home, somewhere between Canterbury and Belmore, nature took its course.

My mother says that a small wafting from under the crocheted trousers was more than enough to signal real trouble. My aunts at this stage had quickly unfurled a newspaper and sat, cowering behind it, as if I had nothing whatever to do with them.

Like all loving mothers, though, Mum proceeded to use whatever she had in her handbag to try to clean me up before we reached our station. However, the lunch must have been too grand, and she had to resort to tearing strips from the newspaper held by my aunts. Unfortunately, so much paper was needed that in the end — it is said — my aunts were trying vainly to remain anonymous, clutching only a limp piece of newsprint about the size of a crossword puzzle.

I have several aunts and even though some of them are not with us any more, I love them all — and always will. ✳

Ken Done with his mother, aunts and cousins.

164

SCOTTISH KILNS, SPANISH HYDRANGEAS

BY JILL PERRYMAN

Australia's own 'Funny Girl', Jill Perryman is one of our best loved and most respected singers and performers. Both she and her husband, Kevan Johnston were acknowledged in the 1992 Australia Day honours list for their services to the entertainment industry and the arts. Today they live in Western Australia. Jill's parents and sister were all in show business, but she owes much to the support she received from her aunt and uncle.

*W*HERE TO BEGIN DESCRIBING our beloved Aunty Anne? Physically she is tiny, and in her younger days she was as round and cuddly as a dumpling. Though more advanced in years now, she is still young at heart and a great giggler enjoying life to the full.

She and my late Uncle Jim had a great deal to do with me when I first left home in Sydney to begin my career, and travelled to Melbourne to join the theatre as a chorus girl. Many times they not only accommodated me but found space for another lost member of the company.

When I married Kevan and we had our two children we had settled in Melbourne, so it was taken for granted that Aunty Anne and Uncle Jim would look after the children (and the dog!), particularly on matinee days which were always a problem. We would drop Tod and Trudy over to stay, and Aunty Anne and Uncle Jim would be waiting at the door full of plans for them: these mature adults would strap empty shoe boxes on their backs as well as the children's, cover their hands with socks for flippers, breathe through straws and belly-roll around the house as deepsea divers.

I could fill a book with my aunt's malapropisms. When friends of hers had returned from overseas, Aunty Anne excitedly told me that the man had worn 'a Scottish kiln in the Highlands' and that in Spain the couple had 'stayed at a Spanish hydrangea'. She also loves the way Princess Di 'wears a cornet' on her head. We all collapse with laughter and Aunty Anne just says, 'Did I get it wrong again?'

Our very favourite *faux pas* is the story of her viewing an exciting western movie on TV. She was trying to explain the entrance of the 'Red Indians' and breathlessly told us '... and *then* over the hill came the red foreskins'!

This darling lady should have had a tribe of children but, due to problems during the birth, her first babe died and Aunty Anne just managed to pull through. There were no other children.

I have experienced much joy reliving some of these thoughts, which come flooding back, and I'm beginning to think that a lot of Aunty Anne has rubbed off on me as I am continually getting words in wrong places and my family say 'that sentence is a real Annie-ism'! ✳

Jill Perryman's Aunty Anne and Uncle Jim (at left) and her parents.

THE LAST OF THE GREAT ARISTOCRATS

BY COLIN STANLEY-HILL

Colin Stanley-Hill is a flamboyant journalist, author and film-maker. He is also Australia's court correspondent with Buckingham Palace — and is sometimes described as 'the mouthpiece of the monarchy'!

'*L*ADY DIANA'S FAME IS IMMORTAL, and her name will go down in history together with Helen of Troy, Cleopatra, Emma Hamilton and all the other great goddesses of beauty.'

So wrote royal photographer Sir Cecil Beaton of my aunt, Lady Diana Cooper. Strong stuff. But with all due respect to Cecil, it does not do justice to the lady I knew all my life, and still love unreservedly. For to me, Viscountess Norwich, or 'the *other* Lady Diana' as she insisted on calling herself after the 1981 Royal Wedding, will always remain a glorious Auntie Mame whose incredible zest for living far outshone her legendary beauty.

I grew up on stories of her unique attitude to driving that would terrorise fellow motorists and pedestrians alike. On one occasion a startled jay-walker was foolish enough to make a rude gesture, and she pursued him down the stairs of a public lavatory in her car, rapping on the cubicle door where he had taken refuge with an imperious, 'Come out, you bounder'!

Other motoring outrages would see her regularly hauled up in front of 'the beak', as she insisted on addressing the judge, and the press would turn out in force for her court appearances, if only to enjoy the way she castigated both the judge and the policeman who had been foolish enough to book her.

'Rubbish!' she snapped at one judge who had timidly tried to admonish her for double-parking her Rolls-Royce: 'We're not all fortunate enough to have a chauffeur, you know...'

She was the last of the great English aristocrats, a lady of such impeccable breeding as to be completely without fear or pretence. A genuine original.

Debrett's Peerage lists her as the daughter of the eighth Duke of Rutland, despite gossip that her real father was the famous sexual athlete Henry Crust — 'who was so beautiful', she once told me, 'he used to play tennis in the nude'.

But whoever was responsible for her birth, there was no question that her mother, Violet, Duchess of Rutland, was also a celebrated beauty in her own right. Curiously enough, Lady Diana was less than impressed with her own beauty, referring to her famous face as 'that boring thing I put my rouge on'.

She was rediscovered by the media when the death of the Duchess of Windsor in 1986 left only two principal players alive from the Abdication crisis fifty years earlier — Elizabeth the Queen Mother, who personified the British monarchy and all it represented, and Lady Diana, one of the closest friends of the then Prince of Wales, briefly King Edward VIII.

It says a lot for the Queen Mum that these two ladies remained good friends, despite Lady Diana's deafening whispers that could almost shatter glass. Like at one royal reception attended by the Queen Mother, when she let out: 'Of course, she married money, you know,' then in the strangled silence that followed, 'and such a name dropper. Always on about that *bloody* daughter of hers...'

Yet the Queen Mother was a regular visitor to Lady Diana's exquisite home in London's Little Venice, overlooking the Regent's Canal, where she would receive pre-noon callers in her white and yellow canopied bed, liberally sprinkled with her favourite peppermints and her favourite 'dawgies', mainly miniature chihuahuas. Alongside a box of sleeping pills she always kept a phial of poison.

The house was a treasure trove of original watercolours and tapestry work by Queen Victoria, its furnishings predominantly English. So when visitors would admire a rare and costly item of Fabergé — court jeweller to the Czars — it would be grandly dismissed as 'foreign imports'. However, a visit from the Royal Matriarch was cause for added concern. For, typical of Lady Diana, she insisted on displaying her multitude of signed royal photographs in the downstairs lavatory, and these had to be removed by her staff lest their location give offence.

Frankly, there was little chance of that, as Lady Diana's standard invitation to use her toilet facilities was to raise one heavily plucked eyebrow and warble, 'wee-wee dear?' — and any titled lady worthy of her tiara would rather bust than admit to understanding what was being offered.

It seemed a miracle that her staff, a young Portuguese couple and their baby — 'thank gawd I like the baby' — not only stayed, but quite obviously adored her. For she would confess to me in their presence, 'they're probably robbing me *blind*, you know'. Once, when there was no response to my repeated tugging of the bell sash, I asked her, 'What can your staff be doing?' She simply raised a jaded eye and said, 'I imagine they're copulating — you *know* what foreigners are...'

As a new and besotted father, I brought my baby daughter to meet her one Christmas and, after extolling the baby's many virtues, confessed there was just one tiny problem — getting her to sleep at night. The answer was a classic: 'Have you ever tried *gin*? — It always worked for me.' And there was no need to snoop at the ranks of crested Christmas cards that lined her chimney-piece; one would invariably come your way the following year — suitably altered and re-signed with her own name. But that was Lady Diana.

Although she has been described as having the most beautiful face of her generation, and was actively courted by the young bluebloods who went off to fight in World War I, the only love of her life was a relatively penniless lieutenant in the Grenadier Guards, Duff Cooper, the son of a surgeon who specialised in operating on 'unmentionable parts'.

Unaware of the carnage that was to come, Duff jokingly wrote to her from the trenches in 1914, 'Goodbye, my darling, I hope everyone you like better than me will die very soon'.

When the war-wounded started to pour in from the front, she was the first to volunteer to work as a nurse at Guy's Hospital, but her sparkle remained undimmed. When asked if she'd mind driving the ambulance from the railway station, she deadpanned, 'I really think the dear boys have suffered enough...'

Their marriage in 1919 was frowned on by the Duke and Duchess who considered their beautiful and talented daughter was far too good for Duff. But he was to prove them wrong by entering politics and rapidly rising to Cabinet rank. Each successive promotion, Diana was quick to observe, was marked by an even grander room when they were invited to the family seat of Belvoir Castle.

Early in the marriage, she became an international stage sensation in Rex Reinhart's play *The Miracle*. It was a curious part because she played a statue of the Madonna that slowly came to life but never spoke a word — which was probably just as well: for Lady Diana had the most unusual way of speaking, her voice a cross between a yodel and a warble, and with an accent so top drawer she appeared to have every one of the Elgin Marbles firmly concealed within her mouth.

She could never have memorised a script; she had difficulty remembering the names of her closest friends, preferring to call everybody 'darling', which she chose to pronounce as 'dulling'. Even her coterie of small lapdogs, she adored but was far too lazy to exercise, were referred to as 'Dawgie 1', 'Dawgie 2' and so on. One of my earliest memories is of her shrieking from the garden window, 'Dulling, take the *dawgies* with you'!

Little wonder this glittering pair became the darlings of the Prince of Wales' set. Edward openly adored her, but Wallis always complained that whereas she had to spend a fortune on clothes, Lady Diana was dressed by such admirers as Balmain, Molyneaux and Poiret for free.

In late old age, Lady Diana suddenly exchanged her couturier originals for pantsuits and a jaunty peaked cap, explaining in one of her deafening whispers: 'Dullings, I've discovered this marvellous shop. It's called Marks & Spencers.' Then in the stunned silence that

Lady Diana Cooper.

followed: 'Princess Anne must have discovered it, too. For she told me that she buys her under-things there...'

Even so, she always retained a distinctive personal style, refusing to follow society's preference for voluminous ballgowns. She once caused an outrage at a Royal Gala by sniffing, 'People nowadays wear big skirts to hide their gin when there is no drink provided — you can see them in their boxes, lifting up their skirts and hauling out the bottles'!

Yet there was one scandal that never touched her. For, despite her extraordinary beauty and the relaxed moral standards of the day, Lady Diana was completely uninterested in sex. She once told my mother, with a baleful glare, 'I gave him a son and that was that'.

Duff, on the other hand, was an enthusiastic womaniser, but by curious coincidence all the ladies he fancied had cow-like names such as Daisy, Molly, Betsie and Poppy. 'Please keep out of the dairy, Duffy dear,' Diana would warble, but secretly she seemed rather relieved: she knew he would always return home. When the number appeared to be getting out of hand she would tell him, 'I think it's time to cull the herd, dulling'.

In 1944 Duff was appointed British Ambassador to Paris, and they arrived with a fighter escort of forty-eight Spitfires. This jewel in the crown of diplomatic appointments has never seen the like of Lady Diana, before or since, and the French applauded her style that brushed away any remaining cobwebs from the Nazi occupation.

The Windsors also returned, and were frequent guests of Duff and Lady Diana. 'How can you curtsy to that woman?' hissed Margaret, Duchess of Argyll, at one glittering diplomatic reception. 'Easy,' said Diana, in one of her whispers. 'I just close my eyes and pretend it's dear old Mary four-fifths' — her nickname for the Queen Consort of George V, and the Duke of Windsor's mother.

I was a very young boy during Diana's embassy days, but she always treated me as an adult, regaling me with stories of when Queen Victoria was 'kicking up her heels around Europe with that dreadful Scottish servant of hers, John Brown — you know, they called her Empress Brown, dulling?' ... and insisting I sit on the only royal throne outside Britain.

My mother was less enchanted. She received an invitation to a grand Ball at the Embassy, and at Lady Diana's suggestion, was dressed by Coco Chanel, who at that time was still in disgrace for her collaboration with the Germans. For some reason, Chanel chose black and designed a ballgown with a huge shawl collar. At the final fitting my mother made the mistake of suggesting that it might disturb her hair, and with one flash of Chanel's cutting shears her blonde tresses hit the floor. She fled in tears to Diana who suggested, 'Why don't you wear the collar *up*, dulling, then no one will notice'!

Apart from being the only lady in black, and feeling not unlike a shaving brush in a frill, the evening was not helped by Lady Diana's insistence on introducing my mother to all and sundry as 'My dear friend Lady Grace, dulling, masquerading as the Bride of Dracula'! As she was to say over the years, 'a little of Diana goes a very long way indeed...'

But age did not weary, nor the years condemn, despite Diana's frequent complaint: 'All my old friends are either dead, dulling, or have lost their marbles. I seem to spend all my time these days visiting the marble-less.' Her spirit remained undimmed.

With her face still swollen from a fall that broke her nose — 'I was carrying two of my dawgies, dulling, so I had to protect them' — she accepted a luncheon invitation from a senior Cabinet minister, disguising her bruising with thick, colourful make-up. A shocked waiter mistook her for a lady of the night, but recognising her illustrious companion led them stiff-backed to their table. An aristocrat of the bluest blood, Lady Diana had no difficulty in handling the situation. With one hand planted firmly at her waist, she swung both hips and handbag the entire length of the restaurant, and received a standing ovation!

Sadly, as with the great ocean liners on which the gentry once sailed, England no longer seems able to produce great ladies like

Lady Diana. 'Now that I'm a matriarch, dulling,' she told me towards the end of her life, 'it seems that I can get away with murder.' The police no longer arrested her for driving the wrong way up a one-way street or for double-parking outside Harrods. Just a friendly caution, 'You should know better, Lady Di'. She almost missed her verbal courtroom battles.

But that didn't stop her whizzing around London in a sporty Mini she called 'My Womb', her hearing aid switched off to the insults of other motorists. On my last white-knuckle ride as passenger, a policeman on point duty dropped to his knees clutching his helmet as she shot past with a whisker to spare, and I glanced across to see the gleam of delight in those famous china-blue eyes.

One of the most marvellous things about my aunt was that she never once told me *not* to do anything. And her single piece of advice down the years was always the same: 'En-*joy* yourself, dulling. *Gawd* knows we'll all be dead long enough...' ✳

AUNT AGGIE OF LORD HOWE ISLAND

By ROSEMARY SINCLAIR

A former 'Miss Australia' and the first female public relations officer to be appointed to any bank in Australia, Rosemary Sinclair was born and raised on Lord Howe Island. She has written, illustrated and published books about the island as well as Bendemeer, Canberra and the Pacific Isles, and is co-founder of the National Association For The Prevention Of Child Abuse And Neglect (NAPCAN). She is married to politician Ian Sinclair.

*V*ARIOUSLY KNOWN AS 'AGGIE', 'Agatha', 'Aggie-paggie' and 'Agapanthus', my aunt Agnes Christian is one very special person. At ninety-two she is not only interested in world events and family affairs, but will philosophise on everything!

She's mad about cricket and sits glued to the television whenever it's on (and to the video, which was a ninetieth birthday gift from her nieces and nephews). Prior to that it was ear to the radio.

Her hearing is perfect, and that presents a problem for the rest of us. She can be way down the other end of the house and hear what we are saying about her! Mind you, all these attributes in one so old are balanced by a less than sprightly mobility. Sadly, her aging legs don't do their job these days and it annoys her no end.

Aggie has always loved entertaining and only recently did we persuade her that she really couldn't keep cooking meals for the masses. We didn't tell her that our concerns extended to the proliferation of cockroaches and mice invading the premises!

She'd have twenty or more people to dinner and think nothing of it. She even *insisted* on doing all the cooking for her ninety-first birthday party. Indeed, for years she supplemented her meagre income as a housemaid at the local guesthouse by operating

'Aggie's Steak Bar' on her own front verandah, while another section of the old family home was converted into a 'granny flat' so she could take in visitors and friends for a nominal rent.

She has lived in the picturesque, albeit pre-fabricated timber house left to her by her father — my grandfather — on Lord Howe Island, for most of her life.

Born on this beautiful 'gem of the Pacific', Aunt Agnes was shipped to a mainland Catholic boarding school at eight years of age, just two years after her mother died. There she was denied access to any family member until her father brought her home three years later. Only recently she admitted to me she was so overcome when she saw her father again she couldn't speak. Her schooling was finished by attending half days at the island school.

She then worked in Sydney for a while, from where she answered an advertisement for household help on a country property at Uralla in northern New South Wales. There, for six months, she worked for a 'dour Scottish gentleman' by the name of Fraser.

Aggie returned to Lord Howe Island, and the pinnacle of her career was her appointment as manageress of one of the island's leading guesthouses — a position she held for many years.

As residents of relatively isolated Pacific islands, there has always been a fairly close community bond between Lord Howe Islanders and the folk on Norfolk Island. It was almost expected, then, that Aggie just happened to fall for a resident of the latter lovely isle during a holiday sojourn.

Her subsequent marriage to Ben Christian, descendant of the famous *Bounty* mutineer Fletcher Christian, lasted little more than a month. She reputedly found him in a compromising situation with another woman, told him to get lost and took the next ship back to Lord Howe. She's been there ever since!

When asked about her husband a few years back she said that 'the worms have well and truly got him' — and this was on national television!

Since the collapse of her marriage Mrs Agnes Christian has spurned many a likely suitor and I fancy she just likes her inde-

Rosemary Sinclair and her Aunt Agnes Christian.

pendence too much. How else could she have enjoyed a reputation as a 'bit of a devil', with all-night parties around the piano and Ag at the keyboard belting out favourites of years gone by. On such occasions she gave the ivories hell with a decidedly unsubtle touch. Certainly, everyone always loved her rendition of 'Put Another Log On The Fire' and, as the evenings wore on, Ag and her friends became more raucous, aided and abetted by frequent sips of her favourite Scotch.

From my parents' house — just across the paddock — we could always hear the goings-on. Next morning, as youngsters, inevitably we would remark, 'Wonder how Ag's feeling today'. It was more a statement than a question.

Mind you, we knew damn well she'd have been up at 5 o'clock and stoked the 'donkey' (a hot water heating facility known only to islanders and outback country folk), cleared the overnight debris, fed the chooks, done the washing — and would be all finished and waiting to greet the first visitors with a cuppa around 8 a.m.

Somehow Aggie just never seemed to tire. What's more, she remembered everything everybody did and said. As we grew up and partied with her we'd just marvel at her enviable ability to keep going while all around her seemed to be 'falling about'.

Certainly, in our eyes, there aren't too many like our aunt.

Now that age and crook legs have caught up with her, Aggie

needs a bit more care and attention than she's been used to. Recently, my brothers, sister and I tried to arrange for a live-in help but she fought like fifty thousand cats and dogs to dissuade us from the decision. 'If I can't do it myself, I might as well be dead' was her philosophy, and so the *status quo* was upheld.

We ring her every other day (thank God for the introduction of the telephone to this tiny isle) and visit her as often as we can — which is never often enough for any of us. Now into her nineties, she can still charm the socks off the best of them and can put up a fight if she feels like it.

She still does the fortnightly grocery order, shipped on the island's trader from the mainland. Vegetables, meat, fruit, and bird-seed for her beloved budgie, feature regularly on 'the list'.

These days Lord Howe is not self-sufficient, most residents getting their supplies from Iluka on the north coast of New South Wales. My now deceased dad was a gifted gardener in his hey-day and kept his sister and many other islanders well supplied with fresh vegies.

They were great mates, my father and Aggie. She, a few years older, just adored him and when he died we thought she probably wouldn't be too far behind him. She sorely missed the regular early morning 'coffee breaks' on her front verandah when the two of them would sit and talk, content in each other's company or chatting over local gossip and national, international or sporting news.

We thought she was 'on the way out', as my dad would say, just before Christmas 1990 — she was really very ill and we prepared ourselves for what seemed to be the inevitable.

Her little bedroom (she keeps the best room for guests!) was afloat with flowers and cards from all her admirers near and far. She certainly has a few! For weeks the phone rang non-stop with queries and best wishes from all over Australia.

One day an old acquaintance called to see her and asked, 'Well, how are you, Ag?'

Her response, 'Well, I'm still here, aren't I?'

And so she is. *

MORE THAN AUNTS

BY HENRI SZEPS

Henri Szeps knew from the age of nine years that he would be an actor, nevertheless he completed a Bachelor of Electrical Engineering degree and a Bachelor of Science degree at Sydney University — though he's acted ever since! Henri is probably best known for his role of the favourite son Robert, the dentist, in ABC-TV's 'Mother And Son', but his credits also include stage and film successes in many parts of the world.

*I*T IS VERY DIFFICULT TO DISLOCATE comedy from tragedy. Pain and laughter are inextricably linked. I have no aunts or uncles in Australia, but I had a foster mother in Switzerland of whom I was very fond. Here is a little anecdote about her which beautifully demonstrates this coming together of opposite emotions.

I was born in a refugee camp in Switzerland, of Polish parents, in 1943. At that time the Red Cross and the Salvation Army had organised vast networks, throughout that country, of families prepared to take in babies at risk. By the time I was eleven months old, sleeping on straw mattresses on wet floors, my mother had seen enough kiddies around us fall ill, and some even die, to decide that I needed to be taken out of there to safety somewhere else.

So, at eleven months I was fostered out to a wonderful family called the Meyers who lived in the small village of Blumenstein in the Kanton Bern. I stayed with them until I was about three, by which time the war was over and my mother was in Paris, living in an apartment. She wanted me back. So suddenly I found myself living with a lady I didn't know, who called herself my mother in a language that I couldn't understand — she spoke French and I spoke *Schwitzer Deutsch*, Swiss German.

Henri Szeps.

When I was about four-and-a-half my mother fell ill and had to send me back to the Meyers again. My first foster mother had died in the meantime, and my foster father, Ernst Meyer, had remarried — a lady from the nearby town of Burgdorf. She is the foster mother I remember and love. I used to refer to her as *Burgdorf Mueti*, mother from Burgdorf. A thirty-two year old son, Martin, also lived with us.

I remember these people as staunch, honest, generous, salt-of-the-earth Lutherans who by taking me in probably saved my life.

By the time I was six my mother was better and wanted me back in Paris again. This time the Meyers didn't want to let me go. They had my future all mapped out — I would be a lay priest. Even then, they had realised my potential in show business.

My mother finally had to come and get me herself. And this time I really didn't want to go. I didn't want to once again leave this cosy, familiar environment for the alien uncertainties and hardships of life with a single parent in a poor area of Paris.

So the day I left was a very sad day for me. And the moment I recall is when I kissed *Burgdorf Mueti* goodbye upstairs. She gave me a big hug, totally enveloping me in her plump arms, probably crying. I turned around, awash with tears, and started down the outside stairs leading from the chalet verandah to the ground. Martin, at the bottom of the stairs, looked up and when he saw me in tears he said, 'For heaven's sake, don't tell me she gave you a spanking at a time like this!' He then roared with laughter at his own wit as he threw my bags into the car. That was the last time I ever saw them as a child. ✳

QUALITY TIMES

BY CARMEN DUNCAN

Carmen Duncan is one of Australia's most talented and successful
actresses ... even though, currently, she is playing the most loathed
woman on American daytime television soap, in 'Another World'.
The Duncan family is spirited, loving and closely knit.

*M*Y FIRST RECOLLECTION, AS A small child, was being flower-
girl for my Aunt Beth — or Bethy, as she was called by those
close to her. I remember getting up in the middle of the night for a
dawn wedding, and that it was fun. But later on, when I was perhaps ten, I stayed with her in Sydney (my home at the time was in
Cooma, at the foot of the Snowy Mountains) and she was so strict
that I ran away. Well, I packed my bags and ran as far as the front
fence!

Somewhere between that time and the time I finished high
school we had made a truce and I was her greatest fan, and she one
of my best friends. I ran crying to her when my first love dropped
me for another girl, and she explained that it was not the end of the
world and that one day there would be someone wonderful to replace him, but to be sure not to settle for second best. I didn't, and I
was married with her blessing and approval. In fact, she spent days
making the wedding invitations, place cards and other wonderful
goodies by hand.

After I was married and wanting desperately to have children,
we were on the phone to each other every day! My darling mother
was overseas at the time and Bethy filled a void in my life. She
taught me to sew, which was a major feat. She taught me to
embroider (mainly roses and daisies for the baby clothes I was
making). She suggested I drink Scotch and water (easier to keep

Paula and Carmen Duncan.

control, less spirits, more water), she taught me that quality of time was more important than quantity.

We had an understanding that bridged time. She had suffered and found pregnancy difficult, as I did. Her children were her life, so were mine — Duncan and Amelia. She had a husband who played a lot of golf, so did I. We shared so many trivial moments, and so many major ones. When she died unexpectedly at the age of forty-eight, I was devastated.

It was the day before my son's first birthday and I almost lost my faith in a God who would take her from us so suddenly, and so cruelly. But I remembered some of the things she taught me; never give in, never give up and *never* lose faith. I didn't. I haven't. When my son was two he told me he'd had a conversation with a woman called Bethy. To this day I believe he did. ✳

ALWAYS A DASHING HERO

BY SIMON TOWNSEND

Brought up in Sydney, Simon Townsend is the name behind the long-running and very popular children's television series 'Simon Townsend's Wonder World'. Today he is still involved in television production and writes for newspapers and other publications.

I DIDN'T MEET AUNT MIN until I was ten because she lived in England. She was already a revered relative, partly because my mother read out her sister's long and newsy letters with enormous pride. But Aunt Min was also held in great awe by me and my brothers as a dashing hero. We had a photo of her shaking hands with the Queen Mother, who presented Aunt Min with a medal for her brave work as an ambulance driver during the blitzes of London. My mother told thrilling tales of Aunt Min hurtling through the devastated streets of London as Hitler's bombs pelted down.

Aunt Min had married a younger man, a raffish Frenchman with red hair who was nicknamed 'Rouge'. This marriage was whispered of with a whiff of scandal. For little kids in Menzies-era Australia, our Aunt Min had the aura of a combined Joan Of Arc and Mae West.

After her divorce, she and her children — Tessa, Tony and Mary, my only cousins — migrated to Australia. They moved into a cottage on the grounds of the big Bondi boarding house run by my widowed mother. For five unglamorous years these two sisters ran a rough and demanding business, right down to toilet cleaning and breaking up fights.

My mother and Aunt Min always stayed close, even when Aunt Min moved away from the city to the Blue Mountains.

In my mother's last years, as her health declined, Aunt Min left

Simon Townsend and his Aunt Min at a celebrity race day in 1980.

her little cottage in the mountains to come and look after Mum. My two brothers and I had left home and married, and we were deeply grateful for the unselfish companionship Aunt Min gave to Mum in those final years. In our eyes, still a dashing hero. ✳

ITALIAN CONNECTION

By CARLA ZAMPATTI

One of Australia's most successful and creative fashion designers, Carla Zampatti has been honoured by both the Australian and the Italian governments for services to those communities. She designs jewellery to complement her collections, and her attitude to fashion is 'just have fun and don't be afraid to try something new'.

I HAVE A VERY SPECIAL AUNT, who is also my godmother. Her name is Zina, and she lives in Italy where I was born and lived as a young child.

Aunt Zina was married but at that time was unable to have children, so I guess I was like the child she had always wished for. We spent as much time together as we could.

I have fond memories of both her and her home, which sits on a gentle, sunny slope in a valley north of Milan. The house is surrounded by vineyards, and Aunt Zina's kitchen was — and still is — the real country variety, with a stone floor and lots of handy shelves everywhere, and always full of herbs, fresh vegetables from the garden, Italian sausages, salami, garlic and all things provincial.

Aunt Zina has always been a wonderful cook. I remember the great big old wood stove going all day. My favourite dish was a wonderful *pizzoccheri* cooked with wonderful buckwheat pastry, spinach, bacon fat and cheese. It was really very, very tasty. In fact, everything Aunt Zina cooked was delicious.

I also remember that coffee was always being drunk, everyone sitting around the long wooden table. And home-made wine was always on the table, though I think when I was little it was mixed with water for me — it wasn't very high in alcohol, anyway.

As a young girl I didn't really cook, but helped in the kitchen

Carla Zampatti.

alongside Aunt Zina, and often foraged in the forest for special herbs and wild plants to put in the salads.

People in that part of Italy have cows for dairy purposes, not for beef, so meat is not really part of the staple diet. That's no doubt why they are so adventurous with pasta and various other dishes. I recall that sometimes we had chicken and sometimes steak, but they were special occasions. Even today, I only like tasty morsels of meat. I could never manage a whole big T-bone steak.

As well, I have memories of eating lots of fresh fruit rather than sweets and ice-cream. It was a very healthy diet, and it's probably where my good health comes from.

My aunt and I were both broken-hearted on my departure from Italy when I was still just a young girl. Happily, Aunt Zina later gave birth to a lovely daughter and now has grandchildren. Because of Aunt Zina and our affection for one another, her daughter is like the sister I never had.

Although we now live on different continents, our reunions — at least once a year — are as if we had never parted. And it's become a tradition that whenever I arrive, Aunt Zina makes a *pizzoccheri*! *

AUNTS, AUNTS AND MORE AUNTS

BY KATHRYN GREINER

Kathryn Greiner was born in Sydney and educated in Australia, London and the United States. She is married to the former Premier of New South Wales, Nick Greiner, and was previously adviser on early childhood services in the New South Wales Department Of Health And Community Services.

*Y*ES, THERE HAVE BEEN A fair few aunts in my life: eight who are directly related; three or four great-aunts and the usual assortment of women who are 'aunts' as family friends.

The three great-aunts, in my mother's family, were always referred to as '*The* Aunts'. Well and truly in their dotage when I got to know them, they lived together in a flat above the shops in the Sydney suburb of Neutral Bay. (Urban renewal being what it is, these shops, and the flat, have long since been demolished.) Every visit to Sydney entailed a visit to '*The* Aunts' for high tea and to be inspected by them to see if life in the USA (where we spent much of our childhood) was corrupting my sisters and me. All three of them were extraordinarily gifted musicians; one had been a governess to a New South Wales Governor's family and was subsequently taken back to London with them, and the other two had been teachers, which was the 'appropriate' career for women in those days! However, they were each strong in their own right and I often wonder what they would have been like if they had been born a generation later.

An example of the possibilities for women of the next generation is one of my aunts, also my godmother, who I'm pleased to say is still alive and thriving, well into her eighties (a true lady does not reveal her age!). She was a career woman in her own right long before it was 'fashionable' — being a buyer for David Jones for many years, before she was head-hunted by Paton and Baldwins, of the knitting wool fame. Hers was a fairly exacting job which she always tackled with gusto and great flair. She also holds the distinction of being the oldest ex-student of Loreto College, Normanhurst, and I think she is still a great role model for the girls currently at the college!

One of the nicest aspects of my extended family is that we number about forty-six on the direct link of the family tree! All

Kathryn Greiner.

very well, I hear you say, but consider what it would be like to marry into this family when you have really known no other relatives than your immediate family. And then consider the real confusion when two aunts married two brothers, which ensures that one particular surname will abound in the family. Even after knowing my family for twenty-five years, there is a glazed look in my husband's eyes whenever I refer to one of my relatives, as I see him mentally finding their position on the family tree. Though I think the most confusing thing for my husband occurs when we travel around New South Wales and find various second and third cousins popping up!

There is a history of strong women in our large and wonderful extended family. I'm very grateful to all of my aunts for the unique contribution that they have each made in their own families, and nothing is so much fun as having my children come home and tell me that they've met so-and-so 'and he says we're related'. And the nice thing is, most of the time we are! ✳

You've Got To Laugh

By Anthony Warlow

Originally from Wollongong, Anthony Warlow attended the New South Wales Conservatorium Of Music which launched him into a distinguished singing career. At nineteen he appeared as a guest artist with the Australian Opera, and by twenty-one he was the youngest principal with that company. He won huge acclaim for his performance in the title role of 'The Phantom Of The Opera' and for his powerful portrayal of the student leader in 'Les Miserables'. He also sang in the international cast recording of 'Les Mis' and has released his own solo album 'Anthony Warlow — Centre Stage'.

*A*S LONG AS I CAN REMEMBER, Christmas was always a favourite time in my year. Our family would gather from all over the country to celebrate the religious and festive season. Christmas morning hailed the arrival of 'the Italian one', a pet name we gave our Aunty Patti. She would arrive laden with gifts, food and wine — but most importantly with a 'healthy tan', acquired on the shores of Balmoral Beach, and an open smile that meant stories and laughter for at least a couple of days.

I recall sitting in awe listening to the tales of her work place. The characters and situations she would end up in, during her time as a welfare worker. Some sad, some hysterically funny, but always entertaining.

Aunty Patti has always been a terrific sounding-board for me. She's a person who shares my obsession with theatre, films and magic, which as a child I would display in front of her at the most annoying times ... though she never minded. She has always been an honest critic of my work professionally, and is constantly watching out for my next role — or for that matter recommending a role or two for the future.

We share the same sense of humour, which has been invaluable at times. Two occasions spring to mind; the Christmas morning we awoke to a heatwave and a broken-down refrigerator (one could only laugh), and the year I decided I wanted to be the next Steven Spielberg ... with video camera at the ready I tiptoed into the bedroom in order to catch her 'waking moments', which were to be edited into my latest masterpiece *Nightmare On Crown Street 3*.

Fortunately, Aunty Patti always could see the funny side! ✳

Anthony Warlow.

MY AUNT 'NUTTIE'

BY JUDY WHITE

Judy White of 'Belltrees', at Scone in New South Wales, is an author and historian, as well as mother of seven children. She holds a Bachelor of Economics degree from the University Of Sydney and a Master of Letters degree from the University Of New England. She has published several books, all of them highly successful.

*M*Y AUNT 'NUTTIE' MACKELLAR greatly influenced my life. She taught me the value of a keen sense of humour, an appreciation of fine cooking, and the enjoyment derived from theatre and dancing.

Airlie Wallace 'Nuttie' Mackellar was born on the 5th of January 1905 at Manly, the beachside suburb of Sydney, while her parents were taking a holiday from the heat at their country home, 'Exeter Farm', at Braidwood. She was a frail baby in contrast to the robust health of her elder brother and sister, my Uncle Ron and my mother Evelyn, who teased her unmercifully about the fact that she only survived thanks to the services of a wet nurse. Later little Nuttie was made to feel the third member of the team and the odd one out; yet she remained a diminutive but forceful character. Perhaps that is how she was called 'Nut', as anyone else would have cracked under such pressure. Her moments of bliss came when the school holidays ended and her brother returned to Sydney Grammar School and her sister to Abbotsleigh.

Nuttie remained 'too delicate' to be sent away to school and was able to return to her make-believe world in which she pretended to be the parent and her parents were her children, 'Peter' and 'Nancy'

Judy White's Aunt 'Nuttie' Mackellar.

(names that stayed with them, replacing their actual names of Jack and Annie Elizabeth). 'Nancy' then became Nuttie's governess in real life; a highly educated and intelligent person, she took her daughter through the Classics at an early age, instilling in her a love of reading and encouraging her vivid imagination.

As a young girl Nuttie also spent many hours in the country kitchen and became a talented and critical cook. She inherited a keen sense of humour from her Mackellar aunts whose quick wit at the dining room table was legendary. She also had a string of pets at Exeter Farm — lambs, poddy calves and a greyhound dog called 'Trimmer' — and was unable to go into a butcher's shop for she identified all hanging carcases as her poddy calves or pet lambs. As well, she helped 'Peter' to muster in the paddocks and in due course became a competent rider, winning camp-drafting events — she even won a silver-handled stock whip at the Sydney Easter Show.

During the Depression of 1930 and the accompanying stock and cattle market crash, the family was forced to move to Sydney. But although my Aunt Nuttie lived in the Eastern Suburbs for many years and set up different business ventures, her early childhood memories of Braidwood and her dependence on her own inner resources stood her in great stead. Her resilience carried her forward; in effect, she'd had little formal education yet she set up two successful businesses, the Jade Green Beauty Salon in the Trust Building on the corner of Castlereagh and King streets in Sydney and later the White Ivy Salon in Double Bay, which had exclusive hand-sewn lingerie, employed many Italian sewers and sent fine pieces overseas. Nuttie was a perfectionist in her work and the trousseau nighties are still the envy of many brides. Her efficiency and understanding of good handwork had been taught to her by 'Nancy' as they had sat and embroidered together for many hours on the Exeter Farm verandah.

Although very small, Nuttie had tremendous energy. She would work all day, attend dinner parties or go to the theatre most nights, and at the weekend would play competition golf. Then in the winter holidays she would race to the snowfields. In my last year at school at Frensham (the boarding college at Mittagong, south of Sydney), she chaperoned me and fourteen friends to the Ski Club at Mt Kosciusko.

Also while I was at school she met me when I arrived at Sydney's Central Railway Station one night, bundled me into her small car, where I changed from my uniform into a taffeta dress, and drove to the Sydney Town Hall to see the finals of the annual Ballroom Dancing Championships. I can still remember my excitement as I watched the dancers glide across the length of the dance floor. Nuttie was a gold medal ballroom dancer herself and gave exhibitions at the Trocadero, often with Nicki Ivanine from the Russian Ballet.

My aunt never married. She had fallen in love at the age of

seventeen with a good looking and charming English jackaroo but her parents forebade her to marry him; and she never truly loved another man. So my sister Jann and I were treated as her children.

In 1941 her brother Ron died suddenly at the age of thirty-nine and in the same year my mother Evelyn divorced my father.

The sisters became very close; they shared the same vital sense of humour and were the life and soul of many parties. I clearly remember being very angry with a school friend and Nuttie calming me by saying, 'Don't worry, darling, what do you expect from a pig but a grunt'. And when I grew older and was bemoaning my looks she would remark, 'Remember, you are only as old as your neck' — a comforting remark from a beautician.

Nuttie loved young people and was often asked to help brides on their wedding day. In the days of little make-up I can still hear her saying, 'We have to be a bit more theatrical for the dull lights in the church, dear', as she made the cheeks glow with an added bit of rouge.

Nuttie really was a vital personality and only operated at high speed. But she also suffered from very high blood pressure and my mother would say, 'Nut, if you carry on at this rate you will have a stroke'. Sadly this sisterly prediction proved correct and Nuttie suffered a severe stroke while working in her shop. She spent twelve years in hospital.

My mother would visit her regularly and their greatest joy was to recapture the old Braidwood stories: how the milkman used to deliver the milk in winter with a drip on the end of his nose; or how the man who kept chickens had a rupture and had to wear a large, leather apron all his life; or how the local dentist would get going with the pedal drill until it was red hot. These were the characters and stories she loved.

Then Nuttie would look up at my mother and smile, and say, 'Evelyn, the nicest thing you ever did was to have my children for me'. Nuttie Mackellar was, indeed, a remarkable and memorable aunt, and for her jokes and her interests that she shared with us I will be forever grateful. ✳

MY AUNT CAROL COOMBE

BY MICHAEL WHITE

Long before grazier Michael White married Judy (née Crossing), their respective aunts — Carol and Nuttie — were great friends. The White family is proud of its association with the same land since 1831. Michael's and Judy's grandchildren are the seventh generation to grow up on 'Belltrees', in the Upper Hunter Valley of New South Wales.

*G*WENNIE COOMBE AND NUTTIE Mackellar were great friends, about the same age, size and vitality. Nuttie remembered going to a shower tea for a mutual friend when Gwen arrived carrying a large straw broom, on which was a label 'Just a broom from Gwennie Coombe'. Gwennie's real interest was the theatre and, although her father was a well known philanthropist and theatre owner in Perth, Western Australia, Gwen chose to defy his advice and financial assistance and went off to London instead. At first the going was tough, but then she got minor roles, changed her name to Carol Coombe and had great offers for leading parts — she appeared in West End plays and gained Hollywood contracts.

Carol Coombe was my mother's sister. She left Australia in 1930 when I was only two years old so during my childhood I could not remember her. However, we established a very close friendship when I arrived in London after the war, in 1949. London was grim, but Carol was full of the joys of life. She had married Ronnie Armstrong Jones and brought up his son, Tony (later to become Lord Snowdon). Carol took us two youngsters to nightclubs and theatres, and then Tony and I toured Europe together, later meeting up with Carol and Ronnie and staying aboard a yacht in the Mediterranean off the island of Porquerole.

Carol loved fun and was apt to do mad things like an exuberant teenager. Yet when we stayed with her at their ancestral home, *'Plas*

Carol Coombe in Hollywood, circa 1940.

Dinas', in Wales, all the servants revered her. She never lost her Australian natural charm.

Carol was deeply saddened by her divorce from Ronnie Armstrong Jones, though later she married an Italian, Beppi Lopez. Tragically, both Carol and Beppi were killed in a car accident on the Appian Way in Rome in 1966.

Carol is buried near the poets Shelley and Keats in the beautiful cemetery near the Porta San Paolo. Perhaps it is dramatic irony that she had played Fanny Brawne in the 1935 production of Dorothy Hewlett's play *Bright Star*, which is about the youthful John Keats. Sometimes Fate does intervene, as Carol Coombe enjoyed her impish appearance and would have hated to have grown old. ✳

197

GREAT AUNTS, ALL

BY MICHAEL KIRBY

The Hon. Justice Michael Kirby — one of the most outstanding members of Australia's judiciary — is a great law reformer, President of the New South Wales Court Of Appeal and public speaker of renown.

*L*IKE MOST MEMBERS OF AN Anglo-Irish family, I was blessed with a close-knit group of people who were most influential in my development. They included my aunts and great-aunts.

As my father was an only child, I had no direct aunts on this side of the family. However, the paternal line did provide a bundle of great-aunts — all too young to think of as 'Great-Aunts', though they were 'great' in other ways.

My great-grandmother on my father's side — who taught my mother how to attend to me, her squawking first-born child — was widowed at quite an early age. She was the salt-of-the-earth. Practical, caring, sensible, industrious. Even though she died when I was quite young, I still recall her most vividly. She had seven children. They were given the names typical of the turn of the century, and rather lovely to my ears: Ruby, Jack, Norma, Gloria, Frank, Anne and Lillian.

Great-Uncle Jack, when only eighteen years of age, witnessed the terrors of World War I. The true extent of the suffering, including that of Australians, in those terrible battles was brought home to me in 1990 when I visited the battlefields in northern France. Row after row of crosses mark the graves of the Australian soldiers who fought on the other side of the world for 'King and Country'. Few visitors attend those manicured lawns nowadays. On Anzac Day there are still official speeches, but for the most part those soldiers sleep in the midst of the farmlands of France. Jack came back from the Light Horse but he was shattered by the experience.

Ruby, the eldest of my great-aunts, was a serious and thoughtful person whom I did not know well. She was a great reader and inculcated reading in her family.

Norma (Normie to my brothers, sister and me) was my father's mother, and hence my grandmother. She was an outstanding person of cultivation, intelligence and sensitivity. She was a person of poetry and literature and she helped to inspire me to enter those realms of gold. My tales of her generosity (and of my neglect, sadly) would fill a book.

Michael Kirby's Aunt Lillian.

The next daughter, my Great-Aunt Gloria (always Aunty Glory to me) was ever an independent spirit and happily is still so. She was one of the early visionaries in the Women's Movement in Australia, like the intrepid Miss Hayes who unsuccessfully applied to be admitted as a barrister in Perth in 1908.

Aunty Glory refused to tolerate a world dominated by men. She was a friend and colleague of Lady Jessie Street, a great leader of the movement for reform. She was against war — perhaps she saw what it had done to her brother. She took part in the International Peace Movement and was a strong supporter of what we would now call social democracy.

Aunty Glory used to travel a lot. My first visions of the big world out there beyond Australia came from the postcards she sent me from foreign parts. These postcards followed the grand trunk route of the Empire. One from Ceylon, another from Bombay, an exotic one from Port Said, views of the Pyramids and of Copenhagen. Aunty Glory stimulated my vision of myself, then a small schoolboy, as a citizen of a wider world.

Aunt Anne — again, really my great-aunt — is also, happily, still alive. She lived in Bellevue Hill when I was a boy. She had married a most cultivated and refined gentleman. I still remember their spacious home when I visited during World War II. Aunt Anne and her husband, my Uncle Gerald, later moved to Turramurra. They and their lifestyle were always my ideal of gracious living. Persian carpets. Beautiful mahogany tables. Fine china. Always a touch of elegance. In fact, Anne was a true auntly figure. And she still is.

And then there was my Aunt Lillian. Tall, shy, beautiful, sensitive Lillian — the youngest of my paternal great-aunts. As children, my cousin Angela and I could not get our mouths around that name. So it became 'Lilyanne', and that is how she signed her letters and cards to me to the end of her life.

Aunt Lillian was a marvellously delicate soul. She was living with my parents when I was born (she was always close to them, and it was the end of the 1930s when times were hard). My mother, ever prepared, had her nightdresses neatly packed with tissue paper months before I arrived on the scene. When the time came she left in the taxi with Aunt Lillian, dropping her off at work on the way. Aunt Lillian said I was a false alarm. Some alarm. When I came into the world, my aunt and her mother provided respectively support and guidance for my parents, so inexperienced but soon surrounded by a growing family.

Aunt Lillian was a highly intelligent woman who learned secretarial skills. She became the secretary to a series of American executives of the Goodyear Rubber Company. Years after they had returned to the 'Land Of The Free' they wrote to her, such was their admiration of her efficiency and grace. When the time came for me to seek my first job as an articled clerk, it was Aunt Lillian who faultlessly typed up all the letters of application. Most of them came back rejected — but it was no fault of hers. I had no connection with the legal profession which was then very largely a family affair. Ultimately, one of Aunt Lillian's letters produced a job. All subsequent applications in my early days in the law were typed by her.

Aunt Lillian never forgot a birthday or an anniversary. She was generous to a fault. She never intruded but was always there when help was needed. When times were especially hard for my parents, bringing up young university students before public grants were available, Aunt Lillian would always dip into her own pocket, matching words of encouragement with practical relief when it was necessary.

She married late, meeting her husband Harold on a visit to Tasmania.

Aunt Lillian became the secretary to the bursar at the Scots College, Sydney. She was very proud of the school. Loyalty was a strong quality of all these sisters. In fact, Aunt Lillian bombarded me with news of the Scots College. I retaliated with the news of my own school, Fort Street High — the oldest public school in the country. She remained with Scots until her retirement. Sadly, her retirement did not last long enough. I deeply regret the fact that a busy life prevented my knowing her better. But is that not common? We neglect our family and friends in the rush of daily events which necessarily gobble up the hours.

My aunts were, and some still are, remarkable women. They were a hardy group, born in earlier, tougher times. They were self-reliant. They read much. They loved poetry. Their lives were an inspiration to me.

A strange beast is the aunt. She is not typically in your immediate family circle. And yet she is not a stranger. You can get to know her as a person, even a friend — if you try. Yet there remain the assumptions and invisible barriers formed by blood and affection. My aunts are no exception to this general rule. Though in every other way they were, and are, exceptional women. ✳

AUNTS REMEMBERED AND ADORED

BY DIANA FISHER

Diana Fisher, radio and television personality and columnist, was born in England but has graced Australia with her bubbling presence for many years. Diana has a wealth of aunts, and, although she was an only child, she is nevertheless 'aunt' to lots of her friends' children in all parts of the globe.

*A*UNTS ... GOD LOVE 'EM! There are those you're born with, those you acquire along the way, those who are borrowed and the one that in due course you become.

My lot all had the most marvellous names, and quite a few that I made up! Like our childhood neighbour Aunty Pussyfoot, because of her fluffy slippers which I delighted in throwing into the garden for her to collect. (Her husband was lovingly known as Uncle Budgie for, as you can guess, he had an aviary full of them!)

My mother's sisters were Aunty Ruth, Aunty Ruby and, the favourite of all, Aunty Venus, the goddess of love, of spring, and the brightest evening star! Aunty Venus was also my godmother, and she was responsible for some of the most memorable presents in my young lifetime ... the first pair of roller skates, the first wind-up gramophone, the first big bicycle and the first ice-skating boots, for she was a champion ice skater and dashingly beautiful.

On my father's side there were aunts in the Davis/Mortimer families like Aunty Maude who lived in the large house on the hill and was the wife of one Alfred Seaward, whom my mother referred to as the old 'box-knocker' — the well-to-do owner of Seaward & Sons, the undertakers! Aunty Maude and Uncle Alfred often took me in their lovely Daimler to Hornsey to some great fruit shop and would give me a penny to buy a bag of fruit!

Then there are the 'borrowed aunts', who are not related but are great friends of the family, like Aunty Nell Coote who lived next door to us. During the war she lived in a large house with cellars in which we slept every night — a rather unattractive, slightly damp 'air-raid shelter'. She was also the most generous of aunts, always giving me the most lovely unexpected presents like 'twenty-one of everything' — from pennies to sixpences, shillings, half crowns and pounds — on my twenty-first birthday. A marvellous gift.

And Aunty Ada — Dora Aylard — who wore her hair in a bun, and with whom I would paint and sew during school holidays.

There were also the 'working aunts'. In London at one time I became a Universal Aunt, one of many, working in every kind of activity and service that the community might want. Through this organisation I met and cared for lots of young children who needed an aunty to get them across London or on to trains and planes for holidays. I also drove elderly ladies to the seaside, helped run the Crane Kalman Art Gallery in Brompton Road, looked after an eminent Harley Street physician, and best of all ran David Niven's life for six months during the filming of *The Guns Of Navarone*!

Of course, one of the things about getting married is that you suddenly acquire a whole lot more aunts. In my case there were fifteen of them on both sides of the Fisher family! [Diana married the Hon. Humphrey Fisher, son of Lord Fisher of Lambeth, Archbishop of Canterbury.] I can't say that I got to know all of them, but I certainly had my favourites. There was Aunty Mosey (whose real name was Decima), married to 'Dosey', and then my mother-in-law Lady Fisher's sisters, Aunt Pen and Aunt Peg. Aunt Peg ran Lambeth Palace and all the activities therein, and Aunt Pen lived in a gorgeous Derbyshire cottage in Repton, where a lot of the Fisher family went to school and grew up. She was a great gardener, a great musician — hummed a lot about nothing much — and was a great giver of unexpected presents, such as her own engagement ring to me, which years later was reset by Andrew Grima, the Queen's jeweller, and which is my prized possession to this day.

All these wonderful aunts bring back so many memories and happy times, they are truly remembered and adored.

Of course, I had a couple of other aunts — Aunty BBC and

Diana Davis then, Diana Fisher now...

Aunty ABC, both of whom I worked for over the years — though they are not the real McCoy! Nevertheless, I had some of the best times of my life with Aunty BBC, working there in Outside Broadcast (Sound) for eight years with all those famous commentators, and later doing all the research for those great Royal occasions, let alone starring in their revues and having my own colour TV program on BBC 2. And in Australia, Aunty ABC, who has given me those great broadcasting moments on radio and television. *The Inventors* for twelve years running, and numerous radio programs with Ellis Blain, Peter Young and that great weekend program with Johnny Hall. So many wonderful memories and happy times.

Now it's my turn to be 'Aunty Australia' to numerous young people who come and stay with me and then journey on, and Aunty Di-Di to my friends' little ones.

Whatever, I just know that aunts are wonderful, loving, caring people, who have added a great deal to my life. ✶

TOTAL DEVOTION

BY FRED DALY

Fred Daly was a Member of the Australian Parliament for thirty-two years and Leader of the House from 1972 to 1975. Since retirement from politics, he has won acclaim as an author, columnist, public speaker, lecturer, radio and television personality, and tour guide.

I'LL NEVER FORGET MY AUNTY ANNIE. She came to live with us in the little country town of Currabubula, near Tamworth in New South Wales, to help my mother — her sister — raise her large family of six girls and five boys.

Aunty Annie had an unhappy early life. A very religious woman, she sought to enter the convent. Her parents, staunch Irish-born Catholics, for some reason or other would not consent to her taking up her chosen vocation. (Strangely, they also withheld their permission for her brother to enter the priesthood — and ultimately he was ordained in his mid-thirties.) Despite an unsuccessful marriage, Aunty Annie was blessed with two wonderful children — a son and a daughter — loyal, devoted and loving. They cared for and protected her, and in later years gave her great comfort as they succeeded in life.

Aunty Annie lived with us for years when I was a very small child. We lived two miles from the town and I vividly recall her making her way each week, either on foot or being 'given a lift' in a horse and sulky by a friendly passer-by, to the local public school to take the Catholic children for a religious lesson. She trained my brothers to be altar boys and prepared us for our First Holy Communion. The local Catholic church was her love and domain. I've never forgotten her devotion to her religion in those very poor days.

I became very attached to Aunty Annie. In fact, I adored her and loved her like a mother. When her brother was appointed parish priest at Dunedoo and she decided to become his house-keeper, I fretted so much for her that my parents consented to my going to live with her for twelve months. I was ten or eleven years old at the time. I took up residence at the presbytery, attended the local convent, became an altar boy and at the same time enjoyed being with my beloved Aunty Annie.

It was at the Dunedoo Convent that an exasperated Reverend Mother told me and another boy, Roger Nott, that neither of us had a brain in our head so we would both probably get into Parliament! And we did.

Fred Daly, aged ten-and-a-half, about the time he went to Dunedoo with Auntie Annie.

Deeply religious, gentle, loving, humble, compassionate; you name the qualities, Aunty Annie had them all. She was the nearest approach to a saint that I've met in my lifetime. Real Mary McKillop stuff!

After the year was up, I returned home and saw Aunty Annie less frequently than I would have liked to.

Aunty Annie passed away whilst living with her son in a large country town. I was then a Member of Parliament. I was present when she was laid to rest. I mourned her passing — a saintly, charitable, gracious lady, never complaining, always helpful, devoted to her faith, family and doing good for others.

I'm certain that my beloved Aunty Annie smiles down on us from Heaven today as I recall my unforgettable memories of my unforgettable aunt. ✻

AUNTY MOLLY

BY NAN WITCOMB

Poet Nan Witcomb lives in Adelaide. As author of the many volumes of 'The Thoughts Of Nanouska', she has delighted us with her sensitivity, sense of humour and great understanding of humanity.

We called her Aunty Molly
she was really no relation —
she lived in a little cottage
behind the railway station —
When we came home from school that way,
she'd often ask us in —
she gave us home-made lemonade
that smelt like Gilbey's gin —
She had a half a dozen chooks,
four cats, two geese and a goat,
and a pair of yapping pekinese
in matching tartan coats.
The miniature menagerie
was shown off with pride,
and we were fascinated
that she let them live inside!
She milked the goat in the kitchen,
'Close to the jug,' she said,
and the chooks would lay an egg a day
in the middle of her bed!

The geese just wandered in and out,
leaving their mess behind,
Aunt Moll would bid us 'Watch your step',
but never seemed to mind.
There were baskets for the pekinese
on either side of the hearth,
and a cat called Lil had kittens
on a cushion in the bath!
We used to talk for hours and hours
of the household that she kept—
we wondered where she ate her meals
and where she washed and slept —
We left that town so long ago,
Aunty Molly must be dead,
so it still remains a mystery—
perhaps she lived in the shed...! ✳

Nan Witcomb.

PART THREE

THE JOY OF AUNTHOOD

THERE WERE TWENTY LITTLE STEPS

A PERSONAL TRIBUTE BY
MAREA STENMARK

*T*O HAVE AN EXQUISITE, NEWLY born babe named after you is a
thrill and cause for jubilation. To be invited to be godmother
brings a sweetness all its own. Godmother. What a beautiful title!
What a compliment! What an honour! Two friends choosing *you* to
be responsible for their precious baby's well-being! How awesome!
How overwhelming! How joyful! So, to be chosen ten times as I
have been, to be godmother for children who have scattered and
now live in many parts of the world, fills me with pride and
pleasure. But to be an aunt is best of all. 'Aunt' — so aristocratic.
'Aunty' — so affectionate. To have the opportunity to play a part in,
to influence, a trusting little child's life is so important that at first
it's hard to comprehend. And many of us do not. We just say with a
deprecating laugh, 'Yes, I am an aunt again'. But just as every birth
is a little miracle, so too is the sensation which comes with
aunthood. In motherhood, extra love is found, immediately, for the
new arrival, and, of course, it's the same with aunts. Could it be that
we are optimists at heart? That we rejoice at life? Embrace the new
challenge? And crave the love which we receive as well as impart? I
believe so.

> From the first to the last, the lot complete
> There were ten little steps and stairs

SO WROTE JOHN O'BRIEN seventy years ago in *Around The Boree Log*.
I always loved that poem and dwell on it now as I write about my
own nieces and nephews. Little steps and stairs indeed. Twenty of

'The Waggaites': Brian, James, Michael, Damien and Caroline.

them. A whole staircase. One might say a spiral special!

My eldest brother Jim and his wife Thérèse (Tess) have five children — four strapping sons now all taller than six feet two inches, well built, smiling, upright, and one beautiful daughter, the last born, Caroline.

First came James Ossian the third. Very affectionate and quick to do things as a baby. He walked early, running everywhere at ten months, he talked early. He was always absolutely fascinated by fire engines and was constantly racing out into the street at the first sound of a siren. Later this interest was transferred to the sport of motor racing. He is a lover of music and sometimes my phone will ring and the conversation will last fully ten seconds whilst he delivers: 'Ree — ABC FM will interest you. 'Bye.' Today he is the father of two fast growing, already tall lads, Andrew and Timothy, and a daughter, Cassandra. Where have all those years gone?

Next came Brian, a couple of years later on. He, too, is a lover of music and the arts, especially Eric Clapton! Brian is not in touch on the minute every minute — far from it — but sometimes about

April or May will come the longest letter from Melbourne, when something he has seen or heard has just reminded him of me. I love that spontaneity and much prefer it to a structured 'I must be in touch with my aunt' type of situation. Today he is financial controller of an electrical components distribution company and father of four — Anthony, Nicholas, Jacqueline and Matthew — and doing an excellent job.

Number three was Damien (Damo). A child with a beautiful nature and looks to match. He hasn't changed really. Damo has a Bachelor of Business degree and today heads The Stenmark Organisation, a marketing sponsorship company, with great integrity and success. He has grown into the kind of man one would have hoped for — he was kind and thoughtful as a child and he still is. As the father of his one and only daughter, Zoë, he's kept on his toes! Just a few months ago identical twin boys entered the ranks, rejoicing in the biblical names of Zachary and Jordan.

The fourth and last son was Michael Thor (the god of thunder) — the Swedish influence again emerging! Physically, Michael is the most like his dad. He, too, is extremely interested in sport and is a keen sportsman himself. At his wedding a few years ago he looked so incredibly like Jim that I did the auntly thing and cried. I also committed the cardinal sin for aunts and told him so — not once, but twice! Mike has a Bachelor of Business degree majoring in local government and is today the administration officer of the Great Lakes Shire Council in New South Wales. Oliver joined the family last year — a lovely laughing child with a will of his own!

Finally, Caroline Mary Thérèse arrived. A source of great comfort and joy to her parents, her mother's companion and loved by the whole family. She married recently and, as she walked up the aisle on her father's arm at Xavier College Chapel in Melbourne, a whole lifetime of memories passed before my eyes. A radiant bride — obviously very happy.

It is a pleasure to sit round the dinner table and listen to them all. Their repartee is clever, witty and pacy. It's never prepared, it just happens. Unkind? No. Funny? Very. They lived in Wagga

Wagga ('the Waggaites') so I didn't see as much of them as they grew up as I did of Tony's and Pat's children who lived closer and were always referred to as 'the Strathfield Stenmarks'.

The Strathfield Stenmarks comprised half a dozen daughters and one son. A lovely family. All these Stenmarks are tall, brunette and have suntanned skin — despite the current trend.

Alison, the eldest, is my godchild. She was the quickest, brightest, most alert little girl. Always responsible and aware that she was in charge of her little sisters. She would march them all off to school at some ungodly hour of the morning; they only lived across the street from Santa Sabina, so they were always at least an hour and a half early, thanks to Alison. Today she is a busy barrister.

Catherine Mary arrived next, called Casey by everyone from a very young age. Always smiling and a 'real little mother' from the time she could walk, she went on to become a nursing sister and Qantas flight attendant. She's married now and is, again, a real little mother to two boys, Oscar and Harry, and a gorgeous girl named Rose. And she's still smiling!

Number three was Susan who always looked fragile, like a little waif. I have a special affinity with Suze as we both have birthdays in March. We are Pisceans and water pals! She was born four days after my twenty-first birthday party, which was held at her home, and I'm sure that party induced her to arrive early! She went on to become a beautiful model, well known on television as 'the Macleans' Girl' (an absolute credit to her dental background!). There were many other ad's which featured her smiling face including several for The Wool Corporation and others for Good One and Glucodin with John Alexander. She then became Channel 7's weather presenter and a TV reporter on *Eleven AM*. Today she is a feature writer with *Vogue Entertaining* and the proud mother of Anatole.

Along came the fourth daughter, Judy Anne Dynamite! At this stage Jim and Tess had four boys while Tony and Pat had four girls and they were talking about swapping wives the next year! Judy's dark brown eyes don't miss a trick. Never have. She is a physio-

'The Strathfield Stenmarks', clockwise from top left: Alison, Susan, Judith, Casey, Antoinette, Paul and Mary-Louise.

therapist, currently doing her Master degree in public health, and lives around the corner from me. In fact, from my kitchen window I know just what she's up to! Harking back, Judy hated getting up early in the morning and going to school so one night she decided to sleep in her uniform to save a little time. The only trouble was, the night she plotted all this so carefully was a Friday. Pity there was no school on Saturday! The best laid plan...

Finally, a beloved son arrived, Paul. Tall, gentle, he looks like his dad. With his wry smile and ability to listen, he is the ideal confidante to his six sisters. Today he is a nightclub proprietor but it seems only yesterday that he would ask his mother as she put him into bed, 'Can I give your hair a twirl?' He made this request, as a child, for years. In those days it was the fashion to have very set looking hairstyles and Pat would always ask her hairdresser to leave a little piece of hair 'out' so she could fix it herself after Paul had given it a twirl. Typical of Pat! And Paul!

Artistic Mary-Louise came next, a dear little girl, the only blue-eyed member of this family. She has had successful showings of her own paintings and is today assistant director of a contemporary art gallery and loving it. She trained at the City Art Institute, now part of the University Of New South Wales. Mary-Louise is the mother of two very, very interesting little boys, Max and Charles. At her twenty-first birthday party this independent young lady proposed a toast, 'Here's to those who wish me well and all the rest can go to hell'!

Antoinette was the final fling in that family. As the expression goes, 'she's been here before'! Very self-sufficient. Nobody can put anything past Antoinetteybear. Today she is living in Japan where she teaches English, is a disc jockey and does some modelling.

So many memories of them all! I can see the first four little girls in Harrods' black and white striped dresses, a present from their great-aunts, coming to our shows. Sitting up as little ladies at the theatre, coming backstage and making straight for the wigs and the lipsticks, trying on the shoes. They were gracious enough to begin with, 'It was a beautiful show, Ree', and then while everyone else was excitedly talking, they would get quietly into the make-up.

Then there is my sister's big family. Anne and John McGlinchey had eight children, beginning with Anne — my godchild, my niece, my friend. Anne possesses many talents — probably too many — so she always had a problem choosing between writing, theatre and arts/law, from which she graduated some years ago from Sydney University. We have 'long deep and meaningfuls' over many cups of coffee together! I remember, distinctly, the joy her arrival brought to the family. My only sister's first born! A new life! A Sunday child — 'blithe and bonny'. And, when she spoke very early, in whole sentences, like 'Daddy's in court', and even sounded the 't', I was thrilled.

Next came Mary Thérèse (Meg). Tiny, yet with the heaviest tread you've ever heard! Crash, bang, wallop and you knew Cyclone Meg was around. A graduate of economics/law from Sydney University, she now lives and practises in South Africa where she is married to a publishing executive. I proposed the toast

The first six McGlinchey children.

at her wedding — hardly believing she was already so well and truly grown up! Meg and I have such confidence in each other that we are partners in a real estate venture.

Enter Michael, the number one son. A beautiful baby boy. Could I be biased? Michael's solemn brown eyes would follow you round the room. He has an associate diploma in leisure studies from the New South Wales Institute Of Technology and makes — and serves, regularly — *the* best cocktails ever. One of the quieter members of the family, Michael and I have long chats. We enjoy each other. He is a good pal of mine, Mike.

The second son arrived, christened John after his father. We used to call him 'Black Jack' with his dark flashing eyes, his quick intellect, his beautiful nature. He sang like an angel, and when he was only ten was diagnosed with leukaemia. Just those few short years ago bone marrow transplants were not performed in this country, so his parents and younger brother, Patrick, who was his donor, went to Seattle in America, where this was done. He lived for five more years, during which time he survived graft versus host disease, meningitis, shingles and pneumonia. He recovered from them all, and we felt sure he was supposed to keep living. He was such a wonderful example and friend to so many people that we were shocked when he died on Australia Day, the 26th of January 1981. It seems fitting that this young man died in the International Year Of The Disabled Person, because disabled he was after all his treatment. We lost a *great* friend when John went.

David was next, a premature baby — almost two months early, so he had to demonstrate in the very first days of life that he was a fighter. Now, in his twenties, he is an arts/law graduate working in a legal firm in the city, on the threshold of his working career. He's newly engaged to be married, yet I can still see him as a little boy, careering round the back garden with a big grin on his face, wearing a huge Lawrence drycleaning bag to keep off the rain!

Number six was Patrick, born when I was living in Canada and six months old by the time I returned. A beautiful looking child, like a Hummell character, interested in everything and everyone. Patrick read newspapers and magazines at an incredibly early age and would insist on telling everyone what was in them! He has always been extremely well informed. An unusual and special character is Patrick. He, too, is doing law, having successfully completed the economics/social science leg of the faculty. Paddy and I will have a trip together one day, I am sure — the only reason we haven't

Danny and I go through 'the rules' at the beach.

so far, although we keep talking about it, is that we remind each other of Patrick Dennis and his Auntie Mame and neither of us can bear the thought of where we might end up! Paddy, as number six, was the youngest in the family for some years, and was known to grumble when he came home from school that 'there are never any babies in our house'!

Well, six years later, Daniel Edward McGlinchey arrived. A real personality boy. The only child of two I've ever known to get up after his afternoon sleep and say to any visitor who was present, with a big smile on his face and his arms extended wide, 'Delighted to see you'! The image of his mother, Anne. When Danny was a little boy I would often take him to the beach at Balmoral, on Sydney's north shore. At the end of summer we were like two little brown nuts. Last thing before setting off I would ask him to repeat the rules of the beach. His little voice would pipe up: 'One, no running away to the island, two, no asking for food — because we have our own — and three, none of that stupid nonsense'. 'That stupid nonsense' incorporated everything from crying or throwing sand to staring at people or splashing water, and was one of the best rules I ever made. Dan and I share the same sense of humour, and we certainly laugh a lot together. Being the youngest of a large family, he is never afraid; there is always someone ahead of him to help. I relate to that, being in the same family position myself. Dan and I play tennis together — singles — and it won't be long before he trounces me off the court! We make each other run, hit hard and enjoy each other. Dan is a house captain and prefect of his school, St Ignatius College at Riverview in New South Wales. We are very proud of him — he has a beautiful heart, Dan Boy!

A couple of years after Daniel was born, Elisabeth arrived. Another special child, she was born with Downs Syndrome. She was a child who brought great joy to the family and to the many friends who took turns to take her to Macquarie University, where she was enrolled in a special program. She was doing so well there that she was about to commence school at Rose Bay Convent, the school attended by her sisters Anne and Mary. A great achievement for such a child. Tragically, she was killed in a car accident a few days before Christmas, at the tender age of five years. Her funeral was on Christmas Eve and many a succulent turkey was ruined while her mass was attended, the church simply packed to overflowing. Christmas will never really be the same again.

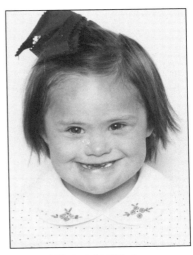

Elisabeth McGlinchey.

The devastation of Johnno and Lissie both dying within a few short months of each other was excruciating. If this is how an aunt feels, I thought, then how can the parents possibly survive. But survive they did. Inspirationally. I don't suppose a family ever gets over those dreadful tragedies but we learn to cope and get on with it, some better than others of us. Both these children had a profound effect on our lives, indeed on the lives of many people, and they will never be forgotten. Of course, in time things returned to normal, whatever that is. I agree with English author Somerset Maugham, who said in the latter part of the last century, 'There is really no such thing as normal'. So, perhaps I should rephrase those words to read, 'In time things returned to usual — or as close to usual as possible' in that family.

Each of the children came to stay with me when they turned seven years old or when they could sleep through the night, whichever came first. They would arrive with their storybooks, to read in the morning until I woke up. They were allowed to go to the fridge and have as much lemonade and ice-cream as they liked for breakfast. Of course we became friends! They became quite used to seeing a fridge where the two most important ingredients were milk (for that essential first cup of tea of the day!) and champagne. In the kitchen when I was preparing a meal they would gaze at me as I sampled every dish. Because they'd all been taught not to touch before the meal was served, they couldn't believe that I was getting away with it. Feeling their eyes on me I would explain, 'Just testing ... to see if it's suitable for the children'! It has become a household phrase and today they all quote it to me — at my expense. Children often have an uncanny knack of knowing an aunt's strengths and weaknesses. Many a night I would escort them — on my back — to bed, delighting them as I rolled, exaggeratedly, from side to side. They referred to the journey — and to me — as 'the Reepy Express'. This 'service' was performed for many years and it was only after several children got on my back at the same time that the Reepy Express called it a day and came to a halt one New Year's Eve. What a relief!

So many endearing childhood expressions! Whenever I was looking for something I'd lost, like car keys, Michael would try to help, long before he even knew what they were, by holding up anything and saying, 'Whattadatsay?' If there were too many people at a get-together, Paddy would exclaim, 'Every Wayne and his dog was there'. I recall taking Alison to the Royal Easter Show where she was interested in the animals. Her eyes out on sticks, she exclaimed, 'Aren't those cows steep!' She changed this to 'hooge' (huge) after that. It was also Alison at her first pantomime who burst into tears when the chorus of tap dancers appeared and began to dance. 'Why on earth are you crying?' I asked. And, in between sobs, she told me she felt so sad for those little girls because they all had wooden legs. Why do they have to grow up? And it was Meg who roared from one end of the house to the other when David was beginning to crawl: 'Mum and Dad, quick! He's up on his foils.' An understandable remark since the Sydney hydrofoil had just been introduced on the Manly to Circular Quay run.

It's almost eerie to me — Dame Edna Everage would call it 'spooky' — seeing my parents all over again in the next generation! My parents' qualities and their foibles are passed on to these young people, some of whom they didn't even meet. Yet, in a smile, an expression, a gesture, the young ones continue the family traits, for better or for worse — though just as long as my parents' integrity

The latest members of the Stenmark family — twins Zachary and Jordan.

and intrinsic values are upheld, I believe it's for better.

Members of a family, to me, are like ferns in a pot. The fern with its roots is placed firmly in the centre of the pot with earth evenly surrounding it for nurturing and warmth. The fern grows, and do we have seven or eight even fronds? Rarely. Some are straight and tall, others grow apart, others need the support of each other. Some fall by the wayside or shoot straight out on a limb. Yet they all come from the same family, with the same nourishment, the same care, the same attention. Why? And a bouquet for those who have joined our family along the way. Thank you for meeting us halfway, for enriching us. It isn't easy entering a big family — it can be very intimidating, overpowering even. But we've been very, very lucky.

Different though the personalities within the family are, they do have one thing in common. They all have a sense of humour. And nary a wimp in sight! I sometimes wish there were a few mellower ones — it would make life a little easier! Whenever I hear someone say, 'she's a Stenmark, all right', I am never sure if it's a good thing or not, and I often suspect the latter.

Over the years my nieces and nephews have developed an extraordinary variety of names for me — Aunty Ree, Aunty Reepo (when the car polish came out), Aunty Arpo (when they couldn't quite manage Reepo), Reepy-deepy, Greeky-Reepy (after a Mediterranean trip), Reeps The Deeps, Reesy, Rio and Reebok (when they thought I was too big for my boots) — but, today, from all of them, it's simply Ree. They all used to refer to my apartment in Stanton Road, Mosman, as the 'Stanton Motel' not only because they were served huge breakfasts there but they ate them on my balcony, overlooking Chinaman's Beach and Balmoral, whilst still in their pyjamas — the ultimate in luxury.

My complaint is having insufficient time to see them all. With everybody so busy we try to arrange a breakfast, but being a family of sleepers-in that doesn't always work out so well. I have a soft spot for them all. Each and every one of them has something special. I also have a friend in each of them and I feel they believe they have one in me. They must think so because of what they tell me! I have always encouraged them, though not pushed them, to talk, and sometimes they tell me things I really wish I hadn't known, but in a large family like ours you have to roll with the punches.

I have different things in common with each of them. With some it's a love of theatre or movies. With others it's the sun and the sea. Sometimes it's a passion for writing and words and music and laughter that unites us. Whilst I often don't like what they tell me they have done, I always love them and, generally speaking, I'm very proud of them. Some of them think I'm hard on them and I suppose in a way I am. But they know it's because I think they are capable of much, and 'to whom much is given, much is expected'. Not for my sake, but for their own and their family's. The approbation of one's nieces and nephews is not easily won. Every aunt, it seems, has to earn it.

Families are funny things. Large families bring great joy and huge responsibilities. When life is going well there are exaltations almost beyond description, excitement, activity, adventure —

everyone is always doing something interesting. But when life is not exactly a bowl of cherries, an aunt weeps for the mistakes, fears for the outcome and dies a thousand deaths for the folly and imprudence which often brings such heartache to parents and the family.

People sometimes say how they envy our large, volatile, impulsive, entertaining, humorous family. But it has to be worked at — no one is in top gear all the time, and perhaps understanding that helps to make us adaptable. We don't live in each other's pockets, in fact the months fly by without our seeing each other, but when we meet up we not only love each other but we like each other, too.

Christmas Day, to me, has always been a magic event — so much excitement, chatter, laughter and sometimes a few tears. Being together is so important. But despite the tiredness occasioned by weeks — no, months — of getting ready and the heat and all the peripheral frustrations, it is a wondrous thing to see family members from the latest baby — sometimes only a week old — to the eldest, with so many disparate personalities in between. And it's a time to remember those who have gone. I hear people talking of rare family reunions held in huge venues in order to contain the numbers and I think how blessed we are to have our happenings so frequently. Annually, at least. Long may they continue!

> There were ten little steps and stairs,
> But the years have shuffled them all about,
> Have worn them thin, and straightened them out
> With the tramp of a hundred cares;
> Ay, and each grim scar has a tale to tell
> Of a knock and a blow and a hand that fell,
> And a break in the line, and a gap, ah, well —
> There *were* ten little steps and stairs.

In my case, twenty! ✳

HUGS AND KISSES

BY MARGARET FLETCHER

Margaret Fletcher, popular radio broadcaster with Melbourne's 3AW and former public relations consultant, was born in Canberra and attended school there before moving to the Victorian capital.

RATHER THAN 'HERE'S TO AUNTS!' we should be saying 'here's to nieces and nephews'.

I just adore and love mine. There is something wonderful about being able to step into their little lives for a time, spoil them rotten, then step aside and let the mums and dads do the tough stuff! Mind you, even though the parents do the tough stuff, I think they appreciate the aunts as well. We are like an excuse for a good time!

My line-up consists of the two 'babies' — a ten-year-old and an eight-year-old — and two 'grown-ups' in their twenties, so I can enjoy two very different parts of the age spectrum.

The most beautiful thing is that in giving all the love, the hugs and the kisses, you get in return the same, twice over.

They also allow their aunt to be unbelievably *wicked*! ✳

Margaret Fletcher at a very special occasion.

AN AMPLE AUNT

BY SU CRUICKSHANK

Jazz singer, comedian, actress, author and all-round entertainer — Su Cruickshank's talent knows no bounds. But she revels in the role of aunt.

S LIDING DOWN MY AMPLE tummy and plopping onto my cushioning feet, giggling, then begging for more. Trampolining on my king-sized bed, cuddles galore and generous wet and sloppy kisses. These are the rewards of being 'Aunt', coupled with the finest of conning, exquisite emotional blackmail and inexorable and unconditional love.

The first born tummy-slider of my lovely brother and his easy-to-love Margaret is Tim, bright, funny and passionate. Timothy is a superlative con-artist and when young enough to have only three or four words under his belt, he would offer to his fully attentive and gushy aunt a smorgasbord of moist and snotty kisses, moments before his grinning plea of, 'Bikkies? Su-Su, bikkies'!

Later on, as a schoolboy, he learnt to poke fun at his very fat aunt. Catching him and his mates laughing at my superb undulations, I challenged him to find one bad aspect of obesity. After some humorous consideration, Tim came back with, 'You take up too much space'! Can't argue with science!

Sweet Amy, a caring and beautiful dreamer who misses nothing. Watching a French-inspired, tongue-in-cheek commercial for 'Le Snack', Amy was heard to comment drily upon the actor's froggy antics, 'Le idiot'! She doesn't need to con her doting aunt, for when she winds around me with her cuddles she can get just about anything she wants.

Sophie is a little like her aunt, lovable, musical and quirky. As a baby she was even more so, chubby with funny fat feet and a

Su Cruickshank with her young nieces and nephew.

healthy regard for her tucker. One mealtime when Sophie was awash with mashed pumpkin, eyes glazed with blissful satisfaction, my brother was heard to sigh, 'Hell, Sophie, I hope you can sing'!

Well? What is wrong with following her aunt into the singing, clowning world of wonderment?

The last Cruickshank, so far, is baby Matthew who, apart from his death-wish leaps and his passion for Walkmans, promises to have the shining glint of madness that seems to permeate my humour-soaked family. Welcome to laughter, Matthew!

Enough of this gushing, Aunt Susan! Ah yes, let me dwell on the beauty of being an aunt — the subject at hand.

I see myself as a part-time parent, without the responsibility of day-to-day nurturing, of knowing that watching television all night, in bed with chocolates, chips and soft drinks, isn't going to hurt — just this once! The pleasure of their well-rounded education and enquiring minds without the hideous expense and endless checking of homework.

All visitors, including nieces and nephews, are rather like fish —

227

they go off after three days. So dear Aunt Fattyboomsticks has the joy of handing them back just as they become exhausted from no proper sleep, develop tummy aches from too many take-aways and are completely insufferable from such indulgence.

My Auntie Mame antics extend far from my family. Most of my friends are blessed with many sproggets and though, as yet, I haven't added to this world, I have always enjoyed children. I have learnt so much from them and hopefully have given more in return. The many, many children in my life have allowed me to be silly, petulant, carefree and funny. Kids look at life from the ground up — positively, hopefully, innocently, selfishly.

The only joy which would surpass being an aunt will be to become a mum — who knows? ✳

AN AUNT'S STORY

BY WENDY FATIN

The Hon. Wendy Fatin, MP, is Minister for the Arts and Territories as well as Minister Assisting the Prime Minister for the Status Of Women.

*A*CCORDING TO A FRIEND OF mine, it is Agatha Christie who did the ultimate disservice to aunthood by leaving the rights of *The Mousetrap* to her nephew. My friend, a veteran aunt, is convinced that this accounts for the wistfully solemn looks aunts receive from the offspring of their brothers and sisters.

In many ways my experience of being an aunt reflects typical Australian conventions. As Tolstoy says at the beginning of *Anna Karenina*, 'Happy families are all alike...' My parents had offered their three children a stable base on which to build our own versions of family life. By the time I was in my early thirties I had four nieces and two nephews as well as two young children of my own. After periods of working and studying overseas, we all returned to live in Western Australia where we moved quietly in and out of each other's triumphs, disasters and mundanities.

So it is really only now that the family has grown up that I can reflect on the experience of aunthood, identifying some of the threads which connect me to the newest member of the family, born in November 1991. James Fimmel, who bears my father's name, is the son of my eldest niece. Seeing James in my house at Christmas time illuminated that web of connection, made me feel the uniqueness of those relationships we too often assume to be smothered by convention.

In the beginning, of course, there was the question of what we called our children. It is one thing to find that the names you have

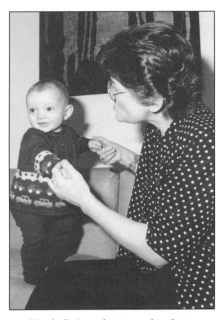

Wendy Fatin and great-nephew James.

selected are shared by next door's pet. (Imagine calling a cat Peter Anthony anyway!) It is quite another to find yourself vying with your sister for an Elizabeth. The result of the contest, I am happy to report, was a tie: she got a Beth and my daughter became Libby.

During the passing of the years, I was not conscious of influencing the diverse collection of youngsters who soon dropped the Aunty from Aunty Wendy. I suspect, however, that I would score rather low in the Agatha Christie stakes. At our most recent family gathering I discovered that their memories of Aunty Wendy insisting on the eating of vegetables has led to at least one permanent aversion to carrots.

Perhaps part of the strength of the bond between an aunt and her nieces and nephews is found in the common knowledge they hold about her brother or sister. Listen to the stories told by people who were brought up living in close proximity to their extended family. For these people, falling out with their mother or father meant packing a bag and leaving home and, for them, the drama was not lessened one iota by the fact that their destination was their aunt's house next door. After all, what better way to console your tearful, indignant young self than to proclaim your outrage to someone who remembers the offending parent at much the same age! Somehow the voice of reason is so much sweeter when it is conveyed with that mixture of loving detachment which lies at the heart of an aunt's caring. ✻

MY LIFE AS AN AUNT

BY PAULA DUNCAN

Paula Duncan lives life to the full. In the 1980s she was queen of the Logies, winning award after award for her impressive television performances. Offstage, too, she has played a variety of roles — wife and mother, fund raiser with the Lorna Hodgkinson Sunshine Home in Sydney, and manager of her own promotions company. A great entrepreneur.

S ITTING HERE IN MY LOUNGE room pondering over my past and gazing at the beautiful unique faces of my nephews and nieces who stare at me through picture frames on my sister's dresser, I have a feeling of sweet warmth, of security and of great pride. All of them are strong individuals with strong principles, and, most of all, they know how to share.

I love being an aunt, though to some extent I try to take a 'back seat' — for, being a mother myself, I know that no one should take over the role of 'mothering'. So what is the role of an aunt? What does it mean? What does it mean to one's brothers and sisters, to nephews and nieces? What does it mean to me?

I was the baby of four children — and a very loved baby. Apparently my darling mother was not too thrilled about having me at the age of forty, but my dear old dad believed I would keep them young. Mum and Dad have always seemed very much in love with each other and have always seemed to share the symptoms of young lovers, experiencing jealousy, tears, anger, passion and fun, not to mention loads and loads of affection.

I remember my childhood very well and the involvement and dependence I had on my brothers and sisters, all for different reasons. They all had very different roles, and still do. When I reached the age of twenty-five, I really wanted them to step aside and look at me for what I was as an adult, but to no avail: I was still 'Baby Doll Face' and have never grown up. I perhaps never will.

My eldest brother, Robert, filled me with so much confidence, love and emotion. He took me to school on the first day and cried as much as I did. I always knew that if the whole world seemed against me, he would still be there with his big arms holding me, loving me. He has the most beautiful children. Three boys by his first marriage and a boy and a girl by his second. In his second marriage he also inherited two other boys.

In the same way Robert and I shared each other's loves, we also shared each other's children. After the break up of Robert's first marriage I became almost like a young wife for a while, a house-keeper, baby-sitter and friend to his children. Each of them so different. Each of them individuals again. They have grown up into handsome men. His eldest, Mathew, has become like a guide and friend to me and we mix socially even now. His second child, Christopher, is a self-sufficient friendly face with a twinkle in his eye that will never leave him. His third son, Stephen, is still like someone I feel the need to protect and care for.

When Robert's daughter, Samantha, was born by his second marriage, I was given the role of godmother. Oh boy, the first daughter and it's me — the godmother — what a joy! I 'adopted' her from when she was a baby and have shared her babyhood and childhood, and, at times, have even shared responsibilities for her, when she stayed with me at weekends. The little boy from this second marriage, Benjamin — the baby fighter, the little hero— has turned into a giant both intellectually and physically. Robert's step-children are also such individuals ... but they always treated me like the good time party girl! The eldest, Frank, became a great social friend and companion to me. Today he has an unusual business, making wonderful pencils, by hand, out of twigs. His brother, War-ren, is a musician (my dream) and a self-made, self-taught achiever.

Robert lived with me for a period, through some good times and bad. Somehow the emotion and love that he poured into me as a child felt so naturally exchanged into the lives of his children.

Then there is my sister Carmen, whom I idolized as a child. I would stay up all night for her, and even take on the role of secretary. She told me the facts of life, she shared her career with me, she was certainly like a mother to me. In fact, ironically, I have always been more afraid to tell her my secrets than to tell our mother. Carmen would not let me get away with anything. I didn't fight with her until the age of twenty-one when I desperately wanted her to look at me as an adult.

When her first child, Duncan, was born, a boy, I felt I had almost borne him myself. The overwhelming joy I consumed was almost the same way she felt about me coming into the world, I guess — I know my mother said Carmen prayed and prayed for me to arrive. Duncan suffered a great deal as a child with epileptic fits, and he nearly died with encephalitis. Once, when he was in my care whilst Carmen was in New York, he was rushed to hospital. I remember praying for God to take my life, not his. A bond was created and I guess we have become like soul mates. He truly knows me with my good qualities and bad. I have the openness to tell him almost everything and I know, no matter how far away our lives take us from each other, we will always be together in spirit.

Then this beautiful baby girl was born, Amelia. She was exquisite from a tiny babe. She was always more Mummy's girl, but according to Carmen she adopted some of my characteristics — determination, perfection, self-sufficiency. It has only been over the past couple of years that we have become very close. I feel more like a big sister to Amelia than anything. Someone who is there when Mum is not around, but someone perhaps who is special, whom she can trust and talk to. We laugh a lot together, we love each other. There you see the role my sister had with me reflecting on my relationship with her children. The sister, the friend, the mother, the idol worshipping — and, funnily enough, they're the children I stay up all night and wait for. Just like I did for my sister. She was my 'other mother' in some ways — and I feel like I am somewhat Duncan's and Amelia's.

Annabelle and Josephine.

Now my other brother, Warren. The rock, the plodder, the backbone, the protector from the background. He is loyal and extremely realistic. Boy, did I need him! I was always apt to go off the rails and enjoy life so much that I didn't accept the harsh realities of survival. It was Warren who became my accountant, and would warn, 'that's all fine, as long as you can afford it'! I could never thank him enough for his help. He was the one who never expected compliments or thank yous. The one who didn't share his feelings as much with me as did the others, but he was always there.

When his eldest child Heidi was born I felt that perhaps by being a security for her I could give Warren something back for the security he gave me. She was deliciously pretty, warm and loving. She was sweet but very insecure in herself, I guess the same way I was (she needed to be loved, like me). I identified with her and we seem like magnets to each other. I have always been drawn to her.

Then this boy arrived, Robert, who was indeed special. Warren was faced with the horrible pain and loss of a child. Why? How could this happen to him? I wanted to kick things and thought how helpless I felt that after all these years of him protecting me I couldn't protect him when he needed me.

In time another son, John, arrived. Strong, determined, and indeed a gentleman, he reminds me of my dad and has inherited so many of his qualities, the best of them being that he is loved by just everyone.

Next a baby girl was born, second daughter, Josephine. A no-nonsense, personality-plus type, she's kind, outspoken, sensitive, innocent and loyal: the replica of my sister-in-law. Josephine has been a strong influence on my daughter, Jessica. She is always there to protect the underdog.

I was wanting desperately to be godmother for one of Warren's children and stood in line with great competition, feeling like it was the only way I could inherit some legitimate responsibility for one of his babies without stepping on toes. I guess I wanted to do for one of his children what he had done for me. It happened: this beautiful warm baby girl was born, Annabelle, and I was made godmother — what a thrill!

To be part of a family like ours is not easy. There is all the emotion that Mum and Dad have always had for each other — love, jealousy, fear, anger, passion, fun, laughter and more love. The fulfilment of being a member of this family is that we all get to see the qualities that we dream of come to life in the lives of one or other of our future generations.

What is the role of an aunt? I am an aunt only by name. I am actually all of those qualities to my nephews and nieces that my brothers and sisters were to me. Rest assured that I could be nothing to any of them without the love and trust of my in-laws. I could not be an aunt if I wanted to take over the parental role.

I see an aunt as a coach standing in the arena and cheering the successes of the team. Enjoying the moments of triumph with my brothers and sisters, and commiserating with them when they don't succeed. Helping out when required, volunteering support and guidance, but never being in charge.

What does my being their children's aunt mean to my brothers and sisters? Sometimes the sense of security and the knowledge that Aunty Pauly is always there. But there can be a sense of infringe-

Paula and her nephew Duncan.

Paula's niece Amelia Barrett.

ment: things have not always been easy in trying to be the 'super aunt'. There's always the quandary of not knowing whether I am needed more as a parent-support or simply as a friend to my nephews and nieces.

What does being an aunt mean to me? A special friend and a chance of new life, the chance to experience childhood again, turmoils of teenage life, the fear of adulthood. A chance to be mad, zany, bossy, warm, affectionate, and not to be judged the way my own children will probably judge me. No real expectation on either side. No relationship like this can exist without a need. I needed to give back to Robert, Carmen and Warren some of the life they gave me. I guess my nephews and nieces want to share some of that past life, too. In this relationship there seems no condition. This relationship provides a good spirit, a ready smile and friendly word, a sympathetic ear and even a shoulder to cry on.

I know my own children, Jessica and Simon, need my brothers and sister to be their uncles and aunt and to share a little of what I was before I married. My childhood perhaps. Possibly to feel free to love without my parental judgement and to know there will always be someone there to talk to if anything happens to me.

I know, however, it is easier being an aunt than a parent.

What does my being their aunt mean to my nephews and nieces? They will all have different answers. They all have different spirits. I really don't know. But I hope our relationship is as rewarding to them as it is to me. ✷

ACKNOWLEDGEMENTS

THERE ARE MANY, MANY PEOPLE who have assisted me with *Here's To Aunts!* and I truly thank them for doing so. I could never have managed without:

Lady Martin who kindly wrote the Foreword.

Margaret Molloy who not only co-ordinated the manuscript but assisted enormously with picking up and delivering of books from libraries, always with a smile.

Margaret Hewlett for additional typing assistance.

Celebrity contributors for sharing their precious memories with us all and for providing irreplaceable photographs of their aunts.

Hat-trickers (eight celebrity contributors who have been in all three 'family' books — *Mum's The Word, Dad's The Answer* and now *Here's To Aunts!*): Ian Chappell, Ken Done, Diana Fisher, Michael Kirby, Gary O'Callaghan, Jill Perryman, June Salter and Carla Zampatti.

Those terrific country aunts, mainly from Warren in the central west of New South Wales, who provided insight into that particular aspect of aunthood.

Sandra and Peter O'Brien of 'Hatton' — that wonderful property where I met with the women of Warren.

Staff at Mosman Library, Sydney, who were unfailingly helpful with this project.

Damien Stenmark for his interest and expertise.

Kim Anderson, Garth Nix and everyone at Angus & Robertson for their invaluable input and for making the publishing of this book such a pleasurable experience.

Pat Kelly of the Australian Broadcasting Corporation Archives for information regarding ABC programs.

Patsy Flint of Aunties And Uncles for providing resource material.

Helen Grasswill, my painstaking editor and stimulating friend who allowed me to express myself (in my own style!).

Bruno Grasswill, artistic director, who designed the book and its splendid cover.

Selwa Anthony, publishing agent, mentor, encourager, friend, negotiator *extraordinaire* — my heartfelt thanks and appreciation ... (I agree with Nan Witcomb who said: 'Selwa would swap a dead rat for a dead possum and somehow make you believe you'd won'!)

And finally, to my family, friends, colleagues, associates and, above all, aunts, my sincere gratitude.

Marea Stenmark

COPYRIGHT ACKNOWLEDGEMENTS

Dennis, Patrick *Around The World With Auntie Mame*, Shakespeare Head Press Pty Limited, London 1958

Eakin, Robin *Aunts Up The Cross*, Anthony Blond Ltd, Sydney 1965

Elliott, Sumner Locke *Careful, He Might Hear You*, Victor Gollancz Limited, London 1963 & Pan Macmillan Australia Pty Limited, Sydney 1983

Greene, Graham *Travels With My Aunt*, The Bodley Head Ltd, London 1969

Grenfell, Joyce *In Pleasant Places*, Macmillan Limited, London 1979

Grenfell, Joyce *Requests The Pleasure*, Macmillan Limited, London 1976

Gielgud, John *Early Stages*, Hodder & Stoughton Ltd, London 1939

Lear, Edward *The Pobble Who Has No Toes* (from *Laughable Lyrics*, 1877), Ash & Grant, London 1977

Magarey, Susan *Unbridling The Tongues Of Women: a biography of Catherine Helen Spence*, Hale & Iremonger Pty Limited, Sydney 1985

Mantle, Jonathan *Fanfare*, Michael Joseph Ltd, London 1989

Moore, Katharine *Cordial Relations*, William Heinemann Ltd, London 1966

O'Brien, John *Around The Boree Log*, Angus & Robertson Publishers, Sydney 1978

Porter, Eleanor H. *Pollyanna*, first published 1927, this edition Harrap, London 1975

Pownall, Eve *Australian Pioneer Women*, Currey O'Neil Ross Pty Ltd, Melbourne 1980

Searle, Betty *Silk & Calico*, Hale & Iremonger, Sydney 1988

Stoney, Barbara *Enid Blyton: A Biography*, Hodder & Stoughton, London 1974

Thomson, Helen (Ed.) *Catherine Helen Spence*, Queensland University Press, Brisbane 1987

Weidenhofer, Maggie (Ed.) *Colonial Ladies*, Currey O'Neil Ross Pty Ltd, Melbourne 1985

Wilks, Brian *Jane Austen*, The Hamlyn Publishing Group Limited, London 1978

Young, Jeanne F. (Ed.) *Catherine Helen Spence: An Autobiography*, W. K. Thomas and Co., Adelaide 1910, reprinted by the Libraries Board Of South Australia, Adelaide 1975

And to newspaper publishers for their assistance, especially *The Sydney Morning Herald*, the *Daily Telegraph Mirror* and the *Australian*.

MOUNT WELLINGTON

A FORGOTTEN CORNISH MINE: 1969-1981

John Hurr

Published by The Trevithick Society
for the study of Cornish industrial archaeology and history

© John Hurr 2021

ISBN 978-1-8384245-0-3

Printed and bound by Short Run Press Ltd.
25 Bittern Road, Sowton Industrial Estate, Exeter EX2 7LW

Typeset by Peninsula Projects
c/o PO Box 62, Camborne, Cornwall TR14 7ZN

Aerial view of mine site in 1975 before development.

Contents

Introduction   1

Foreword by Tony Brooks   2

Chapter 1: The Forgotten Mine   3

Chapter 2: Deep Down   18

Chapter 3: Prospecting and Planning   29

Chapter 4: Rain, Rain, Go Away   40

Chapter 5: Water! Water! Everywhere   46

Chapter 6: Onward and Downward   59

Chapter 7: Preparing for Production   68

Chapter 8: Disappointment and Danger   83

Chapter 9: Hanging On   121

Chapter 10: A False Beginning   137

Chapter 11: Geology   147

Chapter 12: Early History   151

Chapter 13: Later History   158

Chapter 14: Glossary of Terms used in Mineral Dressing   160

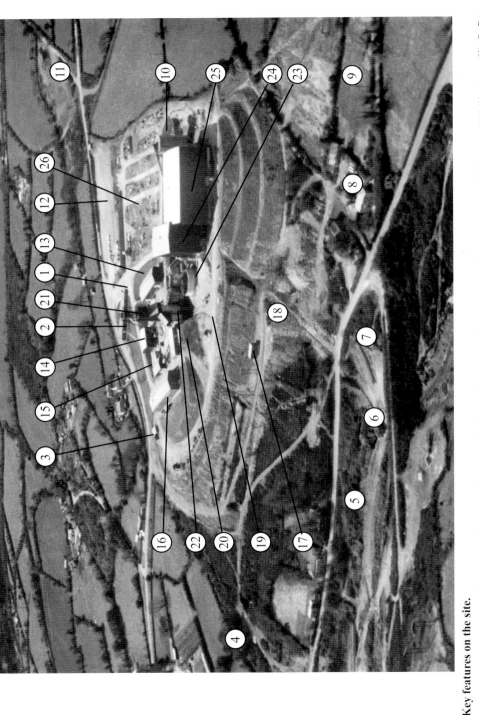

Key features on the site.

1. Site entrance. 2. Administrative office. 3. Robinson's Shaft ventilation fans & underground escape route. 4. Course of Wellington adit. 5. Carnon River. 6. Mill process water pumping station. 7. County Adit. 8. Wheal Andrew Farmhouse. 9. Wheal Andrew Nursery. 10. Fine ore bin. 11. Harveys Shaft and ore stockpile. 12. Car park. 13. Mechanical workshop warehouse. 14. Winder house. 15. Compressor house. 16. Mine office and dry. 17. Electrical substation with two 11kV overhead lines. 18. Process water pipeline. 19. Mine sewage plant. 20. Rock drill shop. 21. Headgear. 22. Waste and coarse ore bins. 23. Thickening plant. 24. Ball mill section of concentrator. 25. Concentrator. 26. Storage and stockpile yard.

Introduction

During the summer of 2002, I visited Mount Wellington for the first time since I had stopped working there about twenty years previously. Wandering around the site, I was struck by the silence and melancholy surrounding the mine. This was understandable following the wide scale destruction caused by the elements and anyone seeking scrap metal. The compressor and winder houses had been dismantled to remove the valuable machinery that had once been installed there, adding to the scene of desolation. It was hard to believe the mine had once offered so much promise for the future.

I have wanted to tell the story of Wellington ever since that visit in 2002. However, later that year I was diagnosed with Parkinson's Disease. Having recovered from the initial shock, I eventually became Chairman of the local PD Society and threw myself into supporting Branch activities. All my other plans were put on hold. At the start of the Coronavirus Pandemic and with all the restrictions we had to endure, my thoughts returned to telling the history of Mount Wellington; or, more correctly, of relating my memories of the mine, from the early days of re-opening in 1969 until Billiton Minerals closed the Concentrator and abandoned plans to continue local mining operations in 1981.

I knew nothing about writing a book, so I sought the advice of Graham Thorne, Publishing Editor for the Trevithick Society. Graham's enthusiasm and encouragement gave me the resolve to begin the project. There were times I wished I had not started, and many days when I was defeated by Parkinson's – but even if it won a few battles, I was determined that it was not going to win the war. It took over a year to complete the first draft, which I handed over to Peter Joseph the Curator and Web Master for the Society. I am particularly grateful to him for writing the chapter on the mine's geology. Pete's skill and experience was evident from the start and I was reassured that the book was in good hands. I would also like to thank my family for their encouragement, and particularly Laura Gulliford, Jason Hurr and my wife Sharon - without their help, this would not have been completed.

Foreword

By Tony Brooks

The author briefly takes us through his time as an electrician at South Crofty and Pendarves Mine before he joined the contracting company, Thyssens, who were sinking shafts at Wheal Jane and at Mount Wellington

In January 1971 he joined Cornwall Tin and Mining Corp who owned Mount Wellington. He was responsible for much of the electrical work on the mine and remained with them until it closed in April 1978. Ultimately Wheal Jane which had been acquired by RTZ, took over the pumping at Wellington. Shortly afterwards he joined Billiton Minerals who had taken over the Wellington mill and some of the surface buildings and were looking at working surface deposits in the Carnon Valley. He left in 1981 to go into private consultancy

Books on individual Cornish mines tend to be written by authors who have little or no actual mining or engineering experience and very rarely have actually worked on the mines that they describe. This book is thus unusual in two ways: that John Hurr worked at Mount Wellington through the period described and that he has written this book predominately from an engineering point of view. This is, I believe, the first time this has been done – and not before time. As every mine manager knows that without the backup of good engineering the mine will not work.

He also gives us a glimpse of the politics of the mine's ownership and the problems of raising sufficient capital in order to progress the mine. Information that one would not find in any published sources.

What is common to all mining operations is that things go wrong – often. Mount Wellington had serious ground problems coupled with high water flows. The author describes at length how he and his team dealt with them. One can almost feel the frustration struggling with recalcitrant pumps and electrics.

Historians tend to write about mines that closed long before living memory. The facts are often well known but information of the people who made the mine work is inevitably lacking because it is not recorded in the dusty pages of the Mining Journal or perhaps the cost books. In this book we meet many of the people with whom John worked some 40 or 50 years ago. Reading his book brings back memories of the visits that I made to the mine and some of the names are very familiar.

Chapter 1

The Forgotten Mine

Approximately 20 years after Mount Wellington closed I was driving from Devoran towards Bissoe, following the route of the old Redruth to Chacewater Mineral Railway. Looking to the north west I could see the abandoned mine and the rusting headgear standing sentinel, overlooking the Carnon Valley. This view has become part of the local scenery since Mount Wellington first opened or, to be correct, reopened, in a wave of optimism during the late 1960s. Now like another monument to the stricken mining industry the mine stands slowly decaying waiting for the final act; courtesy of the scrap yard no doubt. I thought this would be a good time to stop and see what effect the ravages of time may have had on the mine. I heard that some years previously New Age Travellers occupied the buildings and a considerable amount of vandalism had occurred. Preferring to remember the mine in good working order, the thought of seeing this dereliction was also a factor in my reluctance to visit the site. Passing Bissoe I turned up the hill towards Mount Wellington and although feeling apprehensive decided to park the car off the road near the main gate. I could see that the former car park and entrance drive had been blocked with boulders and piles of rubble, presumably to deter the possible return of squatters. It was then that I could see someone moving around inside the security fence so I left the car and went over to the gate for a better look. A few people were indeed walking around, perhaps someone on official business but there was no sign of any vehicles. Perhaps they were former workers so I strained to see if I could recognise anyone. By now they were disappearing behind the old workshop buildings and looked to be heading down the slope towards the large mill complex where the tin ore was formerly processed prior to being sent for smelting. For some reason I thought it would be good to share some past moments with them so I climbed the side railings without thought of trespass and entered the site.

It felt quite weird to return, especially in this manner, after an absence of some twenty years. My attention was immediately diverted to the mine office, adjoining the site entrance and I entered this sad looking building which had been completely gutted with no doors, windows, ceilings or internal partitions. As I wandered through I remembered the large planning office, located at the end of the building, where during that last period of operation the weekly management meetings were held. Those meetings became progressively more gloomy as the inevitable closure of the mine drew closer. I remembered the same building in the early days of the mine when the whole atmosphere was buzzing and a wave of

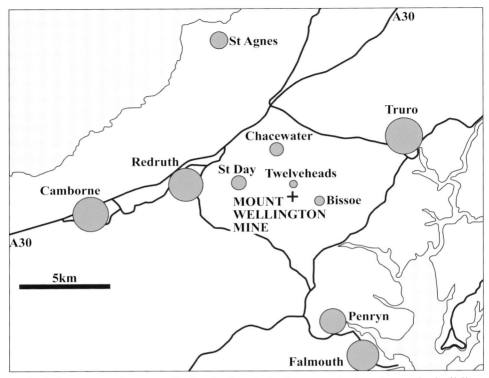

optimistic expectation prevailed as in the start of any great adventure. The building then housed a small specialist workforce with the miners dry or change house occupying one end and offices for the mine management, engineers, geologist, and secretaries in the other half. This was, for a period, where I had a desk, and although in those early days there was little time for sitting I did become involved in the huge pumping problem we encountered. From the very beginning there was always a constant struggle to keep the mine free from flooding. Prior to and during the construction phase of the mine I spent more time in the office designing and budgeting for the electrical installation and even laid out the car park with spaces for 200 vehicles; while in the absence of a mechanical engineer I also became involved with most of the equipment purchase and planning decisions.

Before it got too late I wanted to visit the rest of the mine site which now had a quiet almost haunting feel amongst the dereliction. I could see where the winding engine and air compressors once operated and how the machinery had been removed to be used elsewhere. Passing close to the rusting headgear I could now see the group of people coming back up the slope from the direction of the mill building and I waited as they drew near. I could now see that they were not old enough to have worked here but went to greet them with the usual pleasantries. They were quick to say they were down on holiday and interested in looking over the old mines and were being guided by a former Camborne School of Mines student although he hinted he knew very little about Mount Wellington. The thought occurred to me that probably very few people knew about Mount Wellington or of the struggles faced by a small mining company to develop an operating mine from scratch. They were soon asking questions like "when were the workings abandoned" "what minerals were mined" "how deep was the shaft" "what was the function of that large building" "was the mine likely to be opened again"? and so on. This steady stream of interest further awakened past events and numerous memories which, until then, seemed to lie dormant in my mind. Time, as usual caught up with us and the visitors had to go, leaving me to continue on my way around the rest of the mine site. By now my mind was buzzing with my own personal thoughts and wondering if the whole story should be told. Would it be interesting enough for people to want to read it? I am still unsure but there is only one way to find out.

This is my personal experiences and memories of working at Mount Wellington Mine. Between 1969 and 1981 I was involved as an Electrician, Electrical Superintendent, Energy Manager and Project Engineer with four different companies. I was also lucky to be present when many of the leading characters freely discussed some of the issues that influenced events at the time. I believe that my memory has served me well despite stretching back some 50 years. Regrettably, there were few records available at that time but, fortunately, I have been able to refer to my notes and diaries for that period. I hope that this will provide an informative snap shot of times that are unfortunately unlikely to be repeated. Mining investment is not for the faint hearted and the odds for an exploration prospect to develop into an operating mine are said to be less than 10-1.

Regulation and control by The International Tin Council (ITC) created the foundation for stability and a steady rise in the price of tin. By the 1960s, the upturn in the fortunes of the Cornish tin industry caught the attention of numerous exploration and mining companies. Canadian companies account for 30% of global exploration expenditure and 50% of the worlds publicly listed exploration companies had their headquarters in Canada. These 1500 companies had an interest in 8000 properties in over 100 countries throughout the world.

Stephen Kay, an entrepreneurial mining engineer and his assistant Jack Tindale, a geologist ran their mine promotion business from an office in Toronto, the global capital of the mining industry. Steve Kay was a protégée of Joseph Hirshhorn who had made his millions during the 1930s, trading in mining stocks making him one of the richest and most successful mining entrepreneurs in North America. Joe Hirshhorn provided seed funding for Steve's exploration projects and their business was managed through two companies, International Mine Services Ltd (IMS) and Prado Explorations Ltd. By the early 1960s, Steve Kay joined the swell of mining companies flocking into the County and became interested in the Cornish venture. In 1964, International Mine Services appointed Dr Dylis Jones, an experienced and well-respected mining geologist to oversee their Cornish project. A field office was set up on the site of the abandoned Mount Wellington Mine. Her brief was to help identify and sign up available mineral lease areas for exploration that offered good potential for an early return on investment and where planning approval would not become an issue. Initial funding for this phase of the venture came from private investors, located in the USA.

Mineral rights were successfully negotiated for Cligga, located on the cliff west of Perranporth, and for the Prince of Wales Mine at Harrowbarrow lying to the west of Gunnislake. The third and most important target was the extensive Jane/Wellington mineral lease area which during the 1930s, had been combined and worked as one. Mount Wellington, named after the Wellington brothers who worked the mine in the 1920s, was located west of the Carnon River and lay within the East Cusgarne mineral lease area. This plus West Cusgarne and The Lords of St Day were included in an exploration lease that was successfully signed up. However, the Jane group of mines were located to the east of the Carnon River and their mineral rights were owned and managed by the Falmouth Estates. It was believed that Lord Falmouth was reluctant to negotiate mineral leases with Steve Kay and preferred to deal with established mining companies which could deliver the complete package from exploration through to funding an operating mine. Consolidated Goldfields had the finance and ultimately were able to negotiate the Jane Wheal leases. By 1966 they were preparing the diamond drill programme and carrying out underground renovation to the adit system.

Dylis Jones was also responsible for planning and scheduling the exploration programme and she was assisted by two mining engineers Stan Alder and Terry Nurhonen both graduates of Camborne School of Mines. They were helping Dylis with mapping and recording the diamond drill programme plus logging and storage of cores. Contractors were hired to carry out diamond drilling. After the lease agreements and planning approvals were signed up or in the pipeline, it was decided to put on hold and limit expenditure at Cligga. This kept work to a minimum but enough to satisfy the conditions of the lease. Diamond drilling at Prince of Wales identified a lode coursing east-west at shallow depth indicating good values of tin and wolfram. Plans to intersect this lode by driving a cross-cut in a northerly direction from the vicinity of Watson's Shaft were put on hold. This work was later offered to other interested parties allowing International Mine Services to focus on Wellington. Despite the setback of losing the Jane leases Steve Kay was determined to press ahead and open the Mount Wellington mine. The formation of a new company was now a priority to manage and operate the project and raise the finance necessary for shaft sinking and the necessary underground development to prove the viability of the mine.

Cornwall Tin & Mining Corporation was formed in November 1968 to manage and follow up reports and work identified and referred to as the Wellington

Properties and Cligga properties. The head office was located in USA c/o The Corporation Trust Co, 100 West 10th Street, Wilmington, Delaware. The local address was c/o Mine Office, Bissoe, Truro, Cornwall, England.

Directors:
Chairman J. H. Hirshhorn Callahan Mining Corporation New York
Stephen Kay Professional Engineer Toronto
Arthur Emil Attorney New York
B. Attenborough Toronto
Frank R. Cohen Attorney New York

Officers:
President Stephen Kay
Secretary Frank R. Cohen

A manager was recruited in Canada. James F. Delaney was shortlisted and appointed to manage the interests of Cornwall Tin & Mining Corporation. His background followed a mining tradition that started as a working miner before he studied to gain a degree as a Mining Engineer. Before coming to Cornwall he worked for a contracting firm and managed a project to sink two shafts in northern Canada, near the Arctic Circle. He often said he was lucky working in Cornwall with its pleasant climate, compared to the isolation in the outback of the Canadian mining fields. After Dylis had completed her contract and left Wellington, both Stan and Terry stayed to help Jim Delaney with setting up the mine site and surveys plus detailing a specification for the shaft and inviting contractors to tender for this work. The shaft was to be concrete lined, 4.6 metres diameter and 195 metres deep. There were five levels set at 33 metres apart, Number 1 Level or Adit Level was 47 metres below the shaft collar at surface and there were 16 metres below No. 5 Level to the bottom of the shaft. The shaft was to be named Amy after the daughter of an American doctor who was the principal shareholder but the name Amy was rarely used. Three major companies were in the frame to do the work, Foraky Ltd. based in Nottinghamshire, Cementation Mining Ltd. based in Doncaster and Thyssen (GB Ltd) based in South Wales.

Foraky had recently worked in Cornwall for a consortium that included Union Corporation when they attempted to reopen Wheal Grenville near Troon, south of Camborne. The plan to gain access to The Great Flat Lode by pumping out the flooded workings from Fortescue's Shaft proved unsuccessful. This was due to blockages in the shaft and the large flow of water that overwhelmed the pumps. The mine was abandoned in 1920 and over the years there would have been an untold amount of debris falling in the shaft, as timber rotted and iron pump columns rusted through etc, plus any household rubbish that needed dumping adding to the problem. (During World War II the United States Army had a base on United Downs and some of the abandoned shafts were used to dump unwanted equipment, including jeeps, rather than ship it back to America). Cementation Mining Ltd had also been involved in Cornwall but Thyssen (GB Limited) who were based at Llanelli, in South Wales were favourites to win the contract. At that time, they were well established in the County having sunk Simms Shaft at Pendarves plus they had recently won the contracts to sink No 1 Shaft and Clemows Shaft at Wheal Jane.

During the summer of 1969, I was employed as an electrician with Camborne Tin Ltd. at the recently opened Pendarves Mine. I had previously spent a very rewarding 18 months working at South Crofty. It was a very interesting period in the long history of the mine as a modernisation programme was initiated to take it out of the steam age. An electric winder had recently replaced the old steam whim on Robinson's Shaft and electrically operated shaft signals were introduced. Plans to automate the main pumps in Cook's Shaft were not so successful, much to the relief of the pump men who thought they were about to lose their jobs. A host of changes were made to a variety of machinery throughout the mine in an effort to boost productivity. It was a good time to be at Crofty and a steep learning curve for me but I was well prepared with previous experience of working on industrial installations with SWEB (South West Electricity Board). There was also a special camaraderie and the banter of so many characters was unique to the mine. It was a special place and I had doubts about leaving but ambition drove me to new challenges and an opportunity I thought a new mine would offer. So, with a mixture of emotions after saying goodbye to Tommy May, John Laity, Danny Murry, Frank Webb, Don Harris, Tony Plumb, Norman Skelton, Paul Mankee, Gorden Jeffery the two apprentices Ian Dyer and Frank Partridge and all the other members of the electrical department who I may have forgotten. I left Crofty in July 1969, keen to put my new skills to good use at Pendarves.

One afternoon early in October, I was in the workshop at Pendarves repairing an electric submersible pump ready to be taken underground the following day, I was surprised to see the Thyssen Land Rover draw up. The identity of the driver was unmistakable as the large figure of Willie Knapp, the German Foreman Fitter, ambled towards me. Willie's father a Master Sinker had been in charge at Pendarves and was responsible for laying out the site, but when the shaft contract finished, he returned to South Wales. Willie had permission to take me out to a new site Thyssen were developing and needed help; he advised me to take my hard hat, cap lamp and rubber boots as well as my toolbox. It took approximately half an hour to drive there and on the way, Willie explained the problems they were having with a submersible pump.

During site preparations, it was discovered that the old Mount Wellington adit was blocked due to a collapse of ground. The adit ran approximately six metres below the Bissoe/Twelveheads Road and the ground was very weak. It was important to clear the blockage as mine water was unable to flow out to drain into the Carnon River and backed up in the adit to flood into the mine workings. Plans were made to excavate the weak ground from around the adit collapse and to install 6-foot diameter concrete pipes. The pipes were then covered and reinforced with concrete. E. Thomas Ltd, a local construction firm, had the contract to do the work and were granted permission by Cornwall County Council Highways Department to close the road until the work was finished. To keep the excavation and concrete from being washed out, an electric pump was used to divert adit water.

All equipment on site was hired out from Thyssen Plant Hire, but was maintained by site fitters. Willie was a very good fitter and had tried to repair the pump, but the mystery of electricity got the better of him. As there was no electricity available power for the pump was supplied via a generator that was intermittently tripping out. I followed Willie down over rough ground in what appeared to be a gully; at the bottom there was an opening in which we climbed through into an old stope. At the bottom of the stope we found the adit where we located the pump and generator. I managed to identify the fault and carried out the repairs to get the pump running. The pump was working well and water levels were dropping but we waited until we were confident that the problem had been solved before heading back to Pendarves.

Soon after my visit to Mount Wellington, Bob Mathews, the electrical engineer at Pendarves, gave me a job to install various equipment which included an electric winch, submersible pumps, etcetera, at Bennett's Shaft. Bennett's was a small Ladderway Shaft and was located approximately half a mile north east of Wheal Pendarves. The shaft was directly connected to the flooded working of Wheal Tryphena. The work was designed to gain access and pump out the old working as a precautionary measure to protect the underground levels at Pendarves, which were getting close to Wheal Tryphena. This contract was awarded to Thyssen who brought with them the small wooden headgear that had previously been installed on Mitchell's Shaft at West Wheal Peevor. Jack Symons, a former Underground Manager at South Crofty, but now working for Thyssen's supervised the project with his shift boss Trevor Bulter. The clearances within the shaft were very tight, so Jack had asked Thyssen's Chief Mechanical Engineer, Alfred Hopfenzitz, to fabricate steel brackets to simplify installation. When Alfred came out to measure up and order the steel it gave me an opportunity to talk about possible job prospects. He saw my installation at Bennett's but the best reference came from Jack Symons who allegedly spoke of my work in glowing terms. I think Alfred had also heard of my visit to Wellington from Willie Knapp which I believed would improve my chances of a job. My timing was right, as Thyssen's contract was progressing at Wheal Jane and they needed a site electrician to start around mid December. This gave sufficient time to hand in my notice and finish all my outstanding jobs.

APPENDIX 1

CORNWALL TIN & MINING CORPORATION SHARE OFFERING

SECURITIES AND EXCHANGE COMMISSION

NEWS DIGEST

brief summary of financial proposals filed with and actions by the S.E.C.

Washington, D.C. 20549

(In ordering full text of Releases from SEC Publications Unit cite number)

(Issue No. 69-54)   FOR RELEASE _____ March 20, 1969

TAX MAN OFFERING SUSPENDED. The SEC has issued an order temporarily suspending a Regulation A exemption from registration under the Securities Act of 1933 with respect to a public stock offering by The Tax Man, Inc., of Quincy, Mass.

Regulation A provides a conditional exemption from registration to public offerings of securities not exceeding $300,000 in amount. In a notification filed in October 1968, Tax Man proposed the public offering of 34,500 shares at $2.50 per share. The offering was commenced on November 18 and concluded December 13, 1968. In its suspension order, the Commission asserts that various terms and conditions of Regulation A were not complied with by Tax Man in that, among other things, (a) there was a failure to disclose the name of and stockholdings of a promoter, that a promoter had a right to acquire options, and that the company's president had disposed of some of his stockholdings; also (b) the offering circular contained false statements with respect to the stockholdings of officers and directors and with respect to the rights of officers and directors to acquire stock pursuant to options; and (c) that Tax Man stock was offered and sold during the ten-day waiting period prescribed by Rule 255, without the prior delivery of an offering circular, and by use of written sales material which was not filed with the Commission.

The Commission's order provides an opportunity for hearing, upon request, on the question whether the suspension should be vacated or made permanent.

DROLLINGER SUSPENDED. The SEC today announced that Kyle M. Drollinger, Jr., one of the respondents in an administrative proceeding involving the broker-dealer firm of Abbett, Sommer & Co., Inc., of Fort Worth, Texas, did not seek Commission review of the Hearing Examiner's initial decision in such proceeding. That decision provided, among other things, that Drollinger (formerly a registered representative of and secretary to the firm) be suspended from association with any broker-dealer for 60 days. Accordingly, the Examiner's decision as to Drollinger has become final; and the 60-day suspension of Drollinger has been declared effective as of the opening of business on March 21, 1969.

The Abbett, Sommer firm and two other respondents have petitioned the Commission for review of the decision of the Hearing Examiner, in which he held that the several respondents had offered and sold mortgage note investment contracts issued by Century Trust Company of Dallas, Inc., in violation of the registration and anti-fraud provisions of the Federal securities laws.

CORNWALL TIN PROPOSES OFFERING. Cornwall Tin & Mining Corporation, c/o The Corporation Trust Company, 100 West 10th St., Wilmington, Del., filed a registration statement (File 2-32093) with the SEC on March 17 seeking registration of 200,000 shares of common stock, to be offered for public sale on an "all-or-none", best efforts basis through Shaskan & Co., 67 Broad St., New York. The offering price ($3.50 per share maximum*) and underwriting terms are to be supplied by amendment. The company has agreed to pay the underwriter $14,000 for expenses.

Organized under Delaware law in November 1968, the company has acquired, in exchange for 2,000,000 common shares, three agreements to explore for minerals over an area of 1,670 acres in Cornwall, England. Net proceeds of its stock sale will be used to finance the company's underground exploration and surface exploration drilling programs (principally for tin), and the balance for working capital. The company has outstanding 2,005,000 common shares, of which Joseph H. Hirshhorn owns 55% and Prado Explorations Limited 45%. Stephen Kay is president. Purchasers of the 200,000 shares being registered will acquire a 9% stock interest in the company for their investment of $700,000; present stockholders will then own 91%, for which they paid 19¢ per share.

TRADING SUSPENSIONS CONTINUED. The SEC has ordered the suspension of over-the-counter trading in the securities of Bartep Industries, Inc., Dumont Corporation and Majestic Capital Corporation for the further ten-day period March 21-30, 1969, inclusive.

SECURITIES ACT REGISTRATIONS. Effective March 19: Commercial Alliance Corp., 2-31543 (40 days); Consolidated Edison Co. of New York, Inc., 2-31884; The Echlin Manufacturing Co., 2-31780; Economics Laboratory, Inc., 2-31931; Lee Enterprises, Inc., 2-31630 (90 days); Lyntex Corp., 2-31300 (40 days); Nashua Corp., 2-31682 (40 days); Nippon Electric Co., Ltd., 2-31475 (Apr 29); Orbanco, Inc., 2-30362; Rio Grande Industries, Inc., 2-30845 (90 days); SSI Computer Corp., 2-31970; TRW Inc., 2-31331 (40 days); Utah Construction & Mining Co., 2-31530; White Shield Corp., 2-31312 (40 days); White Shield Oil and Gas Corp., 2-30948 (40 days); Wright Machinery Co., Inc., 2-31072 (40 days). Withdrawn March 19: Applied Technical Services, 2-31456.

NOTE TO DEALERS. The period of time dealers are required to use the prospectus in trading transactions is shown above in parentheses after the name of the issuer.

*As estimated for purposes of computing the registration fee.

CORNWALL MINES RULE BOOK

CAMBORNE MINES LTD.

SPECIAL
RULES

CAMBORNE MINES LIMITED

This book of Special Rules is designed to help you and other workers to keep free from injury. It is the responsibility of every employee to work safely and to achieve this he should have a thorough knowledge of all rules affecting him. This book is to be read in conjunction with the Mines & Quarries Act, 1954 (displayed on General Notice Board). If regulations laid down in the Act are not included in this book it does not mean they don't apply, and any extra rules laid down in this book which may not appear in the Act apply to you whilst you are working for this Company.

"Ignorance of the Law is no Excuse!"

1

GENERAL

1. Every employee must be familiar with the regulations of the Mines & Quarries Act and the safety regulations, and the special rules of Camborne Mines Limited, and comply with them.

2. All employees must wear hard hats and safety boots about the mine, both on surface and underground.

3. Disciplinary action will be taken when an employee:—
  (i) Infringes M. & Q. Act.
  (ii) Infringes Camborne Mines Limited special rules.
  (iii) Fails to comply with an order.
  (iv) Fights or engages in horseplay.
  (v) Is under influence of alcohol or carries alcohol on the Mine.
  (vi) Fails to report an accident.
  (vii) Interferes with anything in or about the Mine provided for the purposes of safety.

4. The Mine must be kept free from litter, scrap timber, broken tools and general rubbish. Place lunch paper, food scraps in the garbage cans.

5. Each shift boss/supervisor is responsible for the safety of all workmen in his section, and any dangerous practices must be reported at the end of each shift to the Mine Overseer or Mine Manager.

6. All persons who may be endangered by work in any area must be warned.

7. No-one shall remove or ignore danger signs.

8. No-one may throw anything down a shaft or manway.

9. All employees should know the procedure to be adopted in the case of accident or fire.

10. Whatever the job, always have a good footing to avoid serious falls and injury.

11. Never tamper with or attempt to repair mechanical and/or electrical machinery. Call the fitter or electrician in.

12. No unauthorised person shall give signals to the winder driver unless an accident has occurred and then only the accident signal.

13. No-one shall interfere with any safety lamp. Each person is responsible for looking after any safety lamp loaned to him.

14. Any person failing to obey an order given in accordance with the regulations or in the interests of safety by any person authorised to do so shall be guilty of a contravention of the regulations.

15. No person shall damage anything provided for protection of underground or surface works, or for the safety of the workmen.

16. There shall be no pushing at any shaft-station. The authorised number of persons to ride in the cage shall not be exceeded.

17. Protruding nails should be bent flat.

18. Do not walk beside a moving train or cross over between wagons coupled to a locomotive.

19. Never work with defective or dangerous equipment. All worn tools or defective equipment must be reported and replaced.

20. Always keep a look out for loose rock. Bar it down where necessary.

2

3

ACCIDENTS

1. All accidents and injuries must be reported to the shift-boss/overseer before the end of the shift.

2. All injuries must be treated by one of the First Aid attendants. After each treatment the attendant must record name, injury, action taken, time of accident, cause of accident, in the appropriate book.

3. Injuries of the following nature must be treated on surface:—

   (i)   Eye injuries,
   (ii) Nail puncture wounds,
   (iii) Gash wounds at joints,
   (iv) Any wound which bleeds profusely.

4. Any seriously wounded person must not be moved by anyone other than qualified First Aid Personnel unless further danger threatens.

5. In the event of the seriously injured person being taken to surface he should be on a stretcher and kept warm with blankets. Sound accident signal at shaft station, phone banksman/onsetter and give him details of the accident. (Injured man's name, nature of accident and injuries and place of occurrence). This will enable the banksman/onsetter to call a doctor and/or ambulance if necessary, and reduce delay.

6. If the accident has resulted in death of the person, nothing should be disturbed at the place of the occurrence before further notice, except for securing the safety of persons and of the Mine.

DRILLING

1. The back and side-walls of the working place must be kept safe and all loose ground barred down.

2. The roof and sides must be washed down and a check made for misfires or sockets. Misfires should be treated as outlined later. Sockets should be cleaned out. If toeholes are under water they must be blown over with compressed air.

3. Holes should not be drilled nearer than 6 in. to sockets. To aid this the burn cut should be alternated from side to side of the face for each round.

4. No holes shall be deepened unless they are unfinished holes from the previous shift, not having been charged with explosive. Confirmation of this should be obtained from the previous shift.

5. Before drilling, the following operations must be carried out:—
   (i)   Top up air-line lubricator with oil.
   (ii) Flush out water line; blow out air-line.
   (iii) Check gooseneck for dirt, fill with oil, connect up hoses.

6. While drilling, the following points should be observed:—
   (i)   Keep steels and hoses out of the way.
   (ii) No-one should stand in front of the machine unnecessarily.
   (iii) Never stand astride the air-leg or inside coils of air-hose.
   (iv) Never use blunt steels. These should be taken to surface daily for sharpening.
   (v)   Stopers should be used on solid staging.
   (vi) Drilling "dry" is prohibited.

7. Pilot holes must be carried ahead of the face and these must be **completed** before drilling of the round commences. The holes should be $1\frac{1}{2}$ x length of round (i.e. 9 ft. long for a 6 ft. round). Off-lode, three holes are drilled; one central and level; one top right-hand corner and one lower left-hand corner inclined upwards/downwards respectively, and outwards at 15°. On lode three holes are drilled; one central and level, one top centre and one bottom centre inclined upwards and downwards respectively (See diagram). Pilot holes should be plugged to prevent charging with explosive.

8. Should a pilot hole hit water, measure the quantity of water being made. If the flow is more than 500 g.p.h., stop drilling and await further instructions. If the flow is less than 500 g.p.h., drill additional pilot holes and if the total quantity is still less than 500 g.p.h., the shiftboss **may** give permission for the face to be blasted.

Calculation of water make:—

A hard hat holds approximately $\frac{1}{2}$ Gall. Thus if a hard hat is filled in 10 seconds the rate of flow is $\frac{\frac{1}{2} \times 60 \times 60}{10}$ g.p.h.=180 g.p.h.

i.e. use the formula $\frac{\frac{1}{2} \times 3600}{t \text{ (seconds)}}$=rate of flow.

9. The water board must be kept near the face at all times in case water is intersected. The telescopic casing pipe is put into the hole to control water flow.

EXPLOSIVES

1. No person shall remove or attempt to remove explosives from the Mine. To enforce this the Manager or persons appointed by him may search persons leaving the Mine.
2. No person shall smoke whilst handling explosives. Open flames must be kept at least 3 ft. from explosives.
3. In any face no hole may be charged without the permission of the shiftboss if any hole in that face has intersected water.
4. Explosives shall be carried only in the approved containers supplied for this purpose.
5. Old or damaged explosives shall be placed in the box supplied for this purpose. The box shall be cleared daily by the shot firer and the explosives brought to surface for destruction.
6. Detonators and fuses may be stored or conveyed together, but must not be stored or conveyed with other explosives, except in the form of made-up primers. Primers shall be made up within a reasonable time of charging up. Detonators shall be removed from unused made-up primers.
7. All detonators and fuses must be kept in the securely locked wooden box provided for this purpose.

Loading and Shot Firing

1. Only persons under the direct personal supervision of a holder of a current valid blasting certificate (shotfirer) may handle explosives or charge faces. Only a qualified shotfirer shall fire explosives. Blasting certificates shall be issued by the Mine Manager.
2. Loading of the face must not start before the drilling of that face is completely finished.

3. Primers must be made up by piercing the cartridge with the special piercer provided and inserting the detonator cap into the hole so made.
4. Explosive must not be removed from its paper wrapping, nor may the cartridge be cut or tampered with in any way.
5. During loading of a face no smoking or naked lights shall be permitted within 50 ft.
6. Only wooden charging sticks shall be used. Powder must not be forced into the hole.
7. Before charging all holes must be thoroughly cleaned out with the blow pipe.
8. All holes must be adequately stemmed and no explosive or stemming shall be removed from any hole unless protruding from the mouth of that hole.
9. Before firing all surplus explosives and detonators shall be removed from the vicinity of the face and locked in the appropriate boxes.
10. For electric blasting only wire supplied by the Manager shall be used for connecting the charges to the exploder. Under no circumstances shall lighting cable, etc., be used for this purpose. The shotfirer must ensure that the wire does not come into contact with any other electrical apparatus or any other electrical circuit.
11. Excess detonator wire must be coiled and not cut to the right length. Detonators must be connected in series.
12. The face must be fired from a distance of at least 400 ft.
13. The shotfirer shall retain the key of the exploder at all times, and the exploder shall only be connected to the shot firing cable immediately prior to blasting.
14. Before firing, adequate warning to other personnel on the same level must be given. Guards must be posted or warning notices displayed at all

8

entrances to the area. The notice must contain the words "Danger" and "Shot-firing". The shotfirer must ensure all personnel have withdrawn from the area, and must have taken shelter himself before firing.
15. Immediately after firing the key of the exploder must be removed and the wires disconnected and short-circuited to remove residual current.
16. After firing the shots the shotfirer, or another competent person, entering on the next shift must ensure, by personal examination, that the area is safe for working to resume. The examination must not take place until at least 30 minutes have expired since the shots were fired, or the air is clear of dust, smoke, and fumes, whichever is the longer.
17. On re-entry after blasting, the sides, roof, face and rock pile must be thoroughly wetted down.

Misfires

(All personnel should acquaint themselves with the notice regarding misfires on the main Notice Board).
1. If a misfire is suspected at the end of a shift it must be reported to the shift-boss so that the next shift can be warned. The shotfirer must post a notice warning people approaching the shot hole of the misfires before he leaves.
2. Under no circumstances should drilling commence at a face if misfires are suspected or known to be present.
3. Powder should not be removed from cut-offs; new fuse should be used to reprime and fire. If part of a hole is left with explosive in it which cannot be conveniently re-fired, the explosive should be washed out with water under pressure, introduced into the hole using a pipe of non-ferrous material supplied by the Manager. Stemming should be washed out using a copper pipe (to enable the hole to be re-primed).

9

LOCOMOTIVES

1. Only persons holding the appropriate certificate will operate a locomotive. Only crew of the locomotive will ride on the train. Unauthorised man-riding is prohibited.
2. At the start of each shift, brakes, lights, controller, gong, sanding device and couplings must be checked. Any defect must be reported to the shiftboss or fitter.
3. No train must be driven at more than 4 m.p.h., or fast walking pace. The headlight and red tail light must be illuminated at all times.
4. The gong must be sounded when approaching corners or working places.
5. The locomotive shall not be stopped by moving the control lever to reverse.
6. All trains should be made up with the locomotive pulling the wagons.
7. When moving a shovel loader with the locomotive, the two should be coupled together.
8. The loco driver is responsible for the safety of the train and should ensure that nothing falls off or can catch walls, chutes, etc.
9. When the loco is left unattended, driver should leave brakes on, control in neutral and the battery off.
10. The loco-drivers must ensure the batteries are taken to surface for charging whenever this may be necessary.
11. Wagons should be coupled up only while the train is at rest.
12. Points should not be changed while the train is in motion nearby.
13. No materials should be carried in or on the locomotive.
14. To re-rail the loco use the proper re-railer or jack provided.
15. No loco should pull more than 8 full wagons.

SHOVEL LOADERS

1. Only persons holding the appropriate certificate will operate a shovel loader.
2. The muck pile must be washed down to keep dust down before mucking with the shovel loader.
3. Before using the loader check that all hose connections are secure and all controls are working efficiently. Report any defects to the shiftboss or fitter. The operator is responsible for the safety and cleanliness of the machine.
4. The loader must not be operated unless the operator is standing on the footplate.
5. The loader must not be operated unless there is adequate clearance on all sides and above the loader.
6. No-one should stand in front of the loader while it is being used.
7. As the loader advances into the muck, check for loose powder, loose rock on the newly exposed walls, large rocks on the pile which may roll down.
8. Do not overload the bucket. Secondary blasting should be used on very large rocks which the loader will not handle.
9. Before moving the loader:—
    (i) lock the upper part with pin,
    (ii) raise bucket using air-motor and support with a bar or drill between the sides,
    (iii) fold step out of the way,
    (iv) bleed air-hoses and remove from spuds,
    (v) loader must be coupled to the locomotive,
    (vi) no-one should ride on the loader,
    (vii) the loader should not be moved at more than walking pace.

11

13

FIRES

1. If a fire is discovered underground every attempt should be made to extinguish it. In the case of oil or electrical fires, water should not be used. Report any fire to the shift-boss/overseer.

2. Don't enter heavy smoke without suitable breathing apparatus.

3. If the fire cannot be immediately extinguished, return to the shaft station and notify the banksman of the type and location of the fire. Warn all other personnel on that level.

4. On receiving notification of an underground fire the banksman will notify the Mine Manager and/or his deputy.

5. All men on the level concerned should be removed from that level. All men underground should be hoisted to surface unless instructions to the contrary are given by the Mine Manager or his deputy.

"Scheme of Transit"

1. Powder shall be taken underground only in the supplied containers marked "DANGER—EXPLOSIVES".

2. Powder and detonators must at no time be in the same conveyance or container.

3. No powder must be left underground at shaft stations for unnecessary lengths of time. It must be moved to the underground working places as soon as possible.

4. Only the onsetter shall ride in the cage with the explosive.

5. No other materials may be conveyed at the same time as the explosive.

6. When moved underground by loco haulage, no other materials should be on the same train.

7. The loco should be separated from the explosives wagon by an empty wagon.

8. Front headlight and rear tail-light (red) should be illuminated and clearly visible.

9. Only a wagon with sides on it may be used to haul explosives underground. Powder must never be transported in the locomotive.

10. All boxes of explosives must be kept underground in the locked boxes provided and used in strict rotation so that they are used in the same order as they are issued.

11. No smoking is allowed near explosives and no naked lights should be placed above or nearer than 3 ft. to any explosives or conveyance that might contain explosives.

12. A train hauling explosives must never be left unattended.

The following general scheme of transit shall be adopted at the mine:—

The explosives for the next 24 hours shall be collected from the surface magazine daily and loaded into the explosives cars which shall be kept at the shaft bank.

The onsetter shall collect the cars on surface and deliver them to the shaft stations where they will be collected by the loco driver. The loco driver shall deliver the explosives to the shotfirer at each working place, who will lock the explosives allocated to him in the boxes provided. Explosive boxes shall not contain more than 100 lbs. explosives each and shall be in laybyes or cubbies and at least 4 ft. from the nearest track. Any explosives not collected shall be returned to the surface as soon as possible.

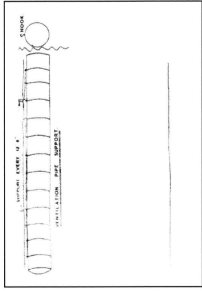

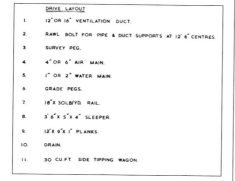

DRIVE LAYOUT

1. 12" OR 16" VENTILATION DUCT.
2. RAWL BOLT FOR PIPE & DUCT SUPPORTS AT 12' 6" CENTRES.
3. SURVEY PEG.
4. 4" OR 6" AIR MAIN.
5. 1" OR 2" WATER MAIN.
6. GRADE PEGS.
7. 18" X 30LB/YD. RAIL.
8. 3' 6" X 5" X 4" SLEEPER.
9. 12' X 9" X 1" PLANKS.
10. DRAIN.
11. 30 CU. FT. SIDE TIPPING WAGON.

16

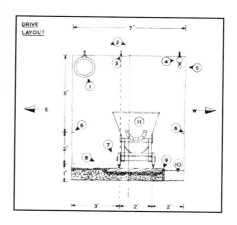

DRIVE LAYOUT

17

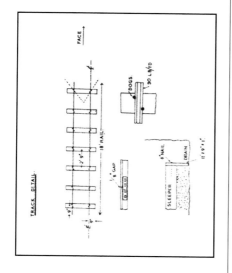

TRACK DETAIL.

18

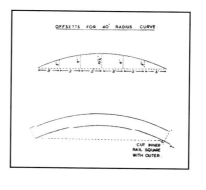

OFFSETTS FOR 40' RADIUS CURVE.

CUT INNER RAIL SQUARE WITH OUTER.

19

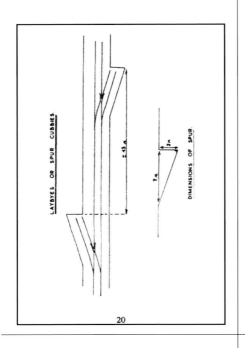

20

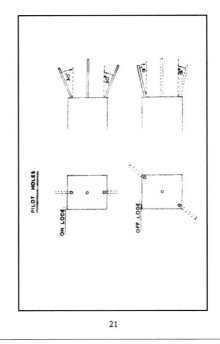

21

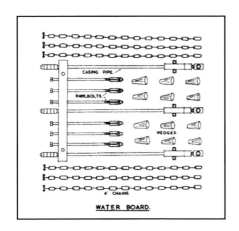

22

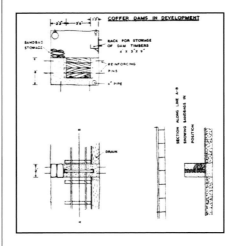

23

16

TRAMMING PROCEDURE

Fig. 1. Loco arrives from tips **pulling** empties. Park empties, leaving space at spur for tramming, sprag empties front and rear. Switch loco. into spur.

Fig. 2. Tram 1st empty beyond spur, bringing loco. behind it.

Fig. 3. Tram 2nd empty into spur. Drive 1st empty to the loader.

Fig. 4. After loading pull full hopper back past spur. Bring down 2nd empty.

Fig. 5. Drive this to the face side of the spur with 1st full and loco. Tram 3rd empty into spur. Drive 2nd empty plus 1st full with the loco. to the loader.

Fig. 6. Repeat procedure until 6th empty is at the loader. Pull 5 full hoppers to the tips.

Fig. 7. Return from tip pulling empties, park, leaving space at spur for tramming, spragg empties front and rear, park loco. to the face side of the spur. Tram 7th empty into spur.

Fig. 8. Fetch 6th full hopper from loader, back past spur. Bring down 7th empty. Repeat procedure as before.

24

17

Chapter 2

Deep Down

Shaft sinking is a job most miners would choose to avoid, but it did not stop a steady stream of men, some having travelled long distances looking for work. Most who tried it did not last for more than one shift, not even the temptation of earning big money would keep them. In 1969-1970 shaft sinkers were paid £8 per shift, which was double my £4 per shift, and this was more than I had been paid at Pendarves or at South Crofty Mine.

Miners worked very hard in the worst conditions imaginable and nobody could say they did not earn their money. Everyone strived to take home the biggest pay packet and valued bragging rights and boasting who could drill the quickest or muck out the most. This banter was carried over to the pubs on weekends, putting smiles on the faces of landlords basking in their new found wealth, while the more sober would pose the question, "Why is it they only talk about mining in the pub and sex and rugby in the mine?". Many a publican would curse, "Those bloody miners, drilling and blasting all night filling the place with smoke and leaving me to muck out on my own". Tin Fever !!

Thyssen's employed over 70 people for their Cornish contracts with Poles, Czechs, Yugoslavs, Germans and Welsh in the majority. It was amusing listening to a Polish accent with a strong, Welsh lilt. Gordon Battersby, a director based in

Site preparation foundations: from left, shaft collar, capstan winch, head gear back legs and sinking winder. Workshop, office and store in background.

South Wales, would visit Cornwall once a month. Fred Beckman was in charge of the Cornish contracts; his office, along with administration etcetera, was at Wheal Jane. He was here for the long term and had recently built his house near Camborne. Dick Gamble was the site agent for Wheal Jane and later left to take up an appointment as Manager of Delabole Slate Quarry. Alan Protheroe, a charismatic Welshman, performed a similar job at Wellington. The two Master Sinkers, Gerhard Timph (Gert) was based at Jane and Heinz Hoffhner looked after Wellington. Both lived in caravans on their respective sites and were on call 24 hours a day. The Saturday afternoon shift was not worked to allow for shopping, as one wag put it, "1 tin of sardines and 7 bottles of Vodka" but a three 8-hour shift rota was in place through the week. There were three German shifts bosses, Vernon, Albert, Wierner, one Austrian, Jacob Priller and two who were local. They each had a crew of four miners, one winder driver, one banksman and one truck driver. There was, of course, the backup maintenance teams who were generally the responsibility of Alfred Hopfenzitz, the Chief Mechanical Engineer, Alfred was my immediate boss and in charge of most things, particularly if they went wrong. Clive Stacey, a jovial Welshman, was Transport Manager, and together with his driver/handyman looked after the vehicles and approximately 25 caravans, which were used for miners' accommodation.

For me the standout character and top personality was Alan "Tiny" Marsh, all 20 stone and 6′ 2″ of him when he was on a diet. I first saw him at Pendarves when he moved from labourer to a trainee miner. He came from the London area and was believed to have trained as a cook. He was a very hardworking man, giving his all to earn the top money, but always had time for a joke enhanced with perfect mimicry; nothing was too much trouble for him, but he did not suffer fools. We thought we had seen the last of him when he was suddenly brought up from underground and Gerhard Timph called an ambulance that rushed him to hospital with a suspected heart attack. Tiny was back the next day asking for a doubler, an extra shift to make up for lost time the previous day. His leg was unmercifully pulled and told he should not eat his sandwiches so quickly.

The equipment needed for shaft sinking, particularly the electrics, was very basic but suffered constant ill treatment, which kept me busy. The mining routine followed a system that had been around for hundreds of years. Drill-blast-muck out but with an additional operation introduced to line the shaft with concrete. Steel shuttering made up of curved panels (in the case of circular shafts) were bolted together in a tube-like structure. It was then made secure to ensure it was lined up vertically before the concrete was poured between the rock face and the shuttering. The concrete would be conveyed down the shaft in a 6in diameter steel pipe with the last one or two sections bolted to a reinforced rubber hose known as a bag. This gave the operator the flexibility needed to direct the flow of concrete around the circumference of the shaft while vibrators were used compacting the concrete

Thyssen GB Ltd. sinking headgear

and fill any voids or air pockets. It was important to prepare thoroughly to ensure that the job was completed in one pour so that strength was not compromised. The amount of concrete was calculated so that a sufficient number of lorries would be ordered and lined up on site ready to off load.

An important piece of equipment was the sinking platform, which was a heavy, wooden, structure that fitted loosely in the shaft, like a cork in a bottleneck. It was approximately 10 feet deep with decking top and bottom. The platform was suspended in the shaft attached by two wire ropes, which were taken up the shaft through the headgear to a winch. The winch was very low geared and raised or lowered the platform very slowly. The wire ropes also served as guide ropes to keep the main winder rope central to the shaft. The platform was made with openings in the deck to allow the bucket to pass through. When being raised from the bottom, the freely swinging bucket had to be steadied by the miners to guide it through the opening in the platform. A crosshead, acting like a yoke, was the means of keeping the bucket from swinging around in the shaft. The bucket and five tons of rock could travel up the shaft at speeds of between 5 and 10 feet per second. There was no room for error with men working below.

Lunch breaks were taken whenever convenient and rarely took more than 20 minutes. This was extended if blasting had taken place and the crews took an extra ten minutes to allow the vent fans to disperse the smoke and dynamite fumes from the bottom of the shaft. Then it was all back down, dropping a man on the sinking platform to connect the compressed air hoses to the cactus grab, clean rock and debris off the platform and lower to a suitable height to enable the shift boss to use the grab. The bucket was unhooked and the winder rope sent to surface to pick up the spare bucket. The winder drivers lowered the empty bucket to just above the platform so as not to interfere with the movement of the cactus grab. When the first bucket was filled, the shift boss rang the signal (pull wire) for the winder driver to lower the empty bucket to a convenient place at the side of the shaft. Then the full bucket was transferred and attached to the hook to be taken up the shaft for the banks man to dump into the waiting tipper truck.

My responsibility was simple; I was part of the backup team that kept the shaft progressing and to keep breakdowns to a minimum with no equipment failure to cause delay. My biggest concern was pumping, and regardless of numerous

Headgear, capstan winch house and winding engine house.

spares, we seemed to be constantly suffering from poor maintenance. I found the biggest problem was the electric Flygt Pump that kept the shaft clear of water. The pump had been introduced recently for use in wet shafts where it could pump over 50gpm at a height of 200 ft. This was a great improvement as previously compressed air pumps were used and discharged water into the bucket. The fitters were responsible for pump maintenance but they were not familiar with the electric pumps. When they got so far the pump was passed to me to complete. This was proving to be unsatisfactory and it was agreed that I would look after the pumps. Dick Gamble thought it would helpful if I could get some practical experience so he contacted the Flygt depot where they maintained their large fleet of hire pumps. He confirmed they could offer practical instruction and also that their repair engineers were all electricians. Dick arranged for me to spend a week at the Flygt Factory in Nottingham undergoing intensive instruction on submersible pumps. I think that in the end it reduced stoppage time in the shaft and must have been worthwhile. I certainly gained from the experience as well as the extra overtime hours due to an increased workload.

I had been with Thyssen's for approximately two months and shaft sinking at Jane and Wellington progressed without major problems. Then I was sent over to Wellington to help with a pumping problem. I knew there must have been some difficulties as Peter Martin, the resident electrician, was a very able man and would not willingly let problems get on top of him. Apparently it was decided to take some samples of the main lode where it passed close to 3 Level. Unfortunately, water started to flow from the lode and was more than the sinking pumps were able to handle, so shaft sinking had come to a stop just below 3 Level. When I got to Wellington the miners had just finished building a dam. Peter had found some cable and was installing it down the shaft, whilst fitters were fabricating a base for the pump and installing pipes in the shaft. My job was relatively simple, to connect the switchgear and starter to the pump motor. I waited for the fitters to finish so I could test the pump, as I did not want to be called back if there were problems. I was introduced to the site agent, Alan Protheroe, who took me up to the office for a cup of coffee. Whilst there, a gentleman popped his head around the door, wanting to know how it was all going. We chatted for 20 minutes or so until the phone went, whereby he was called back to his office and I went back down the site to the workshop. On the way, I said to Alan that he seemed like a nice chap; he said he was and that he was the manager, Jim Delaney. I was impressed, not only had he taken the time to talk, but also he was interested in what we were doing.

The Wellington shaft was completed to 195m by May 1970 and work was pressing ahead on the pump station. A Flygt Pump sat in the drainage ditch to pump water over the dam wall to create a small reservoir with a positive head of water feeding the pumps. Watertight doors were installed on 4 and 5 Levels and we hung a 125hp Beresford submersible pump, rated at 500gpm, near the bottom of the shaft. I was now spending more time at Wellington as more questions were raised regarding future pumping capacity, particularly as we were experiencing greater flows the more we advanced the cross-cut drives north to intersect the lode. It was about this time that Terry Nurhonen left the company; it was believed that the lack of progress on the Prince of Wales prospect contributed to his departure. Stan Alder stayed, but he was not a well man and suffered from angina; an operation in America was said to have been unsuccessful and added to his problems. Meanwhile in Canada, Steve Kay was looking for a geologist; Jack Tindale conducted interviews, and Malcolm Hooper, a young Englishman working in British Columbia, was eventually hired.

Work on 4 Level was proceeding steadily, but conditions were getting worse on five level – it was becoming impossible to support the ground in the fault zone. So a decision was made to abandon the drive and start back with a loop to enable the drive to cut through the fault at 90°, The situation was getting desperate as the make of water began to exceed the capacity of the pump and there was no option but to close the watertight door on 5 Level. As a matter of urgency Alan Protheroe suggested to Jim Delaney that Thyssen's Engineering Department could install a Mackley pump that would be more than adequate to keep the mine drained while 5 Level was being developed. Thyssen's sent an engineer and two men down from South Wales to carry out the installation. However, as mining progressed on 4 and 5 Levels it became obvious that more pumping capacity would be needed. Jim Delaney was not too keen to use Thyssen Engineering again and asked me if I would be able to give him an estimate for the work. I explained the present design did not easily allow extra pumps to be installed and that we needed to beef up the electricity supply if we were to add 2 more pumps. I worked out some rough costs which he accepted and asked me to start. SWEB were able to take the extra load on their system and would make the 11kV connection to a 1,000kVA 11/3.3kVA transformer that I managed to get from J. F. Winder in Leeds. The fitters, under the supervision of Willie Knapp, installed an 8-inch raising main through the shaft. While we were waiting for delivery of the Mackley pumps we used our spare Plueger Submersible borehole pump and installed it in Wheal Andrew Shaft which was located below the mine site close to the Twelveheads Road. We used the Thyssen mobile crane to lower the pump down the shaft, attaching a 4-inch steel pipe and the electric cable to a steel wire rope. The pump was lowered approximately 200 feet down the shaft, enough to reduce water pressure on five level. The Plueger Pump ran well for the first week, but steadily the delivery had dropped off so that by the third week, the flow was reduced to less than 100gpm.

The Plueger was taken out of Andrew Shaft and brought into the workshop to be stripped down for inspection. It was immediately obvious what had happened. The cast iron casing was full of holes caused by highly corrosive water conditions, also the impellers were showing signs of extreme wear. The agents for Plueger came down and offered to replace the pump with a more corrosion resistant materials. Samples of water showed very high acidic levels with a pH of 2.5. Fortunately this was not repeated in the water being pumped from Wellington where average pH values of 4 were recorded. Conditions underground on 5 Level had once again proved impossible as the make of water on the face prevented the miners from working in such wet conditions, in spite of reducing their shifts to six hours. The water that flowed into 5 Level from the west was draining the vast underground working of the old Consolidated and United Mines. This flow was approximately 4 times greater than the flow from the east and was noticeably warmer to the touch. A temporary solution was quickly tried when an airlift replaced the Plueger in Wheal Andrew Shaft. A portable compressor was used to supply air to the bottom of the pipe and a column of air and water was spectacularly shot out on surface. By now with the third Mackley Pump running the water pressure rapidly dropped and with all pumps working it was considered safe to open the watertight door to allow work on 5 level to continue.

It was increasingly obvious that more information was required to understand the effect and characteristics of water movement in our catchment area. A number of shafts were identified that were considered suitable to record rise and fall of water levels *i.e.* those with easy safe access, vertical and free of obstruction. These shafts were located throughout the lease area and included Wheal Andrew, Frederick's, Shears, Davey's, Poldory and Bissapool. I used a simple method of connecting an ohmmeter to a length of blasting wire with two electrodes so that when they touched the water it caused a short circuit, indicating the precise horizon of the water level. The blasting wire was strong enough to attach a weight to enable it to be thrown down the shaft and I could measure off the marks on the wire to a stake driven in near the edge of the shaft. I had a lot of help from Mr Beachamp of Trevince who, at the time, was the official collector of rainfall records; he kindly gave me copies of his reports. There was a regular check of County Adit flows. During wet winters, the water would be too much to flow through the adit portal and back up, even with the second adit which was driven parallel with the original. This back up would send thousands of gallons of water into old workings that we were trying to pump out. All this information would be useful for future pump station design.

Jim Delaney was increasingly asking me for ideas of cost, availability and suitability of electrical equipment and then for general mining machinery. I was allowed to use the desk vacated by Terry Nurhonen with the use of a telephone and shared an office with Stan Alder. We had to employ an electrician for the Wheal Jane site and I took on Mike Webb from Hayle who was available and he soon settled into the job. I was still needed and expected to help when problems occurred at Wheal Jane. I was told this in no uncertain terms after arriving late from Wellington one afternoon following a meeting there with Jim Delaney. A shaft pump was intermittently tripping and the miners had refused to go back down into the shaft as they were about to charge the face with dynamite. They were worried that stray electricity might cause premature detonation, which would not be a good experience if sharing the bottom of the shaft with a box of dynamite. I managed to sort out the problem and was cleaning up my tools when Fred Beckman collared me in the workshop. He drew himself up to full height and wagging his finger an inch under my nose he said "I don't mind if you play golf with Jim Delaney but when I need you here you better come right away". He later calmed down and invited me to the firms staff Christmas Party. Fred's choice of sport was off the mark as Jim and I had no interest in golf.

Lode development continued on 4 and 5 Levels and samples were taken to enable an ore reserve to be calculated. The lode material was hoisted to surface and trucked to our stockpile on waste ground around Harvey's Shaft, approximately 1km south of Wellington. This gave a reserve to feed the mill if the underground could not supply the proposed new concentrator with sufficient ore during the initial start up period. Bulk samples were sent to Mathew Hall Ortech for recovery analysis and concentrator flow sheet design.

There was one last important job to complete before Thyssen's contract was finished. The Mount Wellington Adit ran approximately 100 metres to the south of the 1 Level shaft station and there had never been a connection between them. When this was completed it would save pumping an extra 47 metres with all the advantages of reducing the cost of purchasing pumps and electricity bills. Approximately 50 metres or half way along the drive the ground changed and needed supporting due to the presence of a band of clay. Steel arches and timber lagging was used to prevent a major collapse but the large flow of water pumped from the mine would soon wash out the clay. To overcome this a concrete culvert was constructed through the full length of the adit. A measuring box located on 1 Level station monitored pump and water flows. The pump columns running up the shaft from 1 Level were stripped out and the pipes from 5 Level were now diverted to discharge into the adit.

Finally the watertight doors on 4 and 5 Levels were tested and unfortunately, a leak had been found on 5 Level door that proved difficult to repair. Rather than risk letting the leak get worse a belt and braces method was adopted, where shuttering was fixed in front of the door and a massive plug of concrete poured but allowed all the pipes and valves to pass through.

In Canada Steve Kay was trying to find suitable investors to join him in a deal to finance the completion of Mount Wellington into a fully operational mine. The stumbling block was how much Steve was prepared to part with and he certainty wanted to keep as much of the equity as possible. I wonder now if the TV programme Dragon's Den was running would he be asking for £2.5 M for 40% of the new Company.

The top table section below 1930s California stamps prior to being covered by overspill from the shaft excavation in 1969.

The 1930s California stamps loadings prior to being covered.

Chapter 3

Prospecting and Planning

From the beginning, I seemed to have formed a good working relationship with Jim Delaney and had spent a good deal of time discussing electrical and mechanical requirements for the mine, and I suppose he needed someone to listen and to bounce ideas off. In a limited way, I could talk about my experiences from working at South Crofty, Pendarves and Wheal Jane and this gave him a little local insight and the differences that existed from his own mining background in Canada. I was very pleased that he offered me a job with Cornwall Tin & Mining Corporation in January 1971. However, he had to warn me that he could only offer one month's work at a time with a salary that averaged my Thyssen wages plus free petrol. The secretary, Jenny Mylam had prepared a letter for Mr Richards, the owner of Bissoe Garage, requesting that I be added to the list of those authorised to have company petrol. I later found that "the list consisted of Jim and Malcolm". I did not hesitate to accept his offer and the lack of long term future was similar to my present situation with Thyssen's so it did not bother me.

Now that the underground development was complete and assay samples taken on 4 and 5 Levels, an ore reserve of 1 million tons at a grade of 1% tin would form the basis of a feasibility report – this included the previous diamond drilling results and approximately 2,500ft of driving on the lode. I did not fully understand the economics of mining, but gradually as time went on and Jim's explanation of the importance of 'operating costs per ton', 'investment payback' etcetera, I started to grasp the multitude of risks facing the company.

My role with Cornwall Tin & Mining Corporation continued with a new job title of Electrical Superintendent, but this meant little when there were only five of us employed in the company and multitasking was at times necessary. It seemed strange to see the Thyssen personnel packing up and leaving the site. Saying goodbye to Willie Knapp was a sad moment, particularly as I did not see him again – I believe he started a business importing and exporting antiques from here to Germany. A few years later when the Thyssen contracts were completed Alfred Hopfenzitz made a career change when he started importing and selling German wine in Truro Market.

Jim Delaney was in contact with Steve Kay on a regular basis and once a week he would telephone Toronto; if it was important he would pre-book an early afternoon call to avoid the time zone differences. One morning in February following the previous afternoon's call, Jim called me into his office to say he had spoken to Steve and due to his lack of progress in finding any investment, he wanted to save money and bring the pumps out, close the watertight doors and let the shaft flood. It was agreed that we should leave our two 150hp Beresford submersible pumps fitted with non-return valves and discharging into a 6-inch pipe via a 6-inch Y piece. This would give us a total delivery of 1,000gpm. I would disconnect the cables feeding the 350hp pump motors and the 3300V oil filled (DOL) direct on line starters and all the remaining electrical switch gear. We requested that Jacob Priller, Thyssen's shift boss, stay on with two miners and winder driver to bring the pumps/electric motors out of 5 Level and store them in the workshop. There was one last minute request for Alan Protheroe, to drill ten holes into the lode on 5 level which should help to increase the flow of water from the old workings and facilitate any future attempts to dewater the mine.

I was now deeply involved in planning the electrical layouts, system design and obtaining competitive quotes from four different suppliers and equipment manufacturers. Meetings were arranged with Mines and Quarries Inspectors, planning authorities and SWEB for a new power supply. Further land needed to be negotiated and an agreement reached on price; local landowners and farmers had a tendency to overestimate the value of land, particularly if a "rich mining company" showed any interest.

A potential stumbling block was operating the mine with only one shaft, the standard was set by Wheal Jane with their sinking of Clemow's and No 1 Shafts. In 1862 it was made illegal to operate a mine with only one shaft. Jim was familiar with single shaft mines in Canada and could not agree there was any compromise to safety. He was quite blunt with the Mines Inspector in saying if we were not able to operate with one shaft, then we might as well pack up and go home now. I think I may have added that I believed Pendarves only had one shaft and how did they manage? After further discussion, it was agreed that a second egress could be via a purpose made escape route through the stopes to the adit and out to surface. One more obstacle overcome.

Stan Alder had been working on the shaft and headgear steelwork. This required high precision and accuracy to lay out the shaft steel sets, buntons and guides to ensure the compartments lined up and cages/skips smoothly ran up and down the shaft. A ladder way, pumping columns, compressed air pipes and electrical cables had to be installed and supported in the shaft. There would not be any spare room once all the items were installed; sections and plans would need to be drawn up and an inventory of steel sent out for pricing.

Malcolm Hooper worked on the ore reserves and made a clay model of the proposed mine site. This was intended to show the size of the complete site and proposed dimensions of the buildings. SWEB were very considerate and understood our requirement and our fear of the effect that a power failure would have on the pumps. The existing power supply was an overhead 11,000 volt spur line, which came out from Chacewater. SWEB agreed to look at various options and when were able to give a commitment to proceed, they would get back to us.

Preliminary meetings with Mr Lawson, Mechanical Inspector and Mr Tyrell, Electrical Inspector proved helpful and we worked our way through a number options and ideas, reaching agreement on a start-up programme to satisfy Mines & Quarries Regulations if the mine should go ahead.

Steve Kay had limited success, although when an investor came over with him to visit Mount Wellington nobody was impressed with his lack of interest in the project. Two months later we had a message from Jack Tindale to let us know he would be sending over satellite images that he had obtained from the Space Agency, showing certain anomalies in the Lizard area. These images appeared consistent to a large low grade copper deposit. Jack came with Steve Kay towards the end of 1971, with one of the original shareholder investors, who spent some time with Jim Delaney. Malcolm and Jack discussed the Lizard possibility and agreed that soil samples should be taken on a grid system spaced at 1 metre intervals – this was over an area of approximately 500 square metres. Malcolm found that the land belonged to the Forestry Commission and also British Telecom, who he contacted to get their permission to take the necessary samples. By early January he had the go-ahead, which I thought seemed highly unlikely that any form of mining would be allowed in this area.

The sampling started early in February 1972. Malcolm hired four men, and with myself and Stan Alder, we started this laborious task, which thankfully was during a very dry and sunny period. It was not difficult using a hand held auger to collect about 6-inch of soil, but walking for considerable distances every day began to affect Stan, however he refused to take it easy. We were about a month into the job when Stan called in sick, and a week later we heard that he had died. Stan was a gentleman and we were all sad to hear he had passed away, particularly as the sampling only showed sporadic traces of copper and it all came to nothing.

Back at Mount Wellington, my work continued with costing and evaluating equipment suitability, whilst Malcolm started looking at Cligga. Jim Delaney had applied for outline planning permission for the construction of the mineral processing concentrator, the workshops, winder house, compressor house, miners dry, also including offices for the survey and geological departments. Our existing office was to be renovated for the administration staff and Jim retained his office, where he had uninterrupted views of the site.

One day I was busy at my desk when about 20 members of the Parish Council came into the planning office although it was believed that mining matters were dealt with by a higher authority but they were there to give a verdict on the recent planning application. I was still amazed by the lack of understanding shown by some of the members, who I thought would have at least spent some time to study mining in general particularly as their decision would affect the lives of so many local people and provide so much employment. One lady made a comment which made me smile, she thought it barbaric for the mine owners to send poor miners underground to work in the dark and she could not vote for the application – I did not know best to laugh or cry. We did have the support of the majority of people and Jack Trounson, who came to the meeting and spoke up strongly in our favour. We all owe Jack a huge debt of gratitude for his unwavering support for the Cornish mining industry.

It was looking like a sad ending to the year as Christmas 1972 drew near, with the news that Union Corporation was pulling out of Pendarves. Peter Weeks, the Manager at Pendarves, was friendly with Jim Delaney and we knew the mine had been in difficulties for some time. This was particularly sad as Pendarves was the first new mine to start in the recent revival of tin mining in the country. I had a number of friends who would be affected by this and I could understand what a loss this would be for them. I also wondered if this was the beginning of the end for Mount Wellington, as we had no word from Steve Kay with regards to funding the project. The news from East Cornwall did not improve matters. I happened to see the headline of an article printed in a Sunday newspaper, a picture showed an angler relaxing with rod and line on the banks of a river, with the headline, "Miner's idyllic job". It went on to say that miners working at the nearby tin prospect in Harrowbarrow would leave the mine early to spend the afternoon fishing on the banks of the river Tamar. I showed the paper to Jim, who later mentioned it to Steve when he made his weekly phone call. It was some time later that we heard from the Prince of Wales project that they had no success in intersecting the lode. The company laid off the three miners and closed down the prospect. However, the terms of the mineral lease had to be satisfied before the lease could be revoked. In this case, it was a matter of reinstatement and to ensure that the site had been left safe and secure. It would be approximately four months before this condition was satisfied.

My work continued with costing and availability of mining equipment and the most important item was a winder matching our specification available on the second-hand market, this was causing great concern as we had ruled out purchasing a new winder due to an extended delivery time and also excessive cost. I was told the Wheal Jane winder had cost over £250,000. We were on a tight budget with an added worry that inflation was beginning to spiral upwards. A desperate thought occurred to me, with Pendarves now in the hands of the Receiver, what was happening to the mining equipment and more importantly, the winder. From what I could remember, the winder and headgear would match our requirements and if this became available, we wanted to be first in line to make an offer. Jim and myself made an appointment to visit the mine and talk to the Receiver. We went in the late afternoon when most people had left work to avoid any controversy regarding the reason for the visit. It was explained that no decisions could be made until all avenues were explored with regards to selling as a going concern.

Fortunately, we were pleased to learn much later that South Crofty took over the mine and many jobs were saved.

Our thoughts returned to the question of keeping the mine free from the worry of flooding and the control of pumps with our large inflows of water. I think we had a preference in the choice of pump manufacturers, but we still looked at Sulzer Pumps as a comparison. The Sulzers had proved very reliable at South Crofty, but our experience with Mackley Pumps and their installation at Wheal Jane tipped the balance in the Mackley's favour. The offer from Mackley to keep a complete set of spares available sealed the deal. We would need at least six pumps, each discharging 1,000gpm, driven by 300hp motors controlled by 3300V Direct on Line Vacuum Contractors. The difficult decision proved to be the pump station design. I really thought that we should have a good reservoir to contain the water and to provide a positive head of water to feed into the pumps. The positive head of water above the intake would help prevent cavitation problems, overheating and ensuring the pumps would always be primed during start-up. We also had a very dangerous situation with the proximity of the vast underground workings of the Gwennap copper mines threatening to drown us out if we should accidentally blast into an unrecorded working. I explained this and Jim agreed at first, but then the only way this could be achieved was considered too costly. The scheme involved driving a tunnel approximately 1,200ft from our new pump station below 7 Level to intersect Frederick's Shaft. I believed we would return to this subject if the mine were to go ahead.

I had gone over to Wheal Jane as I was interested to see their compressor installation after contacting Mike Mahafy, their electrical engineer. He was always very helpful when I was working there with Thyssen's and he left me in the very capable hands of Les Oliver, one of his electricians, to show me around. I had known Les when we briefly worked together at Pendarves. He was very experienced and had spent most of his working life in India in the gold mines. They had two Ingersoll Rand Compressors each with an output of 2,000 cfm. They were very impressive and housed in a large building complete with overhead travelling crane. Next Les took me into the winder house which was located adjacent to the compressor, where he was obviously proud to show me their new hoist. It was all very impressive and looked as though money was no object when Consolidated Gold Fields set up the mine. Soon after this visit, I picked up an article about a new concept in compressor design, which moved away from piston to a rotary method of compressing air. Ingersoll Rand had recently introduced their range of Centac compressors, which were originally for use in the food industry because of the clean air that they produced. However, they were now being pushed into all fields of industry, including mining. I could see all the other advantages these machines claimed to offer; they were very compact, did not need to be housed in a large building or have massive foundations or require air receivers. Jim Delaney agreed this would be well worth looking into when the time came and was put into our file system. He was working on the supply availability and cost of rock drills. He had a high regard for Holman's and had used them when working as a miner in Canada – he was most surprised that we could not deal with Holman's direct, but had to go through an agent, particularly as we were virtually on their doorstep. If Jim wanted Holman drills and spares, he had to go through Sydney Williams and his company, PNEU-O-PLANT (Truro) Ltd. I am not sure how this worked out, but I sensed that Jim was disappointed not being able to talk directly to Holman's.

Jack Tindale called and said that Steve Kay was busy and quietly confident he would have some good news for us; in the meantime, could Malcolm contact Ron Hooper, the Mineral Agent for the Duchy of Cornwall, to discuss the outstanding work needed to reinstate the land at the Princes of Wales Mine? Malcolm contacted Ron and arranged to meet on site and invited me to go with him. Once there, we changed into boots, hard hat and cap lamps and followed Ron into the tunnel, which had been driven approximately 100m. Into the hillside. About halfway, we could see a collapse of weak ground, which spilled out over the rail tracks. We agreed a plan with Ron to shore up the sides of the drive using 6-inch concrete blocks and pouring concrete between the block and tunnel wall. We would use some surplus rail track over the top to support the roof. The entrance would be sealed with a substantial concrete block wall. I thought it would be a good idea to get out of the office for a change, so I volunteered to organise and run the job. Malcolm seemed relieved and basically left me to it. Back at the office, I drew up a list of material needed to be delivered direct to site and what needed to be picked up. I hired a pick-up truck for the two weeks length of time I thought the job would take and took on two Redruth men who were willing to spend two weeks working at Harrowbarrow. I telephoned the local Job Centre which gave me the details of people who had previously worked at the mine as I thought that a bit of local knowledge might be useful. Only one was available who I managed to contact and he was willing to come and work with us. He was called Alex Friendship and lived in St Ann's Chapel, halfway into Gunnislake and he proved to be a character. The job was finished to the satisfaction of Ron Hooper, who was willing to sign off the lease. Malcolm paid us a visit and took some measurements, and his reaction summed up how fragile mining could be. He believed that another week and they would have intersected the lode – if there was better supervision, it may have turned out a more satisfactory conclusion.

Preliminary design of the processing plant was being undertaken by Kilborn Engineering, a Toronto based company of engineering consultants. I believed that much of the ground work was discussed with Roy Morgan, who I briefly knew from my time at South Crofty where he was the Mill Manager. Roy Morgan was one of life's gentlemen and got on well with Jim Delaney, and by the time Kilborn came over, Jim was well prepared to discuss the basic design of the concentrator.

In September, Steve Kay returned to Wellington with two men who represented Cargill, who we later found out was one of the richest family owned businesses in the world. They were an American commodity company controlling 25% of the world's grain business and were interested in diversifying into the mining industry. The talks, particularly with Jim Delaney, went well and eventually they made an offer for a controlling interest for 51% of the company subject to a satisfactory and independent study of the ore reserves and re-sampling the lode. They would assign Tom Huxley from Tradex, one of their companies based in Geneva, to be responsible for the project. We were all delighted with this news, it was probably the last chance to develop the mine and it did not matter to us who owned the company. Tom Huxley was an accountant by profession and had very little mining experience, but there was little doubt who controlled the finances. Mining and geological consultants, Maclean & Partners, were engaged to produce independent reports and a feasibility study. Cargill agreed to pay for this, including all costs relating to pumping out our workings to gain access to 4 and 5 Levels.

Jim gave me a free hand to reinstate the pump station and we needed to prove that we were able to pump out within as short a time as possible. I looked forward to the challenge, but realised we were approaching our wet season and all equipment that we put in storage two years ago, was not in the best of condition. We were also worried by the threat of interruptions to power supplies as the possibility of a three day working week was discussed by the government. With coal miners, railway, post office and power station workers coming out on strike, the future was beginning to look grim. As if that wasn't enough, the oil producing Arab nations doubled the price of oil and petrol went from 41 pence per gallon to 71 pence a gallon.

Chapter 4
Rain, Rain, Go Away

With Cargill agreeing to fund the dewatering and the cost of verifying the ore reserves, it was necessary to form a new company to operate and manage the project. So Cornwall Tin & Mining Ltd was registered on the 31st of October 1973 as the operating company for Mount Wellington. After much negotiating, Steve had finally run out of options and the equity of the company was split with 51% held with Tradex and 49% held by Cornwall Tin & Mining Corporation. It was believed that to date, £1,250,000 had been spent in Cornwall and this included a 20% regional development grant from the Department of Trade and Industry. It was estimated that the budget to bring the mine into full production would require a further £2,500,000 – this was to deepen the shaft and develop the underground plus the construction of the concentrator, mining department offices, compressor installation, winder installation, headgear and workshop/stores.

The shaft needed sinking two more levels, with permanent pump station and underground development to meet the demands of the 600 ton per day concentrator. We were all energised by the real prospect of Mount Wellington Mine successfully going ahead. We did not expect the accumulated problems that were beginning to face the country would trouble us – inflation was rising, it went up to 25% but so was the price of tin. The shortage of steel was due to the huge demands of the oil companies to construct their drill rigs and pipelines so that the vast reserves of oil lying deep beneath North Sea could be exploited. The cost of steel increased by over 40%, with availability the biggest problem. Storm clouds were gathering, but here in Cornwall the sun was shining, that was until Christmas when heavy and persistent rain threatened to spoil our party.

I had been given a free hand and full responsibility to dewater 4 and 5 Levels so the appointed consultants could re-sample the lodes and confirm the ore reserve. It took over a month to prepare the site before we could start the two Beresford Submersible pumps and dewater the shaft, enabling us to install the main pumps. It was crucial to maintain the pumping effort once we started and we needed assurance that our power supply would be secure. We were eventually given dispensation by the Department of Trade and Industry and guaranteed uninterrupted electricity supply. I was not entirely confident nor could I trust political statements, so I thought it prudent to hire a generator with capacity to use the hoist or one Beresford pump. This of course would not be enough to dewater but would buy us some time to get the pump man out of the shaft. I had spent hours telephoning around the country before I found one suitable.

It was obvious that just about everyone had the same idea to hire or purchase generators to avoid the effects of the 3 day working week. Eventually I managed to locate J. F. Engineering of Oxford, a company who were importing generators from Czechoslovakia. I gave them a specification for a 250kVA diesel generator and they promised to let me know as soon as possible. We needed Thyssen's agreement to use the equipment that they left on site, and most importantly the use of the winder and headgear, which was critical for us. Thyssen drove a hard bargain when it came down to hire rates. Next, I lined up a team of winder drivers, pump men, banksmen, labourer, fitter, electrician and miner/shaft men, in total 15 men who I thought were needed for the job.

While we were in general discussion with Mr Lawson, the Mines and Quarry Mechanical Inspector, the subject of winding ropes was raised as a legal obligation to comply with Miscellaneous Mines Regulations. This regulation concerning winding ropes required that 6ft was cut off the end of the rope every six months. Under normal circumstances, we should have to change the rope as it had been on the winder over three years, but had not been used in the last two years. Also, if the independent sampling results were found to be unsatisfactory, then the project may not go ahead and the cost of a new rope would be wasted. So we were able to get a temporary exemption for this, providing we carried out ultrasonic or non-destructive testing.

I contacted Hugh Stapleton, the South Crofty Chief Engineer, to explain our situation with regards to rope capping and wondered if Johnny Parker was available to come out to Wellington, to which he readily agreed, and by the following week the job was complete. Johnny Parker was one of Crofty's characters, with his big, black beard and his greeting everyone as, "Alright pard", some even said he called his wife, "pard". He looked the part of a typical miner and he took his responsibility seriously. His preparation was meticulous cleaning the heavy grease off the socket and ends of the steel rope. The white metal had to be melted to the correct temperature and then ladled into the conical socket and splayed out wire. When cold, the white metal fused solidly to the strands of wire encapsulated within the socket, securing the end of the steel rope. After cleaning up and packing his gear away, Johnny signed the M&Q log book before driving back to South Crofty.

The winder drivers relied on the depth indicator, a large dial with a pointer which was calibrated to rotate around like the minute hand of a clock, to show the location of the conveyance in the shaft. When 6 feet was cut off the rope, the marks needed to be reset. The brakes would be applied and the drum declutched to allow the small rotation of the shaft to line up with the new position on the dial. For an exact position, the winder driver would use chalk to mark the drum and confirm this with the man riding on the cage.

Winders have a number of safety devices, the two most important are the over speed and over travel cut out trips. These can be adjusted to activate the winder brakes to prevent the runaway situation, over winding and stopping the cage going over the top of the headgear or crashing in the bottom of the shaft. This is a very simple explanation as there was numerous and sophisticated devices to ensure the safe operation of winders. Now that all the statutory tests complied with Miscellaneous Mines and Quarry Regulations, we could set up the winder with new marks to allow for the rope capping. The 6ft that was cut off the end of the winding rope every six months was to ensure there was a different point of contact on the drum and sheave wheels on the headgear. This prevented the steel strands of the winding rope from crushing due to continued contact at the same point of loading.

The author checking the water pressure at the 4 Level watertight door

Mid-November, and we were ready to start the pumps. I had a commitment from the 15 men who I wanted to employ. I could not give any guarantee for long term employment and I was unsure how long the initial work would last. There were three winder drivers, Mike Tonkin, Ewart Matthews and Mike Jenkin; three banksmen, Tony Hall, Roger George and Vic Peters; three pump men, Phil Jervis, David Roberts and Ian Harris; two labourers, Barry Hocking and David Matthews. David was Ewart's eldest son, together with his other two boys, Michael and Paul had played rugby for St Day. It was a proud father the day they all played together in the same team. I also engaged Winston Edwards our mechanical fitter; one

Collapsed adit.

Below. The start of inspection on the No. 4 Level: Tiny Marsh, Jim Delaney and the Author.

Inside No.4 Level: Author, John Nicholls, Tiny Marsh and Jim Delaney.

Tiny Marsh breaking through the concrete bulkhead of the 5 Level not so water tight door.

Shaft sinking equipment ready to go down the shaft: 5-ton bucket, Cactus Grab; grout pump at bottom left.

Electricians. L – R Peter Martin, Mick Trezona, Frank Partridge & George Gordon.

welder, John Nicholls; electrician, Peter Martin; and shaft man/miner, Tiny Marsh. I had a few more names I could fall back on, as past experience showed that there was likely to be an above average turnover in these jobs. I worked out the rotas for the shift work and decided on 7am – 3pm – 11pm start/finish times. Having briefed everyone, we started the Beresford submersibles at approximately 9am and by midday, the water discharge into the adit at 1 Level was running steady at 1,000 gallons per minute. I asked the pump man to take the bucket (we used the 5 ton sinking bucket to ride up and down the shaft) down every hour to record the water levels in the shaft. I believe I used the right terminology with regards to the bucket, which was a slightly conical shape not always seen in Cornish mines. The kibble was introduced from a very early period, being a more practical shape to haul up and down a shaft. The kibble was shaped like a rugby ball with both ends cut off having a wide belly with narrow opening, which made it less likely the rim would catch in obstacles when being hauled up a shaft.

Peter had prepared the switch gear and starters ready to be taken underground and installed on 5 Level. We needed to control the shaft submersibles from the pump station, so the cables would have to be disconnected and re-routed to allow this. John and Winston had been working on the main Mackley pumps so they could be taken underground as soon as conditions would allow.

We were not disappointed the next day when we came in to work. I arrived early to get the report from the pump man, who was pleased to say the pumps ran well through the night and water level was on the brow of 5 Level station. I went down the shaft with Peter, Tiny and Winston, I confirmed the order of work and was satisfied that we would be able to start the clean up on 5 Level by midday. I then gave Jim the good news when I came back up to find him waiting on the bank. Before we left work that evening, the afternoon shift and pump man were able to control the pumps from 5 Level pump station. To maintain the pumps with a steady and constant flow, we had to feed water into the shaft through one of the 8-inch gate valves that we could gradually open. This allowed the pump man to control the amount of water that we ran into the shaft from the flooded workings behind the watertight door. This was the only way we could use the submersible pumps and if the water dropped too low or rose too high, I had cut-out switches installed with alarms set to warn the pump men.

The shaft was pumped out in approximately 24 hours, but the real work of dewatering the flooded levels behind the watertight doors was about to begin. The main Mackley pumps and motors were taken down the shaft, hung beneath the bucket to 5 Level, where men waited to pull them into the pump station. Here they were roughly assembled on the bed plate and dragged out using pulleys to their original positions in the pump station. They were carefully lined up and when the motor and pump coupling were perfectly aligned it could be finally bolted to the base. The flanges on the discharge and intake pipes were bolted to the pump, and alignment checked again, then, when the electric cable was connected, we were ready to bring the next pump down. It was all going well and by the second week in November we were using all our pumps and beginning to lower the water. We were able to confirm the volume of water being pumped at approximately 4,000gpm by checking the measuring box on 1 Level.

An amusing incident occurred one afternoon when the pump men were changing shift. Phil Jervis was seen leaving the changing rooms heading for the shaft with two huge rubber inflatable inner tubes that were from a tractor tyre. He had a job to get them into the bucket and down the shaft. Apparently, Phil was beginning to get curious about the source of water that was being pumped. This of course invited a wind-up and he was told that he should keep an eye open to check the watertight doors as there were millions of gallons of water ready to pour out into the shaft if they should open. Phil thought that he should get prepared for every eventuality so if this were to happen he could jump in the tube and float up to the surface on the rising water. His fear gradually left as the pressure and water levels that I continued to measure in the surrounding shafts got lower.

With the end of the year drawing to a close we were getting in a good situation to dewater 4 and 5 Levels so that the lode could be sampled. The pumps were performing very well with the water levels dropping steadily and the pressure behind 4 Level watertight door was down to 4psi, approximately 10ft of water. Then all plans were put on hold as we experienced very heavy rain over Christmas, which continued into the new year. Millions of gallons of rain fell on the large catchment area of the mine. By virtue of Wellington's location, this catchment would be similar to the area drained by the Great County Adit, which was estimated to be in the order of 12 square miles.*

When Cornwall Tin & Mining Corporation started at Mount Wellington, the County Adit had been neglected for over 50 years. Evidence of this lack of maintenance was seen in the collapse near the Wellington Portal beneath the Bissoe to Twelveheads road. The remedial work for this short section was important but costly, and very little work was done on the adit from 1969-1978. I don't think we fully understood the importance of this adit system, we were under huge pressures elsewhere and were expected to work within budget, which did not include money or time to maintain the adits. Before we diverted the pump discharge into the 1 Level adit, the water ran into a small settlement dam on surface and then disappeared down the hillside. We probably ended up recycling some of this water as it found its way back down into the Wheal Andrew workings.

Any blockage due to silting or collapse within the 40-odd miles of this huge system would have an impact on the ability of rainwater percolating from surface

*The definitive study of the Great County Adit can be found in the book by Allen Buckley. Mr Buckley must presently be considered the most important historian and prolific recorder of Cornish mining and equal to the legendary figures, A. K. Hamilton Jenkin and Jack Trounson.

to flow freely through the adit. This water would then remain underground, overflowing into the old workings that we were trying to pump out. This then became a liability rather than an important aid to drainage when the mines were at their peak, all pumping into a well maintained adit. Now it seemed we were pumping from some giant sponge with the lode acting like a conduit passing water into our workings. From past records on rainfall and the time it took to infiltrate the ground after dry summers, we thought water inflows would peak at the end of February, or we had hoped so. We thought that with three Mackley pumps at 3,000gpm and a further 1,000gpm from the two Beresford's, we had sufficient capacity to dewater and complete the sampling.

MINE PUMPS

MINE GIANT FIGHTS A NON-STOP BATTLE

One of the water-tight doors in Mount Wellington mine, Bissoe, where water is always the big enemy. To keep it in check, the largest pump in any Cornish mine has been installed. Capable of pumping 2,000 gallons a minute, it is in use 24 hours a day. The other underground pumps together pump 7,000 gallons a minute.

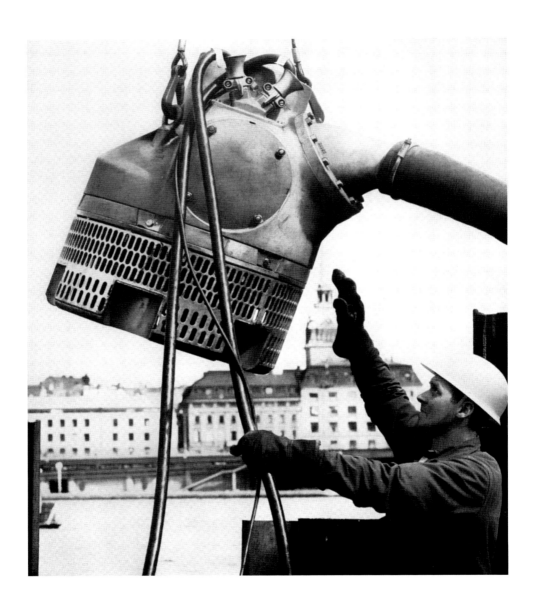

45

Chapter 5

Water! Water! Everywhere

We approached the New Year hoping the rain would ease and the pumps continued to cope with the inflows and to reduce the *in situ* water that filled the vast underground workings of this extensively mined area. However, the rain did not abate and on New Year's Day at 7pm, I had my first call out when the pump man reported that the Beresford Pump had tripped out and he could not restart it. The Beresford's had given us good service and it would be a major blow if we were to lose the capability of pumping 500 gallons a minute. It was disappointing to find the pump would have to be taken out to get repaired. The following notes are a day by day report on some of our activities as recorded in my diary during a period from January to April, a period which was critical to a successful opening of the mine.

The numbers following F and WA opposite represent water levels in Frederick's Shaft and Wheal Andrew Shaft measured in metres from the shaft collars.

Left-right: Phil Jervis pump man, Tiny Marsh, shaft man, Peter Martin electrician (waiting for more pumps).

Tuesday 1st January Pumps running through the day. Called out at 19.00 hours Beresford pump tripping out on overload. Unable to repair. Fault appears to be in the pump motor.

Wednesday 2nd January (F 104.17 - WA 98.5) Pressure 4 Level 8psi, 5 Level 32psi. Taking out faulty Beresford, installing Plueger in shaft. Replace 8″ gate value on bulkhead.

Thursday 3rd January (F 104.76 - WA 99.06) Pumps running okay. Pressure on 4 Level 12psi, 5 Level 25psi. Compressor motor tripped, windings short circuited. Preparing to send off to Electro Mechanical Repairs at Redruth. Thrust bearing packed up on Beresford, sending down to Visick's in afternoon.

Friday 4th January (F 105.36 - WA 101.29) 09.30 hours cable blew out on 1 Level, disconnect and lowered own to 3 Level. Located a replacement 120mm 3 core 250 metres long. BICC in Plymouth. Collected and brought to site at 18.00 hours, installed in shaft by 22.00 hours. Connected 6 inch pipe and electric cable with all pumps back running by 12.30 hours.

Saturday 5th January All pumps running.

Sunday 6th January Two Beresford's off for two hours while fixing rope to cable in shaft. Took Jim Delaney down to 4 Level and opened valve on door.

Monday 7th January (F 106.57 - WA 95.57) Still dewatering 4 Level. Water dripping out of air line.

Tuesday 8th January (F 106.92 - WA 93.71) 12.00 noon water down to 4′6″ above 4 Level track. Water dropped 9″ over a three hour period. Peter repaired damaged cable and hope to run spare Plueger pump off this cable. Heavy rain through last night and all day, rise of 18″ when I measured the shafts.

Wednesday 9th January Opened door on 4 Level, air very bad. Install vent fans, take the air ducting up the drive and leave running. Went to 4 Level with Jim and Malcolm in afternoon

Thursday 10th January Quality of air improving, Malcolm able to organise sampling tomorrow. Maclean & Partners to supervise.

Friday 11th January (F 106.06 - WA 92.17) Amps fluctuation on No.1 and No.2 Mackley, shut down and clean out the intake. After flushing, the pumps run okay. Peter and John fit new rubber seals on 4 Level door. Sampling started, David

Matthews, David Rixon, Ian Harris and Graham Johnson.

Saturday 12th January (F 105.7 - WA 86.83) New Mackley due to arrive today.

Sunday 13th January (F 105.7 - WA 86.83) Taking Mackley down the shaft as a replacement.

Monday 14th January (F 104.58 – WA86.7) Clean up 4 Level and change Mackley pump. Sent 11/3.3kV transformer to SWEB for overhaul. Picked up Beresford from Visick's. The bush that Visick's made would not fit. Pump off all day.

Tuesday 15th January (F103.86 - WA 85.02) Robert Marshall from Visick's re-bored coupling and came down to 5 Level to inspect the key way and pump shaft. John and Peter standing by to install two Beresford pumps.

Wednesday 16th January (F 103.44 - WA 83.09) Continued heavy rain is backing up in the County Adit and water levels have been steadily rising in the surrounding shafts. Installing fourth Beresford pump. Unlikely to open 5 Level door with existing pumps. Checking availability of pumps, motors, transformers, etc.

Thursday 17th January (F 102.62 - WA 82.58) Installing fourth Beresford pump. Water still rising. Situation getting desperate for extra pumps.

Friday 18th January (F 102.21 – WA83) Looking for extra pumps, contact R. F. Winder Second hand Mining Equipment sales at Leeds.

Saturday 19th January (F 101.72 - WA 83.06) Water levels rising in County Adit.

Sunday 20th January Travel up to Leeds, took Winston. R. F. Winder may be able to supply all our needs.

Monday 21st January Arrive 08.30 hours at R. F. Winder premises, find an unused but old Pulsometer pump, which was a standby pump and never left the NCB central stores. This was a 2 stage 580′ head pumping 2,080gpm. The pump looked in good condition and freely rotated. R. F. Winder were able to supply all the items on my shopping list. One Metro Vic 450hp rotor resistance, flameproof motor. Two Reyrolle 200 amp circuit breakers rotor starters.

Tuesday 22nd January Travel back from Leeds. Call into work.

Wednesday 23rd January (F 101.17 - WA 89.35) Went to 4 & 5 Levels with Winston and Peter, new Mackley pump seized! More problems Visick's to work on and finish No.1 pump ready to bring back to the mine tomorrow. Richards & Osborne Transport to bring the Pulsometer and associated gear back from Leeds, charge £185.

Thursday 24th January (F 100.99 - WA 89.74) Located 600ft 8″ pipe at Macsalvors. Sid Knowles Transport picking up to bring to Wellington. S. J. Andrews & Sons to deliver nuts/bolts, flanges and gaskets. Taking No. 1 pump down shaft, running by 12 noon. Bring Beresford out of shaft and take to Visick's. Order 30 cap lamps and charger from J. Miller, Oldham.

Friday 25th January (F 106.15 - WA 91.55) Peter, John and Tiny working in shaft on Beresford. Visick's stripped down new Mackley pump. Winston off sick. Thyssen's helping out with pump parts Alfred came over. Ordered spares for Mackley. Bushes, Impeller neck rings seized up. Able to replace damaged parts from our stock of spares. Beresford lower motor bearing worn pump end free.

Saturday 26th January Tiny and John strip out 2″ pipe from shaft and move cable to allow space to fit 8″ steel pipe on buntons.

Sunday 27th January Contact Ray Jose to come and start welding flanges on 8″ pipe. (Ray is a local self-employed welder and agricultural fitter).

Monday 28th January (F 106.10 - WA 88.38) Tiny, John and David Matthews starting to install 8″ pipe. Detailed Ian Harris, Graham Johnson and Rixon to clean up the adit. Sid Knowles picking up two lengths of 6″ hose from Macsalvors. Hole found in 6″ pipe near 2 Level.

Tuesday 29th January (F 106.1 - WA 87.24) Installing 250 metres 3 core SWA 3300V, 70sq mm cable. Mackley brought back from Visick's. 450hp slip ring motor for the Pulsometer tested at Falmouth Docks, checked out okay. Low reading to earth on Beresford pump motor 0.01 megs, being sent back to Beresford. 15.30 hours, cable slipped from the grasp of one man pulling end of cable through the sub bank. Cable fell through the shaft causing considerable damage. Cable brought into 5 Level. Attempt to make repairs. More problems!

Wednesday 30th January (F 105.21 - WA 86) Generator due today. 120hp compressor motor due back from EMR Redruth. Crane ordered 15.30 hours for Visick's to offload 450hp motor. Visick's to fabricate a bed plate and need to ensure pump lines up with the motor. Non drive bearing on the 350hp motor picked up. Peter called in at 19.00 hours, took the bearing off ready to take to Visick's in morning. New 8″ pipeline in shaft, not plumb – flanges not welded square. Rixon, Johnson and Harris working in adit. Tiny and Tony Hall working in shaft on 8″

pipe. Peter repairing cable.

<u>Thursday 31st January</u> (F 105.62 - WA 83.94) Robert Marshall (Visick's) measuring pump shaft. Hope to get bearing back today. Coupling turned out on lathe. Ray Jose back for more welding, request another welder from Visick's. Rang Mike Webb, need him for electrical work next few days. Peter working on getting bearing back, pumps running 20.00 hours.

<u>Friday 1st February</u> Tiny and Tony continue with installing 8″ pipe. 70sq mm 3 core cable back in operation.

<u>Saturday 2nd February</u> Pumps running okay. Peter, Tiny, John, Dave Matthews.

<u>Sunday 3rd February</u> Peter, Tiny, John and Dave. Installing 8″ pipe in shaft.

<u>Monday 4th February</u> (F 103.01 - WA 76.21) Running out of steel pipe flanges. Send to Plymouth for 24 table 'D' 8″ and 12 table 'E' 8″ flanges and 6 elbows needed by tomorrow. Prepared base for concrete near shaft (Pulsometer).

<u>Tuesday 5th February</u> Concrete ordered for 14.00 hours. Base for Pulsometer completed at 16.00 hours. Pump to be supplied with water from 8″ gate valve on the loading pocket bulkhead.

<u>Wednesday 6th February</u> (F 101.44 - WA 76.42) SWEB complete overhaul of transformer replaced two cracked insulators on HV side.

<u>Thursday 7th February</u> (F 100 - WA 75) Transformer back from SWEB. Peter connecting switchgear 3300V SWEB jointers connecting 11kV HV side to the Transformer. Pump and bedplate taken down to 5 Level and placed on concrete plinth.

<u>Friday 8th February</u> (F 101 - WA 75.23) Start early and disconnect the 2 winch ropes from the platform to use to take the Pulsometer Pump Motor to 5 Level (the weight of motor was approximately 6 tons which exceeded the safe working load of the winder which was rated at 5 tons) I could not risk using the winder for this job so we secured the 450hp motor to the two winch ropes and slowly lowered down the shaft. Motor on the bedplate by 12 noon, to be lined up when pipework is complete.

<u>Saturday 9th February</u> Manoeuvring pump on bedplate.

<u>Sunday 10th February</u> Lining up the pump and motor. 3.3kV 70sq mm cable

blowout in shaft near 4 Level.

Monday 11th February Peter repairing cable in shaft. Continue pipe fitting 8"delivery and 10" suction. Winston our fitter handed in his notice. Hasn't been well for weeks and worried about continuing equipment breakdowns and seemingly lack of progress. Sorry to see him go, he was a good fitter.

Tuesday 12th February (F 92.32 - WA 55.28) Rixon absent again. Asked Alfred H. if we could borrow a fitter. Stopped No.1 Mackley pump to run Pulsometer from No.1 starter. Peter Badjac, an experienced fitter with Thyssen's had been sent over from Wheal Jane to help us. Checked bearing, finished pipework. Started pump, ran very smoothly from 5.30pm – 9.00pm. Cable blew out, Peter Martin made repairs and pump run at 1.30am. Peter Martin watched the pump until 4.00am. Pumping in excess of 2000gpm. Adit not coping with the amount of water. Take down sand bags to adit. Need to clear more of the old Wellington adit.

Wednesday 13th February Men in adit clean up and laying more sand bags to prevent water flowing back. Running Pulsometer on temporary cable.

Thursday 14th February (F 88.92 - WA 53.58) Tiny, David Matthews, Ian Harris and Graham Johnson clean up adit. Peter Martin and John Nic taking damaged cable out of shaft. Pressure on 5 Level rising to 35psi. County adit backed up to highest level.

Friday 15th February (F 86.28 - WA 52.32) Tidy up 4 Level, continue taking out damaged cable.

Saturday 16th February Tiny, John and Peter start on 8 inch pipework new column.

Sunday 17th February Tiny, Peter and John prepare plinth for 2000kVA transformer.

Monday 18th February (F 78.67 - WA 51.73) Ordered concrete for transformer plinth for 2pm. Finished plinth.

Tuesday 19th February (F 78.85 - WA 53.07) Hole in 6" column just above 4 Level, fitted new pipe.

Wednesday 20th February Change over to separate 8" suction pipes for 3 Mackley pumps. Shut down No.2 and No.3 Mackley's to make cable joint on Reyrolle O.C.B. Energised fourth 3.3kV panel and 450hp motor connected. Wired in anti-condensation heater on motor. 8" table 'E' gate valve cracked and replaced with table 'F', picked up from Macsalvors.

Thursday 21st February (F 77.76 - WA 55.63) Call from R. F. Winder, 2,000kVA transformer dispatched from Leeds. J. F. Engineering picked up generator in Dover. Peter finished cable joined on 3.3kV Reyrolle O.C.B.

Friday 22nd February (F 78.30 - WA 60.02) Crane hired from Macsalvors, offloaded transformer onto plinth. Generator on temporary location by winder house. Peter preparing 3.3kV joint on transformer. Leak on 8″ pipe on 5 Level, John to weld new section.
Saturday 23rd February (F 79.9 - WA 63.3) Generator arrived, delayed yesterday, sent to Oxford. Offloaded at 11.00am.

Sunday 24th February Arranged for Frank Partridge to come in. Cable joint on 11kV transformer, Peter jointing 3.3kV side. Shut down supply at 9.00am to change over. Finish and energised at 4.30pm. All pumps running at 5.00pm.

Monday 25th February Peter called in last night at 10.30pm, unable to get power back on. SWEB called, two 11kV fuses blown, only rated at 63A. Power back on by 1.00am with all pumps running.

The author commissioning the Pulsometer Pump installed on 5 Level Shaft Station, February 1974.

Peter Martin and Tiny Marsh checking the flow of balance water on the Pulsometer. Pumping 2000gpm it was the largest pump installed underground in a Cornish mine.

Pressure at 8.00am, 32psi. Pressure at 2.00pm, 20psi.
Running 3 Mackley pumps – 3000gpm. Running 3 Beresford pumps – 1500gpm.
Running 1 Pulsometer – 2000gpm. Running 1 Plueger – 350gpm.

Tuesday 26th February (F 81.87 - WA 73.95) Pressure 10psi, pumping 6200gpm.

Wednesday 27th February (F 83.84 - WA 85.49) Generator running okay, but can't get it to excite. Rang J. F. Engineering, sending engineer. Install 75hp Flygt pump on 8″ pipeline on door bulkhead. Left running. Pressure down to 3psi. Need to close up 8″ valve on Pulsometer pump due to cavitation when pressure drops. Difficult to get sufficient water to pump.

Thursday 28th February (F 85.39 - WA 89.05) Changing Plueger pump. All pumps running overnight. 2 Plueger's – 500gpm, 3 Beresford's – 1500gpm, 3 Mackley's – 3000gpm, 1 Pulsometer – 1200-1800gpm pumping on semi-closed valve to reduce cavitation, affects pressure 6psi.

Friday 1st March Pressure dropping down to 4psi, all pumps running. Need to prepare to dig out concrete on 5 Level door. Tiny to start in morning.

Saturday 2nd March (F 86.51 - WA 91.19) No pressure shown on gauge.

Sunday 3rd March Water approximately 10′ above track 5 Level. Pumps being starved of water.

Monday 4th March (F 90.50 - WA 100.5) Water 9′ above track, need to get more water to pump, increase suction pipe to 10″ on Pulsometer pump.

Tuesday 5th March Thrust bearing on Beresford pump packed up. Stop No.1 and No.2 Mackley's to drain pump station, dam and install 10″ pipe and gate valve. Beresford taken down to Visick's.

Wednesday 6th March (F 92.40 - WA 102.63) Beresford stripped at Visick's, impellors disintegrated. Changing stages and impellors with Beresford, waiting to be rewound. Plueger pump impellors and neck rings worn. Non-return valve worn. Plueger in shaft to be replaced with one on surface.

Thursday 7th March (F 93.42 - WA 103.09) Installed 10″ flange on Flygt pump to connect to Pulsometer. Stayed on all night to watch the Flygt pumping into the suction of Pulsometer.

Friday 8th March (F 94.3 - WA 100.9) Peter and Tiny install Beresford.

Saturday 9th March (F 96.62 - WA 103.05) Running Beresford.

Sunday 10th March Tiny broke through concrete to gain access to 5 Level door.

Monday 11th March (F 98.07 - WA 104.87) Tiny called out at 19.00 hours, 8″ column in shaft dropped after Pulsometer was stopped. Damaged 6″ pipework and non-return valve on Mackley by the shaft. Got the Mackley working by 03.00 hours.

Tuesday 12th March (F 98.92 - WA 105.4) Water down, able to open 5 Level door! Went in on east face, no problem with air. Repairs rubbers around the door. Could see where the leak occurred, the rubber failed to seal on the door frame.

Wednesday 13th March (F 99.93 - WA 105.86) Bearing drive end of Pulsometer picked up. Bearing taken down to Visick's to be re-metalled. D. Roberts, I. Harris, D. Matthews sampling. Tiny standing by the door in case we need to shut up quickly and get the samplers out. Worked on until 18.00 hours.

<u>Thursday 14th March</u> (F 100.69 - WA 106.22) Generator engineers arriving from Czechoslovakia to be picked up from Truro Station. Bearing ready to pick up from Visick's at Midday. Working on to get pump working. Running Plueger in shaft to try and hold water long enough to sample.

<u>Friday 15th March</u> (F 101.63 - WA 106.68) Bearing on Pulsometer back by 13.00 hours. Ran pump okay, water going down. Back in work at 21.00 hours. Water level down, switched off Mackley. Bernard Hallsworth (welder) on loan from Visick's for morning.

<u>Saturday 16th March</u> Start at 06.00 hours with Tiny and Peter to open door. Continue with sampling, door shut at 13.30 hours.

<u>Sunday 17th March</u> Peter and Tiny, D. Roberts and Ian Harris taking samples.

<u>Monday 18th March</u> 2 Beresford's off. Finish taking samples.

<u>Tuesday 19th March</u> (F 105.20 - WA 108.5) 3 Beresford's off, water rising very slowly. Hired JCB from Hydraulic Tin to take B2250 Flygt pump out of the County Adit.

<u>Wednesday 20th March</u> (F 106.67 - WA 109.36) Pumpmen D. Roberts, P. Jarvis, on 12 hour shifts.

We had achieved our target and opened 4 Level and 5 Level watertight doors to allow the consulting mining geologists, Maclean and Partners, to make their reports on the viability of the ore deposits. We could only wait to see if the results were favourable and if Tradex would invest in the mine. I was feeling exhausted after so many callouts and working extra hours but there was no let up as we carried on as if we were going ahead with Mount Wellington. I made a brief summary of the events looking back over the last three months.

From the start of pumping, it took 28 days to open 4 Level and 85 days to open 5 Level. Malcolm Hooper supervised our men over the five days it took to sample each level, all under the direction of Maclean and Partners mining and geological consultants. We experienced 17 major breakdowns that interrupted the pumping, which included electrical overloads, short circuits and motor bearings, while mechanical failures were pump bearings, impellers, pipes and valves etcetera. Of the 15 men I started with, I unfortunately had to sack 3 and a further 4 left for various reasons, but I managed to get replacements. We only lowered the water in Frederick's Shaft by 47 metres, and 67 metres in Wheal Andrew Shaft but this was enough to gain access to the lode for sampling. There could be little doubt that the poor condition of the adit played a big part in not draining surface water, allowing it to flood underground into the old workings.

I later made comparisons with the pumping efforts that took place 104 years previously at Clifford Amalgamated Mines and our own work at Wellington. In the autumn of 1869, Clifford Amalgamated Mines were embarking on a programme to increase their output of copper. This huge concern included the Consolidated and United Mines, which had been the most important copper producers in Cornwall. This was when Gwennap Parish could boast the richest square mile in the world. The mine was well equipped with 20 steam engines and was said to be unequalled on any metalliferous mine anywhere in the world. The bottom levels were flooded and needed to be drained to continue the life of the mine. Similarly to us they started in the autumn during a period of very heavy rain and it took the efforts of eight large Cornish pumping engines to dewater the bottom of the mine. These were:-

Cardozo's	90″ pumping 478gpm	1140ft to adit
Poldory	85″ pumping 887gpm	780ft to adit
Hocking's	85″ pumping 494gpm	1248ft to adit
Taylor's	85″ pumping 520gpm	1380ft to adit
Garland's	85″ pumping 448gpm	1380ft to adit
Clifford	76″ pumping 351gpm	1410ft to adit
Andrew	70″ pumping 520gpm	540ft to adit
Consols	85″ pumping 912gpm	180ft to adit

This gave an average pumping rate of 4,610gpm, but increased occasionally to 5,330gpm. D. B. Barton, in 1966, remarked it was unlikely that pumping of this magnitude had ever been equalled or approached in any other mine or group of mines in the world.

However, on Monday 25th February 1974, we recorded the following; 3 Mackley's pumping 3,000gpm, 3 Beresford submersibles pumping 1,500gpm, 1 Pulsometer pumping 2,000gpm, 1 Plueger pumping 350gpm – a total of 6,850gpm approximately 1,520gpm more than at Clifford Amalgamated Mines.

From 24th February we maintained a pumping rate of over 6,000gpm until the sampling was completed on Monday 18th March. This cannot be considered a true comparison as we had the disadvantage of only one shaft compared with their eight shafts. On both occasions the pumping effort started in the autumn and continued through a winter of heavy rain. Unfortunately for Clifford Amalgamated Mines, the cost of this pumping increased their burden of losses and the mine went into liquidation.

We would never have been able to achieve this without the help of numerous individuals and businesses who all stepped in without hesitation. Peter Visick and the expertise of his employees saved the day on many occasions when pump failure threatened the project. By and large, our own employees were unfailing in their tasks. Peter Martin and Tiny Marsh were particularly good, nothing was too much trouble and they cheerfully went about their work regardless of the difficulties. We also had a great deal of luck in just about keeping a makeshift collection of worn out equipment working. The major contribution to the success of the project was the installation of the Pulsometer pump.

It took just 22 days from the 21st of January, the date I first inspected the Pulsometer in Leeds, to the 12th of February when we started and ran the pump. It should be noted that the Pulsometer stood alone and we had to match it up with an electric motor. Visick's fabricated a bedplate and turned out a coupling, which all had to line up when assembled before taking underground. I also got Visick's to strip the pump to check wear on impellers etcetera. This was found to confirm R. F. Winder's statement of the pump being old, but unused. Likewise, I had the motor taken down to Falmouth Docks to be tested and checked – it would be a disaster if any part of should fail now.

The overall length of pump and motor was approximately 3.3m and could not be located in the already overcrowded pump station. The only place we could install it was beneath the brow of 5 Level station, near the edge of the shaft. Because of the orientation of the pipework, the motor had to sit on the bedplate nearest to the shaft. It also helped when we came to getting it down the shaft, as the motor could be placed almost directly using the winch ropes to take the weight. The motor could then be manoeuvred on the bedplate with chain blocks, hydraulic jacks, sweat and bad language. The pipework was bolted together and, when finished, the motor and pump coupling were checked to ensure perfect alignment.

The motor was purchased second-hand from R. F. Winder in Leeds and was manufactured by Metro-Vickers to a National Coal Board flameproof specification. The crane driver estimated it to weight approximately 6 tonnes. It certainly made the headgear tremble when lifted up by the winch ropes. I am sure that the pump rated with an output of 2,050gpm and a head of 580ft was the largest pump ever installed in a Cornish mine, and the motor by far is the heaviest, most powerful motor installed underground. At the time, the Pulsometer pumped more water than South Crofty, Geevor and Pendarves combined. Pendarves was considered a wet mine at that time pumping between 500 and 600gpm. South Crofty, although pumping from considerable depth, rarely exceeded 600gpm and at times, found difficulty in providing their mill with sufficient water to process their tin, while Geevor was considered a dry mine, pumping approximately 300gpm

The longer we waited to hear from Tradex for their official response to the consultant's report, we believed our chances started to look favourable. So, to get a head start, we began to chase up on some of the immediate requirements needed for the mine. This included making trips "up country" to check on winches and hoists suitable for sinking the shaft and opening up 6 and 7 Levels, a pump station and loading pocket. We were running out of ideas, but eventually I contacted the National Coal Board and a Mr Lomas, with the grand title of Deputy Area Store Purchasing Manager. Mr Lomas was based in Stoke-on-Trent and very helpfully pointed us in the direction of available winders.

However our waiting was nearly over as Steven Kay wanted Jim to travel to London for a meeting arranged for Thursday the 4th of April. We all felt fairly confident but at the same time very nervous. Cargill had not wasted any time in making a decision it took just 2 weeks to evaluate the sampling and reach a conclusion.

Chapter 6

Onward and Downward

Thursday 4th April 1974, Jim Delaney joins Steve Kay and Frank Cohen in London to represent Cornwall Tin & Mining Corporation in a meeting with George Mitchell and Tom Huxley, who flew over from their Geneva office to represent Tradex. The meeting had been arranged to finalise their agreement and sign the legal documents for a joint venture to bring Mount Wellington Mine into production. Before Jim flies back from London, he manages to telephone to break the good news to us. There was a huge feeling of relief to be given the green light after many months wondering if we were going to be made redundant. But this time gave us an opportunity to plan all aspects of setting up the mine infrastructure, checking availability of specialized equipment, notifying services, gaining outline planning approval and getting quotations. We were now in a position to press ahead with ordering equipment and services particularly those with lengthy delivery times that could ultimately delay production targets. Inflation was still high and we would need to confirm quotations before placing firm orders.

Our biggest concern was the lack of available winders that would be suitable for our requirements. I had made contacts within the National Coal Board, who in the past had been a good source of second-hand equipment. I also talked to M. B. Wild to see if they were able to convert a single drum to a double drum winder. There were three winders that the Coal Board had available, which we wanted to inspect as soon as Jim returned from his London meeting. Our flight to Leeds took us via London where we met a David Wilson who showed us around, but unfortunately the winders did not meet our specification so we returned to Newquay empty handed. I went back to Mr Hall at M. B. Wild for a quotation, estimate for delivery, the speed and pay load of the conversion. As they were original builders of the hoist in 1954, they were able to supply this information at short notice. To purchase the winder from the NCB, we had to put in a bid, of which I was clueless what would be acceptable or even its market value. So, I got the help of Mr Lomas, who said this equipment could not be released before a thorough inspection was made, which he authorised right away. A few days later he telephoned to inform us the report on the hoist was favourable and a bid of £12,000 should secure it. After discussion with Jim, we sent the cheque off and within two weeks we had confirmation that our bid was successful. Mr Richardson from M. B. Wild would organise the removal of the winder from Sneyd Colliery in Stoke-on-Trent to their Birmingham works. They were to make an immediate start to build our winder.

Almost a year earlier, 18 miners were killed in a horrific accident at Markham Colliery, near Chesterfield. Twenty nine miners were being taken underground for the start of the morning shift. Halfway down the 1,407ft deep shaft, the winder went out of control, failing to respond to the driver's efforts to stop or slow it down. It was estimated the conveyance hit the bottom at a speed of 29ft a second (27 miles an hour). The empty cage travelling up the shaft ran out over the sheave wheels at the top of the headgear. The winding engine house looked as though a bomb had struck it and completely demolished the building, however the driver was lucky to escape serious injury. A public enquiry later completely exonerated the driver, but certain electrical and mechanical recommendations became statutory.

M. B. Wild and GEC collaborated to ensure the hoist had the latest statutory and recommended safety features built into the conversion. We were later given the bad news that the steel for the new drum shaft was unattainable due to the demands of the booming oil industry. Getting a tip from Consolidated Goldfields, the steel was eventually sourced from South Africa. The specifications of the hoist gave us a winding speed of 18-20ft per second and a payload of five tons. It was a bit unique as it had a central bearing, which was retained when the conversion of single drum to double drum was made. This did not have too much significance to the fleet angle, as we were able to position the winder where its location gave us the optimum angle of between 1 and 2 degrees. The angle between the centre line through the lead sheave wheel and the centre line of the rope to the drum, is known as the fleet angle. Any deviation from the optimum will impose undue stress on the steel winding rope.

The design and plans of the winder house together with the dry/mine office building, the compressor house and workshops would be given to Crendon Buildings for final confirmation of price and supply dates. This company was more familiar with supplying agriculture buildings, but fulfilled our requirements at reasonable cost. The L shaped concrete beams were in filled with concrete blocks and rendered to approximately 5 ft above ground level. The roof and sides were clad in dark green rubberised steel sheets to comply with Cornwall County Council planning approval.

Talks with the SWEB engineers led by Geoff Stubbs were brought to a satisfactory conclusion with a commitment from us to consume five year's worth of electricity. This satisfied their need to recoup the capital cost of bringing in a dual supply from their Baldhu substation. This gave us maximum security of what was in effect an 11kV ring main with overhead lines spanning the Carnon Valley into our substation. These were brought into our circuit breakers with the metering equipment connected via bus-bars with 11kV distribution around the mine site. We discussed the system with Mr Tyrell, the Mines and Quarries Electrical Inspector, who fully approved our plans. He reminded us of our responsibility for all future installations, particularly after the Markham Colliery tragedy, which I thought was

Rope capping in preparation to development underground. Left to right: Phil Jervis, Mike Matthews, Roger George, Barry Hocking, David Avery, Nick Barsch, Bernard Hallsworth.

obvious given the circumstances.

Gordon Battersby, the Thyssen's director in charge of the Cornwall area, came down from Llanelli and brought Fred Beckman, well known for his tough negotiating skills, to discuss the shaft sinking plans with Jim Delaney. Jim wanted to hire his own miners with minimum supervision from Thyssen's. He particularly wanted Alan Protheroe to run the shaft sinking and to hire the equipment which was specific to the job. Apparently the negotiations were quite tough as Gordon thought he had Jim over a barrel with the hint that they could use the headgear and sinking hoist on another job. However, Jim had years of contracting experience and was resolute in his argument to use the Thyssen sinking equipment; they eventually agreed a mutually acceptable arrangement to start the shaft sinking as soon as possible. The 150hp sinking hoist needed complete overhaul to comply with latest regulations and new rope to place the existing one, which was now past the statutory time for use. Gordon Battersby was sending his engineers, David Morris and Barry Ward, down to work on the winder and we would liaise with Mr Lawson, Mines Inspector. All work had to be carried out while maintaining the availability of the hoist to access the pumps and pump man on 5 Level. By mid-June, the work on the hoist was complete. Rod Jarovick, Thyssen's electrician, ran through the final safety checks and signed his report for the Mines & Quarries Electrical Regulations Log Book. A Humble type detaching hook was fitted while stress calculations and drawings were made available to be checked by Mines and Quarries Inspectorate. Alan Protheroe and the team of shaft sinkers were now able to start to take the shaft down below 7 Level.

The contract to build the concentrator was awarded to Kilborn Engineering. They were based in Canada where they carried out the majority of their work. Karl Freitag, their Engineering Director, flew over from Toronto and brought with him Bill Harvey, who he had put in charge of the project. Jim Delaney brought in Roy Morgan for the meeting to discuss in detail flow sheet design and construction of the 600 ton per day concentrator. Kilborn were to manage the project with Bill Harvey and his small team of surveyor and civil engineers overseeing the contractors. This was to be Bill's last project as he was nearing retirement, so he intended to come over with his young wife and baby son. Kilborn were going to use the Wheal Andrew Farm House for their site office and it was to be fitted out for that purpose. Following the meeting, they flew back to Toronto to prepare preliminary drawings.

I was determined to plan and install all the electrical work on the mine, but this was not the usual way Kilborn operated and they advised against it. They were understandably worried about trusting an individual to keep up with the work load and ultimately holding up the project without recourse for compensation. I

Start of survey by Kilborn Engineering in preparation of excavations to construct mine infrastructure.

needed to prepare my case carefully.

We were fortunate to have had the recent experience of pumping large volumes of water which helped us prepare for the whole question of mine drainage. The question of breakdowns could be answered simply by installing sufficient pumps to have a reserve of approximately 50%. Mackley Pumps assured us they would always keep in stock enough pump spares to build a pump. We would benefit from having a large reservoir where the water levels remained above the intake pipes feeding the pumps. This positive pressure should eliminate cavitation and the risk of running dry on start up. The biggest risk came from the vast body of water that lay in the old workings above our 6 and 7 Levels. If miners were to blast into unrecorded workings it could drown us out. I broached the subject again with Jim, who had been uncertain to commit to a project that involved driving a tunnel 360 metres long from below our 7 Level horizon into Frederick's Shaft. Cost was the reason for his reluctance, but now the arguments for this certainly outweighed any thoughts of cost savings and the scheme was adopted.

By the beginning of July, the mine started to take on a different appearance. The shaft sinking slowly stuttered down and reached 6 Level by the 2nd of August 1974. Progress gathered pace as the sinking crews gradually improved their performance much to the satisfaction of Alan Protheroe and the shift bosses. Tiny Marsh who was a leading figure with us during the pumping exercise was taken on as a shift boss. Peter Thomas came to us from Crofty while a few others I remember were Paul Kaston, Mike Allsopp, Ted Hatch and Trevor Butler.

The excavators and heavy earth moving equipment made short work of removing the rising ground where Thyssen's originally had their caravans. This was the area where the new workshops and warehouse building were to be located. The overburden was used as infill to level the sloping ground for the site of the new mine office and miners dry complex. The reinforced concrete columns, beams and block work was completed, followed with the side cladding and roof. The intricate winder foundation had to be delayed until the final drawings from M. B. Wild were available. However, before the walls and roof of the winder house could go ahead, the new drum, shaft and bearing pedestal had to be assembled.

I had a trench dug and lined with concrete block which ran around the site, linking all the buildings with the services needed to run the mine. These included compressed air, water, electricity and telephone. I was mindful of the need to prepare my plans and electrical scheme for the concentrator installation. I had until the 11th of September to write a report for Kilborn's Electrical Engineer, Frank Hampshire, who was coming over from Canada for a meeting. I had been informed by Bill Harvey that he would be bringing with him preliminary drawings and a bill of quantity which I was eager to see. In the meantime we needed to ensure the ongoing pumping and mining operation was maintained and required men with the necessary skills.

Micky Trezona had just served his time as an electrical apprentice at South Crofty. He came to me looking for a job, which I thought showed his initiative. He had a good personality and was well suited for maintenance work, so I was happy to employ him. At this time we were without a Mechanical Engineer so it was left to me to keep on top of maintenance so I employed three fitters and a welder. The fitters were David Avery, Nick Barsch and Duncan Fallow, who all had mining experience and wanted to work at Wellington. Bernard Hallsworth was a top class welder, who had worked with us before having been on loan from Visick's, we knew his work and he wanted to join us. A number of men started looking for work as word spread that Wellington was starting up. I was most surprised to get a visit from a character I knew from playing rugby, who was a very good miner having gone through the training school at South Crofty. Nick Worrall came to Wellington looking for a job on surface as he was not keen to work as a shaft sinker, but would like to start mining when the shaft was finished. I asked Nick if he could drive a JCB as there was a vacancy and he readily accepted the offer, but unfortunately during his first week, he somehow managed to clash with Malcolm Hooper and he left. Nick was later to prove his ability by opening up Wheal Concord and had Jack Symons to manage the mine. It was seven years later that I had a phone call from Jack, asking for help with a pump breakdown and I was pleased to be able go over and make the necessary repairs to get them running again. After coming up from underground, Jack then invited me across the road for a cup of coffee in the cottage they used for an office. I met up with Nick and following small talk, I'm afraid to say rugby was the subject, he offered me a job. He wanted me to carry out the weekly winder maintenance and sign the M&Q log book. Unfortunately, I had to turn him down, but he pinned a consultant's label on me until I found somebody to do the job permanently – all of that is another story.

Unfortunately, Alan Protheroe and the sinkers were cursed with the presence of the Wellington Fault and weak ground conditions, which the shaft intersected around the 7 Level. The collapse and run of ground at the bottom of the shaft resulted in delay and the huge amount of concrete needed to complete 7 Level Station increased the development costs and knocked the budget sideways. The crews worked over the Christmas and into the New Year. As work on the mine progressed, the need for senior staff and department heads became important for managing the increasing workforce. Interviews and recruitment was conducted on both sides of the Atlantic. The first appointment was made by Tom Huxley from the Geneva office, this position was for a Chief Accountant and one that tied the financial control close to Tradex. Jim Delaney was responsible for recruiting Harold Wing for the job of Surface Superintendent, Roy Morgan as Concentrator Superintendent and the Chief Chemist whose name I can no longer remember. Malcolm Hooper and myself were already engaged, but Malcolm managed to move into the role of Mine Superintendent; I thought that Alan Protheroe may have stayed on as he had good man-management skills. Steve Kay conducted interviews in Canada for mining personnel and hired Leo Reitveld as Senior Mine Captain, Art Ball as Mine Captain, and a number of shift bosses to help with training up miners. It was interesting to note that Art's brother, Jimmy, worked at South Crofty as a motor mechanic. Phil Askew, another of Steve's appointments, told me a few days after arriving to take up his position as Mechanical Superintendent, he thought he would be in charge of the surface and electrical departments. He was unhappy with this situation, which may have contributed to his early return to Canada.

I carefully prepared for the visit in September of Frank Hampshire, Kilborn's electrical engineer as I wanted to discuss my plans for the electrical installations on the mine. Frank had been a former employee with the LEB (London Electricity Board) and he was interested in our supply contract with SWEB. He was satisfied with the security of supply and compliance with regulations, including the earthing system. Frank returned to Canada in support of my proposal to hire sufficient electricians to carry out the installation for all the mine infrastructure. We then could choose the electricians most suitable to keep on a permanent basis to eventually carry out the equipment maintenance. Those who did not match our requirements would be offered the many jobs that would become available throughout the mine. I had no problems in finding electricians when needed and could activate the tried and trusted Cornish communications network. A few pints in the pub was an enjoyable means of spreading the word, providing the participants were not too enthusiastic and woke up next morning forgetting where they were the night before.

Eric Harding from Ingersoll Rand came down to discuss the advantages of their new Centex air compressors, which we thought would be ideal for us, but we were unable to make a commitment to purchase at that time. We made contact with him when we knew the mine was going ahead. He offered to take us to see the compressor under operating conditions in the confectionery industry in Berkshire. It was an offer we could not refuse so Ingersoll Rand arranged the flight from Newquay and Eric met us at Heathrow to drive us to the Mars headquarters and factory at Slough. We were impressed with the installation and how it neatly fitted within the building. We were treated to a splendid lunch before returning home. They were keen to get their new range of compressor operating in a mining environment and they did not want to miss this, their first opportunity.

Weak ground associated with the fault in the vicinity of 7 Level continued to cause huge problems, which seriously delayed the underground development programme during the early part of 1975. Ground support became impossible over wide spans and the pump station had to be redesigned. The pumps could not be positioned either side of a central aisle, but were now located in two narrow chambers with room for five pumps in each. The loading pocket was the means to fill the skips to a maximum of 5 tons of ore to be taken to surface and automatically dumped into the coarse ore bin. The loading system was redesigned and a conveyor was now used to deliver the rock from the ore pass to the skips. Even the relatively small chamber for the electrical substation proved a problem due to the very wet conditions, and I was not prepared to risk installing the high voltage equipment until we were sure it was safe to do so. Steel mesh and rock bolts sprayed with a reinforced cement supported the roof and the substation dried sufficiently to bring down the panels of 3300V direct on line vacuum contactors used to start the pumps. Auxiliary supplies of 415, 240 and 110V were transformed down from the 3300V ring main circuit, feeding the eight pump starters through bus-bars and isolating switches. The two shaft cables were PVC double armour 120mm rated at 3300V. They were clamped with steel backed hardwood blocks bolted to 1 ⅛-inch steel rope at 10 metre intervals and secured to the shaft on the steel buntons.

The first building ready for occupation was the workshop/warehouse, which was partitioned to incorporate the offices for the Surface, Mechanical and Electrical Superintendents. So, after being in the 'top office' for five years, I found myself down with Harold Wing and Phil Askew close to the hub of activity on the mine site. Soon after Micky Trezona started, I hired two more electricians, Frank Partridge and George Gordon to prepare the groundwork for the mine and surface installations. My old office space was taken by Nigel Deacon, our new accountant, who gradually found his feet with the unfamiliar activity of the mining industry. Harold Wing's appointment bucked the trend of employing younger men, he was in his 50s when he started with us but was very experienced and had managed a quarry at Long downs near Penryn. He also had a small nursery and would supply the mine with trees in accordance with the Cornwall County Council planning requirements which required a fair amount of landscaping. Phil Askew, whose wife originated from Camborne, came from a background of open-cast mining where he supervised the maintenance of very large dumper trucks, grab shovels and excavators.

Lunch times were generally taken in the King's Arms at Chacewater where Jim liked to drive us down for a pint and ham sandwich. Ivan Jenkin the landlord of the Pub and his wife had looked after us all the time we had been coming for lunch. A table was always made available for us in the main bar, while the smaller side bar with large murals painted on the walls depicting underground scenes, was the haunt of the Wheal Jane staff. One lunch time, Ivan came to us with a surprise request, he was intending to leave his pub and hoped we could give him a job on the mine. Jim thought there would be a vacancy in near future for a Drill Doctor and he would let him know in the next few weeks. The Drill Doctor is an affectionate term for the men who maintained the compressed air rock drills and kept the miners' drill steels and bits sharp. Ivan was delighted as the long hours of running a pub started to play havoc with his health. I was pleased to see him start his new job sometime following the spring of 1975.

As time passed, I began to notice a slight change in the lunch time atmosphere, with more intense conversation replacing the previous relaxed banter. The change was inevitable as problems underground caused delays to the mine programme, which could prevent the concentrator from operating due to a lack of ore, which in turn would create cash flow problems. I also noticed a number of personality clashes as disagreements between senior staff started to surface and egos were being bruised. But I became far too busy with the electrical installation I was about to undertake to let this affect my work, and lunch times at the King's Arms gradually fizzled out. We were all hoping that the underground development would make up the lost time and get back on schedule during 1975.

Chapter 7

Preparing for Production

Cornwall County Council granted planning approval in September 1974 for the construction of the concentrator building, ore bins, tanks and conveyors. There was also permission for the workshop, compressor and winder house, plus the miners offices and dry buildings. An extension to the height of the headgear and extra back legs to strengthen it was also approved. Further applications were granted during 1975 for a sewage disposal plant and change of use for the Wheal Andrew Farmhouse into offices. There was a later application in October 1976 for the erection of two explosive stores on United Downs. The Wheal Maid Valley was the site of the tailings dam, which gained planning approval during 1975.

My programme of electrical installation work now included all the mine infrastructure, the underground and concentrator. I was able to engage the electricians over a gradual period as equipment and services for the completed buildings became available to us. I used Mick Trezona, Frank Partridge, led by the more experienced Peter Martin, for the underground installations. The eight pumps were each driven by 300hp motors at 3300V and started by Direct on Line vacuum contactors which was controlled with HV switchgear in the purpose built underground electrical substation. Power for the auxiliary circuits was transformed from 3300V to 415V, and supplied the sump pumps, loading pocket conveyor, facilities for charging the battery operated locomotives and 240/110V for lighting. The battery charging stations were provided on the levels.

Once the shaft had been completely furnished and the steelwork with all the gates fitted, we proceeded to install the electric shaft signals. This was generally a universal system that relayed a series of coded signals by means of push buttons to activate an audio/visual (bell and light) indication, that instructed the winder driver to move the cage to the desired destination in the shaft. A system of fail safe electrical interlocks was used to prevent the conveyance from moving if the shaft gates were open. In the event of emergencies (loss of power), the system was backed up by a simple mechanical device known as a "knocker", that was operated by a pull wire – that extended from the winder house to the bottom of the shaft – the same code of signals were used. Telephone communication was set up in the pump station on all levels and taken up the shaft into the mine office, winder house, workshops and security guards office. Security was manned around the clock and provided emergency cover, 7 days a week.

The workshop was the first building to become available for us to install the electrics and we were ready to start at the end of November 1974. I specified that all buildings were to be wired using single core cables within galvanised conduits and trunking. To carry out this work, I needed electricians with industrial experience, particularly for the electrical installation in the concentrator, which would be ready for us to start at the beginning of May 1975. A nice gesture from Micky Trezona came at Christmas 1974. He had cut a furze bush and tied it to the top of the headgear and wired in some lights around it. He told us it was traditional

Electricians (left to right)
Front row: Frank Partridge, Micky Trezona, Mervyn Skinner, John Kellow, Peter Stewart
Back row: Geoff Bray, Vince Holland, Alan Pyatt, Author, Peter Martin, Mike Woodley, John Triniman, ? George Gordon

for mines to do this and he did not wish to bring bad luck to Wellington. Looking out from Jim's office on a dull winters afternoon, it certainly brightened up the Christmas week and I could see that Jim appreciated the thought.

I was fortunate to be able to pick the type of men who I thought would be ideal for the job. The next person to join us was George Gordon, who had good references having previously worked at Castle-an-Dinas Quarry. As equipment and buildings needed wiring, I hired more electricians, John Triniman and Vince Holland, who started early in April 1975. They needed mates to help them, so I brought in John Kellow, Peter Stewart and Mervyn Skinner, who I believed were steady workers and would be ideal to bring into the maintenance team later when needed. John was the first to be given a maintenance job and he took on the responsibility of looking after the miners battery operated cap lamps – from then on, he was known as "Cap Lamps Kellow". My preference was to recruit electricians who I thought would be able to adapt to maintenance or installation work.

We were aware of the delays caused by difficulties in modifying the winder but could not adjust our programme to compensate for this and hoped we could make up the lost time in the future. Further delays were experienced in our hoisting capacity when it was discovered that we had to reduce our payload. During the previous shaft sinking were able to use a 5 ton bucket but now we were hoisting from below 7 Level and the weight of the extra 70 metres of the wire hoisting rope pushed it over the safe working load for the Thyssen winder so now we had to

Vince Holland and Mervyn Skinner installing ladder rack, cable support systematic.

use a 2 ton bucket. The area at the front of the shaft where rock from underground was discharged into a truck to be dumped off site, was now excavated to build the waste and ore storage bins. The fitters had to reposition the dump chute in the headgear around 90° to allow the truck to back into the side of the headgear to receive the rock from underground development, while lode material was stockpiled in our storage area around Harvey's Shaft. The increased height of the headgear was necessary to enable the new 5 ton skips to travel up to the dumping point and automatically discharge their loads into the storage bins. Our skips were made from a steel alloy in an effort to reduce weight and had man riding facilities above the rock compartment. We had three built, two in permanent use and one in reserve – I believe we had one quote at £15,000 each.

We were very concerned when Ingersoll Rand telephoned to say they had difficulties in supplying the compressors with 3300V motors and that they could only get 415V motors which came from Italy. I was very cautious of starting a 550hp motor on a 415V supply. I contacted Gordon Jelly, the Klockner Moeller engineer to see if they had any issues with supplying switch gear and star-delta starters for 550hp motors. They assured me they could build the panels and controls and match the delivery times for the compressors. There was an embarrassing moment when Ingersoll Rand came to commission the system and could not get the compressors up to speed before they tripped out on overload. It was fortunate I had Gordon Jelly standing by, but there were still some very stressful moments before he found an extra overload relay that was incorrectly set. After that, we had no problems with delivering compressed air at a pressure of 100psi.

More men were being taken on, but it was increasingly obvious that there was not enough skilled miners to work the mine. The staff members who joined us included Chris Burton, Mine Geologist, who took Malcolm Hooper's job after Malcolm became the Mine Superintendent. Chris Burton's assistant was Dave Kneebone, a local man with practical mining experience. The Mine Engineer was

Tim Warner, who was in charge of the Survey Department. Derek James, who was brought in as the second Mine Captain, came to us from Geevor. John Pressdee, a Welshman who spent some time in Canada gaining experience in Mineral Processing, became Roy Morgan's assistant in the Mill, and John Fleming started as our Chemist/Metallurgist. Nigel Deacon's administration department engaged Roger Scoley as an Assistant Accountant and Ron Mallet was the new warehouse manager.

Bill Harvey and Kilborn Engineering were on top of the concentrator construction programme and by February 1975, the foundations for the fine ore bin and the ball mills were complete. I had been impressed with the performance of George Gordon who demonstrated his electrical skills during the previous four months that he had worked for us. I now needed hands on supervision for the day to day work in the Concentrator and George was the obvious candidate. The steel frame started to rise out of the ground and by May, this was covered with cladding which allowed us to start the first fix of the electrical installation. This was no easy task due to the height and span within the building. To overcome this, I purchased three very large extension ladders and a scaffold tower to allow us to reach up sixty-odd feet to the ceiling. It was necessary to install lighting first, as the cladding completely closed in the building with no natural lighting. We were all surprised with this feature and Bill Harvey explained to us that this was a standard Canadian

design as most of their mines were located so far to the north to have many daylight hours, so windows did not warrant the extra cost. The lighting load was approximately 50KW made up from 8 x 1000W and 75 x 400W high bay mercury discharge lamps, plus office, laboratory and exterior lighting. We now needed more electricians and were joined by Terry Bray, Geoff Bray (not related), Michael Woodley and Alan Pyatt.

The lack of skilled miners was a tremendous worry as underground development fell behind schedule. The programme would require a steady feed of

Don Hennings, A. B. Wibe (engineer), Author, George Gordon and Peter Martin in a discussion on the advantages of ladder cable rack support.

ore through the commission stages of the concentrator increasing to the designed throughput of 600 metric tonnes per day. The ore from underground would be supplemented from the stockpile which had been expected to grow at a faster rate. Wheal Jane appeared to solve their problem of labour shortages when the mine invited Derbyshire lead miners to come and work in Cornwall. The forward thinking Consolidated Goldfields were able to offer the incentive of family housing on the Wheal Jane estate at Threemilestone. This attracted a community of miners down to Cornwall, but Wellington did not have the means to offer these incentives. However, the idea sparked a plan to bring over miners from Canada. Steve Kay organised a number of interviews through agents for Hard Rock Miners to work in England at a Cornish Tin Mine. It was believed that up to 60 men were signed up for a short term contract. A plane was chartered to fly the miners into London. I am not sure how it was intended to get them from London to Truro but at the end of the day it did not matter. Apparently, vast quantities of alcohol were consumed during the flight and scuffles broke out, so the authorities sent them back to Canada. The much needed help did not materialise and the scheme was an embarrassing failure. Following the Canadian fiasco, a training scheme was set up and two experienced miners were used as instructors, which was said to have been worthwhile. It was after this that Malcolm was sent to the top office and Leo Reitveld took over as Mine Superintendent.

The plan to distribute the multitude of cables from the control room in the Concentrator to the individual motors was made possible by the use of heavy duty galvanised ladder racking supplied by A. B. Wibe of Watford. This system was perfect for our application with the ladders coming in a variety of widths and at six metres long offered good support and flexibility to add extra cables if needed. It was generally agreed that Vince Holland and his mate, Mervyn had done an excellent job installing the cable support system almost without incident. The building was 20 metres high and to reach the roof beams, I used our extension ladders. Near the end of the job, Mervyn was working at the top of a ladder when he was overcome, for the first time, by an attack of vertigo and froze, hanging onto the ladder and unable to move. It took a superhuman effort to reach him as we feared he would panic and fall. Vince and John Triniman managed to get one of the ladders up beside Mervyn, which John climbed to get close. Vince climbed up behind Mervyn and after a while, they managed to slowly get him down. Nobody was hurt, but we could not risk allowing Mervyn to work on ladders, so we later moved him underground to maintain the battery operated locos.

The area around the loco charging stations required it to be well ventilated, but as more ground was opened up, demand for clean air through the mine increased beyond the capability of the portable fans. The mining department needed to improve air conditions and Amy Shaft was to be the main upcast shaft to remove noxious gases, dynamite fumes and dust. Robinson's Shaft was used to force clean, fresh air down through the stopes and levels. This shaft, located approximately 100 metres to the south of the new winder house, was a part of the emergency escape exit that ran through to the bottom levels. The shaft was named after R. C. N. Robinson, a onetime director and consulting engineer at Wellington when it was a working mine during the 1930s. Then the shaft was equipped with an electric winder and steel headgear, which was the main hoisting shaft, having been enlarged with three compartments in 1935. Harold Wing organised his mason, Dick Evans, to build a collar around the shaft and we installed a large electric fan which was fitted over the shaft. This forced air down the shaft into the mine, which needed a number of wooden doors fixed like air locks so that the flow of air could be directed efficiently to where it was most needed.

We had completed most of the electrical work on the buildings and underground, and were now focusing on the concentrator but there were still some issues outstanding. I thought we could use an all-electric system to provide hot water for the washing and miners showering facilities in the dry building. However, I was getting too many complaints and there was nothing worse than coming up from a day's work underground to find the water was not hot enough. I called the local heating engineer in to convert to an oil fired hot water system that satisfied our hot water requirement. The dry was designed on the Canadian style where you would enter the changing area, undress and put your clean clothes in your locker then walk through to the drying area, where working clothes were hung on racks to dry out. After changing into their underground clothes, the miners could walk through to collect their cap lamps and pick up their brass tag showing their individual number. This simple measure allowed the shift bosses to identify who was underground and was essential in the event of accidents.

During the run up to Christmas, I had a call from Don Henning, the salesman (or Commercial Marketing Manager as he preferred) of A. B. Wibe, the suppliers of the ladder cable support system. Don wanted to know if he could write an article on our installation for the *Electrical Contractor*, a monthly trade magazine. I said he was welcome to come down, but it would be best to wait until February when our work would be nearing completion. February arrived and Don Henning called to say he was bringing Tony Rea with him who was the editor of *Electrical Contractor*. We spent a pleasant afternoon going around the mine to view the various points of interest, with a running commentary from me. Don had brought a photographer with him and Tony Rea was busy taking notes. I was surprised when Jim Delaney called me into his office sometime in April, as he had just received some copies of the *Electrical Contractor* that had arrived in the post. Jim, trying hard not to smile asked if I had been misquoted on some of the statements made in the article, which of course I had but was unable to answer having difficulty keeping a straight face. He was of course referring to the first paragraph where I got carried away in stating that Mount Wellington would be the largest tin producing unit in Europe. I hoped that our friends at South Crofty and Wheal Jane did not read this.

March 1976, and we had completed all but a few of the last minute jobs to finish the electrical installation and were ready to commission the equipment. The basic design and function of the concentrator was the separation of cassiterite (black tin or tin oxide) from the waste material. The following seven mineral processing techniques is a simple description of the main equipment used to recover the cassiterite in preparation for transportation to the smelter.

Slurrification: this was the means where sands, muds and slimes are mixed with water to create a pulp that can be pumped into the thickener.

Thickening: this is the process of making the pulp thicker and is achieved by pumping the pulp into a large circular tank where the solids begin to settle. The thickened pulp is pumped from the bottom of the tank and clear water overflows the top.

Grinding: in this process coarse material is ground to liberate fine cassiterite. Grinding takes place in a tubular mill which is half full of steel balls. As the mill is rotated, the steel balls are lifted and drop on to the material, which then passes out the other end of the mill. There are three ball mills, the largest is driven by a 350hp motor.

Classification: there are two types of classification, screening and cycloning. The screening is used on relatively coarse material and separates the feed material into an oversize and undersize. The cycloning is for the finer material with the pulp being pumped under pressure into the cyclone. The material is separated into two sizes, with the larger material passing out of the underflow and the finer out of the overflow.

Gravity: this process is where the coarser material is treated and is equipped with Holman shaking tables installed in a space saving configuration, one on top of the other. The table moves back and forth across the diagonal and water flows at right angles to the motion. The feed is introduced at the head motion corner and moves down the table and across to the opposite corner. Cassiterite (tin oxide) is about 2½ times as heavy as the other associated minerals and is not washed so far down the table by the water. It is collected separately from the other material at the far end from the feed.

Flotation: this is a method of selectively separating different minerals. Chemicals known as reagents are added to the pulp to activate the required mineral and make it water repellent. Fine bubbles of air are then mixed with the pulp in the flotation machines and the activated mineral sticks to the bubble and floats to the surface to form a froth. The froth is then scraped off the surface of the flotation cell.

Filtration: this is a method to remove the water from a pulp to give a dry solid and is used to dry the final concentrate. The concentrate is then sent off to be smelted to tin metal, known from ancient times as white tin. The waste or tails were pumped to the Wheal Maid Tailings Dam. It requires a skilled workforce to operate a process plant, otherwise the losses soon become unsustainable. The mineral processors are not always given credit for the work that is done, sometimes under difficult circumstances.

The ore from underground passed through a cone crusher before being stored in the fine ore bin, it was then conveyed into the concentrator to begin the lengthy process to separate the tin from waste material. Bartle's (Carn Brea) Ltd, a small specialist steel fabrication firm, located in North Street, Redruth, put in a bid to make and install the five conveyors needed for this process. Their Managing Director, Tom Reed, came out to Wellington to reassure Jim Delaney and Kilborn they were capable to meet the specification and that they were a subsidiary of BICC, a large electrical manufacturing company, which would guarantee their work.

Whilst modifications to increase the height and strengthen the headgear were taking place, most of the underground work was suspended. This provided the time to furnish the shaft with steelwork, which was designed with a layout to accommodate three compartments, two for the conveyances and one ladder way. The services were located around the circumference of the shaft and included 4 x 8″ pipes to pump mine water, 1 x 8″ pipe for compressed air, 1 x 4″ pipe for clean water that was pressure fed into the rock drills to suppress dust. Two electrical cables for the pump motors and cables for shaft signals, lighting and telephones. Unfortunately, this work delayed the underground development and preparation of the stopes.

With the tailings pipeline laid from the concentrator to Wheal Maid Dam, we were ready to start the commission phase of the concentrator equipment. We had installed Flygt B2250 high head pumps in the culvert leading from the County Adit. The water flowing from the County Adit would always be sufficient to supply the needs of the concentrator, even in the driest of summers. The commission period proved difficult, particularly for the supervisors who had to contend with numerous mechanical failures, which reduced running time and the ability to fine tune equipment. It was noticeable that many of the operators were unable to understand basic plant operation. The concentrator was designed to process 600 metric tonnes of ore per day with a recovery of 1% tin, this would leave 540 tonnes of waste to be disposed of and permanently stored without risk to the environment. This waste material, known as tailings, was pumped in the form of slurry approximately one mile from the concentrator to a dam located in Wheal Maid Valley. The construction of the dam was a major undertaking and designed to settle out and prevent the fine sands, slime, toxic materials and heavy metals from contaminating the overflow of water that would enter the stream that joined the Carnon River.

A culvert was built in the valley with towers that were adjustable, ensuring clear water could overflow into the stream as the dam filled with tailings. Waste rock from the underground workings was trucked in by road to build the embankment. Within a few weeks of the dam being used and the tailings being in contact with the culvert, it was discovered that a major problem had occurred in the structure of the concrete. The tailings, heavily contaminated with sulphides, reacted with water to produce sulphuric acid, causing the concrete to disintegrate, thereby rendering the culvert unusable. There was some dispute about who had overlooked to ordering or specify any sulphide resistant cement. However, with the old culvert removed and the new one in place, the Wheal Maid tailings dam was finally available for use.

The situation on the mine and underground was no better, with continuing niggly equipment breakdowns. Phil Askew, our Mechanical Superintendent, was under considerable pressure from Roy and Leo and became increasingly disappointed with the situation and saw no alternative but to leave. The demands of the mining and concentrator departments led to the reorganisation of the maintenance, with the foreman John Taylor and his five fitters and one welder working in the mill and reporting to Roy Morgan. Eric Williams, the Mine Mechanical Maintenance Foreman, had five fitters, four welders and two semi-skilled fitters within his scope of responsibility and reported directly to Leo, the Senior Mine Captain.

At the start of 1976, the price of tin on the London Metal Exchange was $5100 per metric tonne and climbed at an unprecedented rate throughout the year to a high of $9300 in January 1977. This helped management to offset the worry of overspending the budget. Kilborn Engineering completed the concentrator contract in March and with the plant commissioned, Bill Harvey returned to Canada. Before leaving, he expressed his satisfaction in the high standard of work the electricians carried out and the considerable sum of money that was saved by doing it ourselves. I thought it did not seem so long ago that it had taken considerable persuading to be allowed to do this.

Although I felt a tremendous sense of satisfaction in successfully planning and completing an installation of this size, I was thinking I would never have an opportunity within the electrical field to experience the challenge of this work again. With tin production in sight, Jim Delaney wanted operating budgets updated. These were to cover the 18 week period from January 12th to May 30th 1976 and for a full year starting June 1st 1976 and finishing May 31st 1977. The accounting system at Wellington was based on a four week period with 13 periods in a year. Department Heads submitted their best estimated operating costs for the two periods. The underground manpower was expected to gradually increase by the end of May 1977 when it was believed to reach 180 and together with surface manpower requirements, came to a total of 275 men. The operating budget for labour and materials was expected to be £2,664,145. My budget for the first 18 week period was £18,555 for labour and £5,190 for material making a total of £23,745. For the first full year the labour costs were £61,591 with material costs of £40,669 making a total of £101,660. The full budget reports can be found in Appendix 7

My concern now was to develop a planned maintenance programme from what had been a mixed demand for installation and breakdown repair work. My choice of men to keep was made easy as some of the original people had or were intending to leave. George Gordon fancied the excitement of going to Nigeria for a road building programme with ARC. Frank Partridge found the security of a job as an electrical fitter with South Western Electricity Board more to his liking. Mike Woodley returned to London and Alan Pyatt was believed to work as a jobbing electrician in Truro. Unfortunately our top man, Peter Martin eventually left and went up north to join Thyssen for shaft sinking in Yorkshire but came back to start his own successful business. "Cap Lamps" Kellow, who was very conscientious and not afraid to confront miners twice his size and half his age if they mistreated his lamps, stayed with us. Mervyn Skinner was also pleased to continue with his job of looking after the battery operated locomotives. Peter Stewart was another man I wanted to keep, he had been a tremendous help to me keeping on top of the installation paperwork, from delivery notes to recording maintenance schedules, and I wanted him to continue. I asked him what job title he would like, but not to expect a pay rise, so he came up with Electrical Inspector as it sounded more important than an electrical maintenance clerk. Peter was a highly qualified First Aider and was later to organise the mine's First Aid Team which became part of the Mine Rescue Team.

ELECTRICAL CONTRACTOR

Electrical installation at Britain's newest tin mine

by Tony Rea

In mining and ore processing the electricity requirements for driving the many motors needed can be considerable. The nature of the environment in which the electrical services have to be installed can pose problems. This article describes aspects of the electrical installation at the Mount Wellington Mine, Bissoe, Cornwall, shortly to be brought into commercial operation by Cornwall Tin & Mining Ltd.

Although Britain has been a tin producer for time immemorial, most of the tin used in the country nowadays comes from abroad. This reliance on imports could be dramatically reduced when a new tin mine and ore processing plant at Bissoe, between Falmouth and Truro, becomes fully operational later this year. With an expected annual output of 200,000 tons, the Mount Wellington Mine will be the largest tin producing unit in Europe. When its output is added to that of other tin mines in Cornwall Britain's imports of the metal could be halved.

Development of the mine and construction of the processing plant have been carried out by their Canadian financed owners, Cornwall Tin & Mining Ltd. Commissioning of the mine and plant now being undertaken is the culmination of ten years of planning and construction work which started in 1966 with exploratory drillings to determine extent of the tin in the area.

The mine comprises a 300 metre deep shaft that serves seven underground working levels. At each level mined ore is conveyed by battery driven locomotives to subsidiary shafts down which it is tipped to the bottom of the main shaft. From there it is then

Conveyors at Mount Wellington were supplied by a BICC company, Bartles (Carn Brea).

hoisted up to the top in 5 ton skips.

On the surface equipment associated with the operation of the mine are a shaft head hoist, air compression plant conveyors for shifting the ore to the processing plant, and a variety of control and switchgear.

The ore processing plant contains mills, sifters and shakers, and concentrators which between them crush the ore, separate out the tin and make it into a concentrate ready for smelting.

Commercially exploitable quantities of zinc and copper are also extracted. Traces of gold and silver are often found in the ore from this area but they have no commercial significance.

Two 11kV ring mains

Electricity to the site is supplied from the South Western Electricity Board system via overhead line. From the jointly owned Board/company main substation the power is fed round the site via two 11kV ring mains. One of these serves the mine and associated surface equipment, the power being transformed down to 3.3kV in three transformers. The other 11kV ring main serves the process plant and other surface buildings through four 11kV/415V transformers.

Mr John Hurr, Cornwall Tin & Mining's electrical superintendent, told *Electrical Contractor* that the 11kV distribution system was not commonly used in mines in Cornwall but he had chosen it as being more flexible and providing greater system security than the 3.3kV networks commonly used.

Total maximum demand for the whole site is 3.3MVA.

Underground the main installed electrical load is provided by eight 300 h.p. electrically driven pumps installed at the foot of the bottom of the shaft. Their main function is to keep the mine as clear of as much floodwater as possible. Even during the dry months at least three and possibly four pumps will be needed to be kept in continuous operation. During the wet months a maximum of five is likely to be needed. Eight have been installed to provide standby pumping capacity in case of failure, and there are plans to install two more.

The pumps are capable of pumping water at a rate of 1,000 gal/min through a height of 213m. Because the mine is situated in a hill the floodwater does not have to be pumped to the top of the shaft. It is fed into a duct that runs through the hillside to discharge it into a neighbouring river.

Because it is vital to keep the pumps going at all times a 250kVA diesel generating set has been installed at the shaft head to provide standby power for two 150 h.p. submersible pumps. At the present this is the only standby generating plant installed on the site.

Unlike coal mines, tin mines do not contain flammable gases and so it is not necessary to use flameproof electrical equipment. However the moisture laden dust

John Hurr, electrical superintendent at Mount Wellington (centre) with Don Henning, marketing manager, AB Wibe Ltd (right), "Electrical Contractor's" editor, and cable support system.

produced in the mining process can have a deleterious effect on electrical equipment and so special enclosures are needed for the motors and control gear installed underground.

In addition to the power supplies for the floodwater pumps the only other electricity supply underground is for the chargers used for the locomotive batteries, communications systems and the minimum of permanent lighting.

Compression load

All drilling and excavation tools and equipment are pneumatically operated. As also are the few conveying equipment installed underground. Compressed air for the pneumatic operations is provided supplied from two fully automatic sequenced controlled compressors installed on the surface. Each is driven by a 575 h.p. motor and has an output of 2100 c.f.m.

Also connected to the mine's 11kV ring main is the load to the 450 h.p. hoist used for hauling up skips of ore from the bottom of the shaft, and also for lifting the workforce up and down. The hoist, originally built in 1954, has been converted from single to double drum action and is powered by a refurbished 3.3kV British Thomson Houston motor. GEC provided technical assistance in the renovation of the hoist and motor to ensure that they met the recently introduced new safety requirements for mine hoists.

In the processing plant the main electrical load is provided by 150 motors ranging in output from f.h.p. to 350 h.p. and having a total capacity of 6500 h.p. Among the function of these motors is to drive the various mills, shakers and concentrators as well as pumps and conveyor belts. In addition there is a lighting load of over 50kW. This is made up from 75 × 400W and eight 1000W high bay mercury discharge lamps and 30 × 125W m.b.f. fittings. For exterior lighting 200W linear sodium floodlights were used.

Control equipment

The distribution boards and motor control starters and switchgear for the various electrical plant are installed in two separate sections, one covering the electrical load from the mine and associated surface equipment and the other section for covering the ore processing plant and ancillary buildings. Similar equipment is used in both sections.

The main distribution boards and control panels are of the heavy duty type built of steel sheet but with transparent cover to allow for "walk by" inspection of the moulded case circuit breakers that protect the distributed load. The breakers are fitted with adjustable thermal overload and instantaneous magnetic trips. In addition there is a busbar coupling switch that provides a breaking capacity of 65kA rms.

Protection and power supply for direct on line starters of from 40 h.p. to 350 h.p. and for 575 h.p. Star Delta starters for the compressors are provided by motor operated circuit breakers in similar high duty panels to those used for main distribution board. Direct connections are fed from the distribution board on the main busbars of the motor starter panels, and the outgoers from these panels are located at the bottom of a plinth section. Because the management of the mining company wanted to minimise the space taken up by equipment the panel for the 575 h.p. starters is built around three sides of a rectangle.

For motor starters up to 40 h.p. totally insulated boards are used. The incoming supply for these is via 1000A busbars in the upper enclosures, and each section has 400A vertical droppers. A feature of this equipment that had special appeal to Mr Hurr is that any starter can be exchanged at any time without the need to isolate other drives, and that if desired two or three starters of one frame size can be replaced by a starter of a larger size, or vice versa, thus enabling modifications to a supply system to be carried out with the greatest of ease.

Mr Hurr was also attracted to this particular equipment because it met with his requirements that the distribution equipment should be combined with the starters.

Each starter comprises a main load switch and a contactor with thermal overload protection, backed up by BSS 88 fuses. Selected starters are fitted with ammeters, or with current transformers for remote ammeters, while all have stop buttons and a "running" light. As with the panels for the large starters, all connections are made through the base plinth.

Totally insulated transparent fronted modular enclosures house suitably arranged terminals for connection to the respective starters band carry the remote push buttons and ammeters for showing the state of operation. Ancillary equipment includes limit and float switches with individual key operated push buttons and "stay on" stop buttons at strategic locations round the plant. All metal mounting plates and flanges are

Power cabling and wiring of the main switch panel in the mill.

Part of the main distribution board in the mill.

bonded to earth to conform to the earthing requirements of the Mines and Quarries Inspectorate.

Cables used in the mine and processing plant range in diameter size from 0.5mm^2 to 630mm^2. The 3.3kV and low voltage distribution and control cables are p.v.c. insulated, s.w.a. and p.v.c. sheathed. These are manufactured to BS6346/69 but with conductivity of armour wires not less than 50 per cent of that of any one conductor to meet with Mr Hurr's request that they should comply with the Mines and Quarries Regulations.

In the processing plant the 16,000m of armoured cables installed are supported by Swedish made ladder racking. Commenting on the choice of cable support systems, Mr Hurr is reported as saying that the whole range of systems available was considered and that for the particular requirements of Mount Wellington ladder racking was selected.

"Experience has proved we made a very wise choice. In addition to its weight/load carrying efficiency the 6m racking lengths and comprehensive choice of accessories offered with this particular system made the installation of a catwalk easy compared with past experiences. Moreover the saving in time and labour has made a significant cost factor contribution. This has been very pronounced in view of the 5m and 20m elevations we had to contend with, coupled with the widespans between the framework of RSJs to which

---

Tin mining in Britain is concentrated in Cornwall. The annual production is about 3,500 tons, compared to a world total of 180,000 tons. The consumption of tin in Britain is around 12,000 tons.

Only recently has the tin mining industry in Britain revived after the slump in the 20s and 30s when mining stopped almost entirely because it was not economical. The mines had to be made very deep and extend out under the sea and it was cheaper to import from places like Malaysia where the tin is found closer to the surface. But in the last few years the price of tin has doubled, from £1,500 per ton to £3,000 per ton.

Tin is used for a variety of different applications. In Britain 50 per cent of tin consumption is in tin plate and 30-40 per cent in solder. Traces of tin are used in a number of different processes, for example in p.v.c. to prevent yellowing and preserve clarity, in vinyl wallpapers and for agricultural purposes. Though very small amounts are involved, tin is a vital part of the process.

---

the racking support arms were clamped" Mr Hurr said.

To reduce overall electricity consumption and therefore electricity bills extensive power factor correction equipment is to be installed. Six 95kVar capacitors are for instance to be used to correct the consumption of six of the eight floodwater pumps installed at the bottom of the shaft. In addition there will be 570kVar of 3.3kV capacitors and 620kVar of 415V capacitors. Of the mv capacitors some will be used for individual correction of the larger motors. The smallest motors will be corrected by an automatic correction unit.

Mr Hurr is confident that the elimination of the penalty charges imposed by the South Western Electricity Board on its industrial tariff resulting from the use of power factor equipment will lead to an early recovery of the capital cost involved.

The future

All electrical installation work on the site was undertaken by Cornwall Tin & Mining's own electrical staff, under the supervision of Mr Hurr, who was responsible for designing it. This approach was adopted as it was felt that because the installation was unique it was best for the company to keep direct control. Furthermore Mr Hurr felt that it would be very helpful

Interior of the concentrator plant.

for the maintenance and running of the plant for these functions to be carried out by the men who actually installed the equipment.

The installation has been carried out within a budget based on cost estimate prepared by Mr Hurr with reference to his previous experience in mining installations and figures made available by consultants. All equipment has been supplied as a result of competitive tendering. Price has not always been the main factor in the choice of particular makes of equipment. Technical requirements, reliability, the provision of back up service and above all delivery were also important factors in determining the choice.

Much of the equipment was supplied via ITT Distributors Ltd at Camborne, including most of the cables and the power capacitors. Mr Hurr has nothing but praise for the service offered by the branch and in particular its efficient documentation which made his own accounting work that much easier.

After having been involved in the designing and installing of the whole plant project for three to four

Refurbished BTH motor and winch drive the shaft head hoist.

11kV three core main cable looping in and out of two 1MVA transformers and lv p.v.c. single core cables.

years Mr Hurr sees the future as a complete change from contracting to maintenance work. There will, however, be much for him to do in his position as electrical superintendent. There will be the supervision of the planned maintenance schedule and the work order system which he has recently introduced, as well as the inspection, repairs and overhauls. A provision of the Mining and Quarries Regulations requires that earth continuity and insulation testing is carried out at intervals not exceeding six months.

Mr Hurr feels that a system which can plan, estimate schedule and direct the activities of the electrical department will help to keep costs down and the plant running efficiently.

For a project designed to help reduce Britain's adverse balance of payments there is much need for it to run as smoothly and efficiently as possible. Mr Hurr is determined to see that the electrical side at least plays its part in this.

Manufacturers of equipment and plant.
BICC Power Cables Ltd ⎱ 3.3kV and low voltage distribu-
BICC General Cables Ltd ⎰ tion and control cables, power
⎰ capacitors
BICC Components Ltd, cable glands, soldering lugs
AB Wibe Ltd, ladder racking
Klockner-Moeller Ltd, mv motor control and distribution equipment
Brush Engineering Ltd, motors
Crompton Parkinson Ltd, motors
Distribution Transformers Ltd, transformers
Long & Crawford Ltd, switchgear
Thorn Lighting Ltd, lighting
GEC, motors
Dorman Smith, distribution panels
Square D Ltd, control gear
Simplex-Power Centre Ltd, trunking
Martin & Lunel, plugs and sockets

Photos on page 38, bottom page 39, centre 41 and top of this page by BICC.

Circle reader inquiry no. 26

Chapter 8

Disappointment and Danger

Vince Holland and Mickey Trezona were detailed to carry out winder maintenance which had been scheduled for Saturday mornings with prior agreement of the mining department. On that particular weekend it was planned that a spillage crew were organised to come in and clear the bottom of the shaft of the build up of material that fell from the loading pocket into the shaft. The clean up crew had come into work early to ensure any water in the shaft was pumped out before they were able to remove the spillage. To help easier access a steel mesh panel which was part of the safety barrier was removed leaving an opening into the shaft. The spillage cleanup crew then went up to surface to prepare for the task of digging out the build up of muck in the bottom of the shaft. Meanwhile Vince and Mickey were making their way down the shaft working on the signals which was part of the winder maintenance programme. They arrived at the loading pocket with Vince leading the way around the side of the shaft but he did not notice the mesh panel had been taken off. Vince continued and fell into the open shaft landing on the spillage pile approximately 40ft below the loading pocket. What started as a routine Saturday morning where we had our time slot for winder and signal maintenance, ended up with reports of a horrific accident. That afternoon I received a message to phone the mine. I eventually managed to get through to the security office who got Peter Stewart, our First Aider, on the line. By now, I was fearing the worst, but Peter assured me that although Vince had multiple fractures, his injuries were not life-threatening. He then briefly explained what had happened. Mickey saw Vince disappearing down the shaft and could see him sprawled out on the build-up of spillage and immediately raised the alarm. He had fallen approximately 40ft and tried grabbing the steel buntons on the way down, which was the reason for breaking his arms and the bones in his fingers but it was believed to have the effect of breaking his fall and probably saved his life. Vince was in extreme pain and it was with great difficulty that they managed to get him up the shaft and into the waiting ambulance, taking him to Treliske Hospital. There would normally be 4 or 5ft of water in the shaft and if Vince had fallen into this, he would have drowned before the rescue team reached him. Vince eventually made a full recovery and returned to work on Monday 21st February 1977.

The 1976 annual report prepared by Steve Kay for the Cornwall Tin and Mining Corporation shareholders, was cautiously optimistic for the future prospects of Mount Wellington Mine. The following is a summary of the letter dated 24th of January 1977. He stated that the mine had started production and was on the

Double deck shaking tables in the foreground, Mozley Tables upper left.

way to operating at full capacity. During the past year, the surface plant including the 600 metric ton/day mill, the hoisting, workshop and administration facilities were completed and the underground development of the mine, which had been delayed, was now commenced.

It had been expected that underground development would have been completed sufficiently to support a mining and milling operation by the end of summer 1976, but certain water problems prevented this. Water from the old United Mines situated some 1200ft to the west, infiltrated the lower levels of our mine making it costly and difficult to operate. By September, it became necessary to give priority to driving a tunnel from the bottom of our mine to intersect the United workings and thereby make it possible to drop the water level in these old workings through our pumping facilities.

We are now back on schedule and have begun commercial production testing with the mine and mill operating at 3,000 tons of low grade ore per week. So far we have made six shipments of tin concentrates to the Capper Pass Smelter. Full production of 1% grade tin should be reached when the underground development is finished, which is expected by June.

The mine staff has increased to 220 men and I am happy to report that our training programmes have been successful in turning out competent, local miners.

Tin prices continue to rise due to an imbalance between supply and demand. Tin has moved from $3.03/lb as of December 1975, to $4.85/lb to date.

I was beginning to sense a certain unease within the mining department and was apprehensive when I had a call from Jim Delaney inviting me to join him for a visit underground. He particularly wanted to go down to 2 Level where the brothers, David and Michael Matthews, were working. At the time, I was not aware of the reason or of the consequences for this visit, or why Jim asked me to accompany him. After a few words with the brothers and a cursory inspection of the lode, we went back up to surface. On the way, I detected an air of despondency when Jim admitted that it was not looking good – he was following up a report from the geology department with concerns of low grade ore and the lode being uneconomical to work. During the 1970 exploration phase, 2 and 3 Levels had not been developed as it was presumed that the lode would carry similar grades found in the adit and the lode samples on 4 and 5 Levels. This logic was accepted when the feasibility study was carried out in February 1974, but now would create a major setback to production and a shortfall in the ore reserves. I would never know why Jim asked me to accompany him, but I believe this marked a major

Double deck shaking tables with flotation cells in the background.

The mine's ball mills.

turning point in the future of the mine.

On the 7th of March, a few weeks after our visit underground, Jim promoted Leo Reitveld to Mine Superintendent in an attempt to improve productivity. Malcolm Hooper was moved to the administration office, but I was not sure what his responsibilities were. It was no coincidence that Steve Kay and Jack Tindale came over from Toronto a few days later on the 11th of March, but we could only guess the reasons for their visit.

The mill and underground were still dogged by a variety of breakdowns that were occurring all too regularly, this hindered the continuous operation of the plant needed for the efficient recovery of tin concentrates. One particular breakdown had serious consequences for the plans of Harold Wing and temporarily inconvenienced the people living in the village of Twelveheads. Before taking the job of Surface Superintendent Harold was developing his hobby and had set up a small nursery. He had discussed this with Jim Delaney and it was agreed that he would cultivate some of the land attached to Wheal Andrew Farmhouse. The idea was to bring on and provide shrubs and trees that were to be planted around the mine to comply with the landscaping proposals as part of the Cornwall County Council Planning Approval. The breakdown occurred outside the mill on the side of the hill overlooking Wheal Andrew when during the night a joint on the tailings

Mike Woodley connecting the circuits control panel in the mill sub station

pipeline parted and tailings were pumped down the hillside and flooded across the road. While this blockage of the road only caused a day of inconvenience to the traffic into Twelveheads, the damage to Harold Wing's nursery was one of total devastation. The weight and flow of the tailings swept through the plots uprooting all of the plants and finally covering the ground in 2ft of grey mud. All of the saplings that were due to be planted around the mine to help hide the building were destroyed. All of this was due to the bolts securing the pipe connection being incorrectly fitted.

During the week that Leo took over the Mine Superintendent's job, Roy Morgan was adding further equipment in the mill to improve the efficiency of the plant – new slimes, table, screen and spirals were installed. Following discussions with Flygt engineers, we decided to revise the layout for the process water pumps from single stage to a two-stage system. A small holding tank was built into the hillside above Wheal Andrew Farmhouse, where water was pumped from the adit in the first stage and from there it was pumped directly into the mill. This gave a more secure supply of water to the mill and a greater flexibility of the available pumps.

More ominous signs followed the previous meetings when Tom Huxley and George Mitchell arrived from Geneva on the 29th of March. At the next staff meeting in April, Jim Delaney announced that Malcolm Hooper was leaving at the end of May. His next statement made me feel very sad as he said he would be going at the end of July. Jim's replacement, Mike Davies, would be taking up his appointment in the last week of June, giving a month where Jim could acquaint him with the mine. There were two more appointments, one which directly affected Harold Wing and myself; Mike Maynard was appointed as the Mine Maintenance Engineer with responsibility for the Mechanical, Electrical and Surface Departments. For the last six years I had reported to Jim Delaney the Mine Manager and now I was losing a friend and contact with the top office. The other appointment was Rudi Reckhart, who replaced Leo Reitveld as the Mine Superintendent. I thought that this was a welcome change of supervision styles; where Rudi had a quiet, authoritative presence, Leo by contrast was loud and tended to provoke argument. Mike Maynard was another timely appointment who eventually brought the fitters together and organised a preventative maintenance strategy. After university, Mike spent some time in South Africa where he became a member of the Association of Resident Engineers, but took this opportunity to return to work in this country.

For me, it was a sad occasion when we attended Jim's leaving party – I owed so much to him for giving me the job that fulfilled all my ambitions. He was a caring, thoughtful man who did not suffer fools gladly and was proud to call himself a miner. He treated everyone equally regardless of qualifications, valuing a person's ability to do a job above all else. He would say, "If you could hack it, you can

Conveyors, ball mill, coarse ore bin and headgear.

The Mill steelwork with the fine ore bin foundations in the centre of the picture.

The coarse ore bin in front of the headgear.

The winder drums being assembled on their bed plate. The reinforced concrete beams to the centre right are for the construction of the winder house once the installation is complete.

Duncan Fallow and Derek Semmons (fitters) installing the winder (note the central bearing).

do it". One of his favourite stories was about the very highly qualified expert Mill Manager who travelled the world lecturing on his innovations to improve the efficiency of mineral processing. The company always encouraged him to give these talks particularly if he travelled abroad and was away for long periods. As soon as he had left, his mill foreman, who had years of experience and very little education, would tweak a few valves and they soon found recovery would improve.

The arrival of new management confirmed the company's commitment to overcome the difficulties at Mount Wellington and to remain involved in the mining industry. A project that Tom Huxley looked at was a tin prospect located in the foothills of the Bolivian Andes. He decided it needed further investigation and proposed to send Mike Davies, Mike Maynard and geologist Chris Burton to Bolivia and prepare a feasibility report. They were away for almost two weeks and upon their return, Mike Maynard gave me his version of the trip. The mine was in a remote location, approximately 10km from the nearest town. The mine site was served by a dirt track and there was no electricity supply. A variety of diesel engines provided power to run the machinery, the diesel was brought to the site in 45 gallon oil drums on the back of Land Rovers. This was stockpiled to get them through the rainy season when the track would be washed away. The owners of the mine were desperate to get investment to develop the site and to improve the infrastructure. While the project looked promising with a high grade tin deposit at shallow depth, Mike Davies considered the risks were too high to invest, particularly in such a remote place.

A rivalry, not always friendly, between fitters and electricians, developed into a sporting challenge with a game of 5-a-side football played on Tuesdays after work. We made reservations for the sports hall at the Carn Brea Leisure Centre and this became a regular event. I was usually roped in at the last moment to make up numbers. Soon after arriving at Mount Wellington, Mike Maynard indicated his willingness to play and was invited to join us and immediately demonstrated a talent for the game. During this time, I became friendly with Roger Scoley our assistant accountant, and we discovered a mutual liking for the game of squash. We decided to take this further and arrange a game, but this was a very popular sport at this time and we could not find a free slot that suited us during the evenings. We thought we could manage to get away for an hour during our lunch break. This was a relatively quiet time and we could make a regular booking for an hour at midday on Fridays. We occasionally overran the hour if it was a tight game and incoming players knocked the door to announce their arrival and the occupants were expected to leave. One lunch time we heard the knock, but in an effort to finish a tightly balanced game, we carried on. It was not long before the door was knocked again, this time louder, so we immediately finished and opened the door only to come face to face with Mike Davies and Nigel Deacon, Roger's boss. I was not sure who was surprised the most, but embarrassment turned to smiles as we all saw the funny side of the "squash meeting".

With the mine beginning to get established, a more serious and very important team was practising and learning new skills to enter the annual Mine Rescue and First Aid Competition. This took place during the summer with the venue alternating around the mines. There was fierce competition not only between teams, but also the participants where some mines were able to enter A and B sides. Although Mount Wellington were keen and practised hard, they did not have the years of experience gained by South Crofty and Geevor. Although we were behind the other teams, we were not despondent with our efforts and believed that in time we could beat South Crofty, Geevor, Wheal Jane, Pendarves and ECC Ball Clays near Newton Abbot, to win the trophy. With all the activity taking place outside of work, it was a natural progression to discuss the formation of a club. So, on the 5th of January 1978, the inaugural meeting of the Mount Wellington Mine Social Club was held in the Carharrack Sports Club. There was a reasonable attendance with those present voting in Derek James as Chairman and Peter Stewart as Vice Chairman. Never wanting to lose control of finances Nigel Deacon insisted on becoming the Treasurer and Roger Scoley became our Secretary. The privilege of becoming members of the Mount Wellington Mine Social Club gave us associate status with Carharrack Sports Club and an invite to help reduce their stock of beer was duly complied with.

Now that the social club was up and running, we were able to obtain insurance cover for sports injury, which gave us the opportunity to arrange rugby matches against other mines. Mark Oliff from South Crofty called, so between us we were able to agree a date on which to play. This fixture list went on to include Pendarves Mine and Wheal Jane – the games were to be played on Sunday mornings as Saturdays were ruled out, because most players were playing for their clubs on Saturdays. Next I managed to get hold of Mike Williams who agreed a fixture with Pendarves on Sunday the 19th of February, we also had a fixture with Wheal Jane on Sunday 12th of March. Unfortunately, the weekends we were due to play Pendarves Mine and South Crofty, the weather changed and we experienced storm force winds and heavy snow falls. The game against Wheal Jane was played at St Day, the Wellington team made up with the bulk of players provided by St Day RFC. Wheal Jane relied on the Truro second team for the majority of their players, with the two rivals fairly well matched. After a hard fought game, not always within the rules, Wellington lost by one point, scoring two tries, one conversion and one penalty. Only in the dying moments of the game did Wheal Jane go ahead scoring a try, which everyone except the referee clearly saw a forward pass, with the final score of Wellington 13 and Wheal Jane 14. Enjoying the after match banter over a few beers, the referee came in for some leg pulling with shouts of, "Ref, when are you starting your new job at Jane?"

Tradex were determined to keep Mount Wellington running and were carrying the financial burden on their own. Steve Kay and his shareholders had given up any hope of making a return on their investment and seemed resigned for substantial losses and played no further meaningful part in the final months of the mine. No stone was left unturned to find tin deposits within our lease areas that were a ready source of ore to feed the mill. A series of costean trenches were excavated on United Downs in order to expose the possibility of lodes outcropping in this area. This was achieved using bulldozers and scrapers similar to that used in highway construction. A small exploration team was set up, led by Derek James and his geologist David Kneebone, to access shafts within the target areas.

The first shaft to be investigated was Sampson's located on United Downs. A crane was used to raise and lower a two-man cage that had been specifically designed and fabricated with all the built-in safety requirements in accordance with Mine and Quarry Regulations. Non-destructive testing of the lifting eye and shackle met with the approval of the inspectorate. The cage was approximately 7ft long and 2ft square with a simple design using 3-inch heavy gauge angle iron for the frame, which was formed into a point on the top and bottom.

On the 9th of January, Tom Huxley came over from Geneva to gain first-hand knowledge of the work in progress. The early results of the exploration programme would have been disappointing, but the next targets located at Wheal Moor, Whiteworks, Poldory and Wheal Squire were believed to be more promising. Underground, the problems continued to be disappointing with the number of breakdowns and mistakes causing too many stoppages and call-outs. It was a nightmare trying to overcome:

- Unable to tram ore on 4 Level due to loco failure (loco left with flat battery). Sent fully charged loco to 4 Level only for the next shift to send the good loco back up, leaving the one with flat battery underground.

- Bottom of shaft flooding, pump reported not working. Electrician called out to find pump working okay, but a gate valve had been closed, stopping the flow of water.

- Electrician called out when the winder was reported to be on stop. Tested out okay, it was found that the shaft gate was left open on the loading pocket with the interlock preventing the winder from moving!!

There was better news in the mill with the installation of the flotation plant on target for starting at the end of the month. The instrumentation added to flotation cells controlled acid valves and reagent feeders. Nature conspired to force us to shut the mill down on February 18th, with strong winds and heavy snow storms causing interruptions to the incoming power supplies.

The continuing breakdowns and call-outs were casting an atmosphere of gloom within the maintenance departments. At the end of February, Mick Trezona came to see me and wished to hand in his notice to leave. This was disappointing news as he was one of the first to join us and over the last four years, he had developed into a first class electrician. His cheerful personality would be missed.

Derek James and his team continued with the exploration targets. Wheal Moor was investigated but did not show signs of significant tin reserves. Poldory seemed to offer hope of a small tonnage of ore, as did Wheal Squire. It was found that sections within Wheal Squire were flooded and needed to be pumped before access could be gained to investigate the shallow workings. I hired a portable generator to provide power to a pump that we had as a spare at Wellington.

At the beginning of the Second World War, Jack Trounson reported on the Cornish Mining Industry and presented suggestions within various scenarios in which tin production could be increased. It seems uncanny that the following extract could apply equally to Mount Wellington in 1978, as it did to Whiteworks Mine in 1938. Unfortunately, time was fast running out for the exploration crew and the investigations at Whiteworks Mine was left unfinished.

The small Whiteworks tin mine, standing a little to the north of the once celebrated Gwennap United Mines, is a further proposition that merits immediate attention at the present time. Operations on a small scale were carried on here for a year or two, but were abandoned in 1938, as the price of tin was temporarily very depressed. Only one lode was worked, although there are at least two in the mine. The workings consisted of 4 or 5 levels extending at the most about 240ft from east to west and connected by short cross-cuts to a small vertical shaft. The bottom of the latter was only 230ft from surface and by reason of the free drainage provided by the Great County Adit in this area, the mine was dry and did not require any pumping plant. The bottom level, however, encountered water and had it been possible to sink deeper, pumping would undoubtedly soon have been necessary.

The lode here is very unusual, consisting of a clean and easily separated cassiterite in the gangue of soft white banded "killas" or clay-slate rock. It is exceedingly easy to mine, crush and concentrate, and a considerable area was stoped out during the short period that the mine was in operation. The lode strikes slightly south of west and north of east and dips steeply to the north, and it is stated that some of the stopes on it were over 10ft wide when breaking down the mineralised walls as well as the lode proper.

The actual milling recovery of tin was low, but it must be explained that all the ore mined by the late company was little more than the "leavings" of the old men who, at some very distant period, had worked the lode in a most peculiar and selective manner. The old miners had apparently picked out the richest "leaders", leaving small holes and an extraordinary ramification of small and irregular workings in every direction. The late company never reached the limits of the old men's workings either laterally or in depth, but it was generally thought that if they had had the cash resources to sink below adit level, they would have been able to develop the lode below any point reached by the old men and that, in consequence, the nett tin content of the lode would have been found to be far higher than in the shallow workings above adit level, where the old workers had found it profitable to "pick out the eyes".

At the time Whiteworks was abandoned early in 1938, it was estimated that £5,000 would have been sufficient to enlarge the shaft and sink it a further 100ft in order to get well below adit level and in view of the prospects as they appeared then, the property now seems worthy of the most serious consideration. Incidentally, although all plant has been removed, the mine is quite close to Mount Wellington mill and the latter could be brought into immediate commission for handling the Whiteworks ore. Some modifications in the flow-sheet would undoubtedly be necessary, but the very simple nature of the Whiteworks ore would make it an eminently easy one to dress.

Rumours were beginning to spread further gloom as it was thought that Consolidated Goldfields were wishing to pull out of Wheal Jane. It was known for some time that accumulating losses were unsustainable. Management seemed to change at regular intervals, but this turnover did little to bridge the ever widening gap between profit and loss. Whatever decisions were made at Wheal Jane would have a direct influence on the future of Mount Wellington, which in any event did not seem encouraging, so I needed to take stock of the situation and consider my options for the future.

All of this was overshadowed with the tragic news we received on Tuesday the 21st of March when Danny Bowden lost his life. Danny was a surveyor working on 5 Level when he walked across a stope that contained a large percentage of fine material. He had got partway across when he began to sink down and was unable to grab anything to prevent submerging deeper into the stope. He was beyond the reach of his mate, whose frantic efforts could not stop Danny from disappearing beneath the surface. By the time the alarm was raised and his body had been recovered, it was too late for it was found that Danny had suffocated. This quiet, well liked man was the first and only fatality at Mount Wellington and his death was a very sad reminder of dangers working in the mining industry.

CORNWALL TIN & MINING CORPORATION

Annual Report 1976

CORNWALL TIN & MINING CORPORATION

DIRECTORS	J. H. HIRSHHORN/New York, New York *Chairman of the Board* Callahan Mining Corporation
	STEPHEN KAY/Toronto, Ontario *Professional Engineer*
	ARTHUR EMIL/New York, New York *Attorney*
	B. ATTENBOROUGH/Toronto, Ontario *Partner in Tom & Barnt Limited*
	FRANK R. COHEN/New York, New York *Attorney*
OFFICERS	STEPHEN KAY, *President*
	FRANK R. COHEN, *Secretary*
	J. D. S. BOHME, *Assistant Secretary*
HEAD OFFICE	c/o The Corporation Trust Company 100 West Tenth Street Wilmington, Delaware
MINE OFFICE	Cornwall, England Bissoe, Truro
TRANSFER AGENT	Bankers Trust Company New York, New York
SOLICITORS	Farber and Cohen New York, New York
AUDITORS	Richard A. Eisner & Company New York, New York

The cover is a photograph of Cornwall Tin's plant situated in the rural countryside of Cornwall, England near Truro showing the shaft headframe and milling facilities.

CORNWALL TIN & MINING. CORPORATION

President's Letter

January 24, 1977

To the Shareholders,
Cornwall Tin & Mining Corporation.

The English tin mine in Cornwall has started production and is on its way to operating at full capacity.

During the past year the surface plant which includes the 600 metric ton/day mill, the hoisting, the shop and administration facilities was completed and the underground development of the mine, which had been delayed, was commenced.

While we had expected to complete the underground development sufficiently to support a mining and milling operation by the end of the summer of 1976, certain water problems persisted which delayed this objective.

Water from the old United Mine workings situated some 1100 feet to the west infiltered into the lower levels of our new mine making it difficult and costly to operate. By September it became necessary to give priority to driving a tunnel from the bottom of our mine to intersect the United workings, and thereby make it possible to drop the water level in these old workings, through our pumping facilities.

We are now back on schedule and have begun commercial production testing with the mine and mill operating at 3,000 tons of low grade ore per week. So far we have made six shipments of tin concentrates to the Capper Pass Smelter. Full rated production at 1% grade tin should be reached when the underground development is finished which is expected by June.

The mine staff has increased to 220 men and I am happy to report that our training programs have been successful in turning out competent local miners.

Tin prices continue to rise due to an imbalance between supply and demand. Tin has moved from $3.03/lb. December 1975 to $4.85/lb. to date.

Respectfully submitted
on behalf of the Board of Directors

Stephen Kay
President

CORNWALL TIN & MINING CORPORATION

Tin in 1976

World tin mine production and consumption increased three percent and ten percent, respectively, as the world economy improved, according to the Bureau of Mines, U.S. Department of the Interior. Restraints on tin exports from major producing nations were removed by the International Tin Council (ITC) at the end of the second quarter after the ITC had sold over 17,000 metric tons from its buffer stock. The ITC revised the tin price range three times during the year, for a total increase in the floor and ceiling price of 19 percent and 20 percent, respectively. The Fifth International Tin Agreement came provisionally into force July 1. The United States ratified the Agreement on October 28, marking the first time the United States has joined a metal commodity agreement.

U.S. consumption of primary and secondary tin increased, with the total domestic consumption up 16 percent over the 1975 level to 64,700 tons. Major uses for tin were tinplate, 31 percent; solder, 28 percent; bronze and brass, 14 percent and chemicals including tin oxide, 10 percent. Consumption of tin in all major end uses increased over that of 1975. U.S. brass mills consumed about 800 tons of primary tin and 210 tons of secondary tin compared with 1975 levels of 481 tons and 244 tons, respectively.

Most of the Nation's tin supply came from overseas sources such as Malaysia, Thailand, Bolivia, and Indonesia, and from recycling. About one-fifth of the tin used in the United States in 1976 was reclaimed from scrap at 15 detinning plants and 160 secondary nonferrous metal processing plants. U.S. mines in Alaska, Colorado, and New Mexico provided less than 100 tons of tin during the year.

The only primary tin smelter-refinery currently operating in the United States is the Texas City, Tex., facility of Gulf Chemical and Metallurgical Corp. In the first 10 months of 1976 the smelter received 3,548 tons of tin-in-concentrates from Bolivia for smelting. In addition to concentrates, the smelter processed tin containing scrap and residues for secondary recovery.

The General Services Administration (GSA) continued sales of surplus tin during the year. Sales from January to November totaled 3,501 tons compared with 569 tons for the same period in 1975. At the end of November, 2,846 tons remained available for disposal. On October 1 the Federal Preparedness Agency (FPA) set a new stockpile goal of 33,021 tons, a reduction of 8,129 tons from the prior objective. . . . . . .

This review was taken from the Mineral Industry Surveys, U.S. Department of the Interior, Bureau of Mines, dated December 20, 1976.

CORNWALL TIN & MINING CORPORATION

BALANCE SHEET

ASSETS	August 31, 1976	August 31, 1975
Current assets:		
Cash	$ 7,892	$ 29,853
Account receivable — corporate joint venture		17,367
Other current assets	1,980	2,210
Total current assets	9,872	49,430
Investment in and subordinated amount receivable from corporate joint venture (Note B)	2,222,007	2,637,930
TOTAL	$2,231,879	$2,687,360

LIABILITIES

	August 31, 1976	August 31, 1975
Current liabilities:		
Notes payable — shareholders (current portion) (Note C)	$ 75,000	$ 75,000
Accounts payable and accrued expenses	52,598	50,179
Accounts payable — affiliates	12,858	9,750
Total current liabilities	140,456	134,929
Notes payable — shareholders (long-term portion) (including accrued interest) (Note C)	371,137	436,585
Total liabilities	511,593	571,514
Commitments and contingencies (Notes B[5], C[2] and F)		

Shareholders' equity:
(Notes B and D)

	August 31, 1976	August 31, 1975
Capital stock — common — authorized 4,000,000 shares, $.01 par value each; issued and outstanding 2,555,400 shares	$ 25,554	$ 25,554
Additional paid-in capital	2,292,742	2,292,742
(Deficit)	(598,010)	(202,450)
Total shareholders' equity	1,720,286	2,115,846
TOTAL	$2,231,879	$2,687,360

The accompanying notes to financial statements are an integral part hereof.

Attention is directed to the foregoing accountants' report.

CORNWALL TIN & MINING CORPORATION

STATEMENTS OF OPERATIONS AND DEFICIT

	Year Ended August 31, 1976		Eleven Months Ended August 31, 1975 (Note G)	
Income from management services (Note E)		$ 30,000		$ 27,500
Expenses:				
Management fees (Note F[3])	$ 18,000		$ 16,500	
Officer's salary (Note F[4])	12,000		11,000	
Interest expense (Note C)	9,552		13,281	
Net foreign exchange loss (Note B[3])	343,135		114,533	
Other operating expenses	42,873	425,560	30,217	185,531
NET (LOSS)		(395,560)		(158,031)
(Deficit) beginning		(202,450)		(44,419)
(DEFICIT) — END		$(598,010)		$(202,450)

(Loss) per common share is based upon 2,555,400 shares outstanding during the year ended August 31, 1976 and a weighted average of 2,477,191 shares outstanding during the eleven months ended August 31, 1975.		$(.15)		$(.06)

The accompanying notes to financial statements are an integral part hereof.

Attention is directed to the foregoing accountants' report.

Auditors' Report

The Board of Directors and Shareholders
Cornwall Tin & Mining Corporation

We have examined the balance sheets of Cornwall Tin & Mining Corporation (a Delaware corporation) as at August 31, 1976 and August 31, 1975 and the related statements of operations and deficit and changes in financial position for the year ended August 31, 1976 and for the eleven months ended August 31, 1975. Our examinations were made in accordance with generally accepted auditing standards, and accordingly included such tests of the accounting records and such other auditing procedures as we considered necessary in the circumstances.

The Company's current liabilities, which totaled $140,456 at August 31, 1976, were substantially in excess of its current assets, which totaled $9,872 at that date.

In our opinion, subject to the Company's ability to obtain additional working capital through borrowing or sale of additional capital stock or both and subject to the realizability of the Company's investment in and receivable from the corporate joint venture described in Note B, which is dependent upon the attainment of future profitable operations of a mine under development by the joint venture, the financial statements enumerated in the first paragraph hereof present fairly the financial position of Cornwall Tin & Mining Corporation (a Delaware corporation) at August 31, 1976 and August 31, 1975 and the results of its operations and changes in its financial position for the year ended August 31, 1976 and for the eleven months ended August 31, 1975, in conformity with generally accepted accounting principles applied on a consistent basis.

New York, New York
October 27, 1976

RICHARD A. EISNER & COMPANY
Certified Public Accountants

CORNWALL TIN & MINING CORPORATION

STATEMENTS OF CHANGES IN FINANCIAL POSITION

	Year Ended August 31, 1976		Eleven Months Ended August 31, 1975 (Note G)	
Financial resources were applied to:				
Operations:				
Net loss		$ 395,560		$ 158,031
Items included in determination of net loss not providing (requiring) working capital: Loss on foreign exchange (Note B[3]): Decline in value of deferred subordinated receivable from corporate joint venture due to change in rate of exchange	$(415,923)		$(409,054)	
Less deferred gain on sale of assets	67,861	(348,062)	288,567	(120,487)
Interest on long-term debt not currently payable (Note C[3])		(9,552)		(625)
Working capital used in operations		37,946		36,919
Payment of long-term notes payable to certain shareholders		75,000		75,000
Reduction in deferred gain on sale of assets due to accrual of liability for stamp duty (Note B[2])				30,254
Total		112,946		142,173
Financial resources were provided by:				
Sale of capital shares (Note D)				300,000
Regional development grant received from the British Government (Note B[2])		67,861		67,915
Total		67,861		367,915
(INCREASE) DECREASE IN WORKING CAPITAL DEFICIENCY		$ (45,085)		$ 225,742
Increase (decrease) in components of working capital deficiency:				
Current assets:				
Cash		$ (21,961)		$ 11,794
Accounts receivable from corporate joint venture		(17,367)		14,407
Other current assets		(230)		2,210
		(39,558)		28,411
Current liabilities:				
Notes payable — bank				(175,000)
Accounts payable and accrued expenses		2,419		9,446
Accounts payable — affiliates		3,108		(31,777)
		5,527		(197,331)
(INCREASE) DECREASE IN WORKING CAPITAL DEFICIENCY		$ (45,085)		$ 225,742

The accompanying notes to financial statements are an intergral part hereof.

Attention is directed to the foregoing accountants' report.

CORNWALL TIN & MINING CORPORATION

NOTES TO FINANCIAL STATEMENTS

(NOTE A) — Significant Accounting Policies:

[1] Foreign currency translation

Funds on deposit in the United Kingdom and other assets and liabilities related to the Company's participation in a joint venture in that country (Note B[1]) are translated into United States dollars at current exchange rates. Translation gains and losses are charged to current operations. Accounts stated in Canadian dollars are included at par.

[2] United Kingdom Regional Development Grants

The Company has received certain regional development grants from the United Kingdom Department of Trade and Industry in partial recovery of its expenditures for mining exploration in Cornwall, England, prior to the start of the joint venture described in Note B[1]. Since such grants were made at the discretion of the Department of Trade and Industry, the Company accounted for them only as they were received. Prior to the start of the aforesaid joint venture (October 31, 1973), the grants had been recorded as deductions from the Company's deferred exploration expenditures. On October 31, 1973, these expenditures were transferred to Cornwall Tin & Mining Limited ("Limited"). Subsequent to that date, grants received ($67,861 in the year ended August 31, 1976 and $67,915 in the eleven months ended August 31, 1975) were credited to deferred income from the transfer (Note B[2]). The Company does not expect to receive any additional regional development grants.

(NOTE B) — Investment in and Subordinated Amount Receivable from Corporate Joint Venture:

[1] The Company, through its ownership of 49% of the capital stock of Limited, is engaged in a joint venture to finance the development and exploration of certain mining properties known as the Wellington property and the Cligga property, respectively, in Cornwall, England. Development of the Wellington property is to include placing a mine in production on that property. The Company's investment in Limited and a subordinated receivable from Limited of £1,249,020 (Sterling) arose from a transfer to the latter of certain of the Company's assets on October 31, 1973. The receivable was initially recorded by the Company at the U.S. dollar equivalent ($3,046,984) of the aforesaid amount of £1,249,020 based on the rate of exchange prevailing on October 31, 1973. This amount exceeded the Company's carrying value of the assets transferred by $250,906 and the latter amount was credited to deferred income.

[2] Deferred income from the transfer was (1) increased by $67,861 during the year ended August 31, 1976 and

$67,915 during the eleven months ended August 31, 1975 to reflect regional development grants received in those periods (Note A[2]) and (2) decreased by $30,254, representing the estimated liability for stamp duty expected to be assessed by the British Government on the transfer of assets to Limited.

[3] The deferred subordinated receivable from Limited of £1,249,020 is reflected in the balance sheet at August 31, 1975 and August 31, 1976 at its then-current dollar equivalents of $2,637,930 and $2,222,007, respectively. These amounts give effect to a significant decline in the U.S. dollar value of the British pound sterling during those periods. The decline in each period was charged first against deferred income, and the balance against operations as follows:

	Eleven Months Ended August 31, 1975	Year Ended August 31, 1976
Subordinated receivable at beginning of period	$3,046,984	$2,637,930
Subordinated receivable at end of period	2,637,930	2,222,007
Gross loss on translation of pound sterling	409,054	415,923
Less deferred income (below)	288,567	67,861
Net charge to operations	$ 120,487	$ 348,062

Deferred income (Note B [1]) is summarized as follows:

	Eleven Months Ended August 31, 1975	Year Ended August 31, 1976
Balance at beginning of period	$ 250,906	$ -0-
Development grants (Note B[2])	67,915	67,861
Stamp duty	(30,254)	
Loss on translation applied (above)	(288,567)	(67,861)
Balance — end of period	$ -0-	$ -0-

[4] The Company's subordinated receivable from Limited is to be repaid by the latter out of its future earnings on an equal basis with advances aggregating £1,300,000 made to Limited by the company holding a 51% interest in the joint venture. Both of these obligations of Limited, however, are subordinated to loans aggregating £1,650,000 made jointly to Limited by an agency of the British Government and a bank and to additional loans subsequently made to Limited by the bank (Notes B[5] and H). These lenders hold first liens on all of the assets of Limited; and no payments on account of advances or dividends may be made to Limited's shareholders while these loans are outstanding.

[5] The Company and its co-venturer have guaranteed to the agency of the British Government and the bank referred to in paragraph [4] above completion of the project to place a mine into production on the Wellington property. In addition, they have agreed that, if additional funds are required for that purpose, they will supply such funds in proportion to their respective holdings in Limited. In this connection, the Company and its co-venturer, in February 1976, individually guaranteed repayment to the aforesaid bank of an additional loan commitment of £2,000,000 made available by the bank to Limited. Reference is made to Note H with respect to an additional bank commitment to Limited guaranteed by the Company subsequent to August 31, 1976.

(NOTE C) — Notes Payable — Shareholders:

[1] In November 1970, the Company borrowed, without interest, an aggregate of $600,000 ($150,000 each from its two major shareholders, Prado Explorations Limited ("Prado") (the majority shareholder) and Mr. Joseph H. Hirshhorn ("Hirshhorn"), and $300,000 from five stockholders who own an aggregate of 124,000 shares. The notes are repayable in sixteen equal consecutive quarterly installments from July 1, 1974, and are subject to prepayment in amounts equal to 50% of the Company's net earnings in each three-month period. The notes are subordinate to all subsequent indebtedness of the Company for the purposes of bringing the Wellington mine up to a tin-producing stage and of constructing a tin mill at the mine site.

[2] The Company is obligated, at the request of the holders of not less than 50% of the aforementioned 124,000 shares of common stock, to file and cause to become effective, at the expense of the Company, one registration statement under the Securities Act of 1933 with respect to all or any of such 124,000 shares. In addition, the holders are entitled to include, at the expense of the Company, all or any of such 124,000 shares of common stock in all other registration statements filed by the Company under the Securities Act of 1933 on forms which will permit the inclusion of such shares.

[3] In July 1974, Prado and Hirshhorn waived payment by the Company of current and future installments payable on the notes held by them (aggregating $300,000) until such time as the Company earns sufficient income to pay such installments; unpaid installments bear interest at the prime rate as established by the First National City Bank of New York City from the due date of each respective installment until the date it is paid.

(NOTE D) — Sale of Capital Stock:

In June 1975, the Company sold 100,000 shares of its then unissued common stock to three subscribers for the sum of $300,000. Of this amount, $1,000, representing par value of the shares sold, was credited to capital stock and the balance ($299,000) was credited to additional paid-in capital.

(NOTE E) — Income from Management Services:

Pursuant to the joint venture agreement of October 31, 1973 (Note B), the Company is to provide the joint venture, for a ten-year period, with such management services as are required and is to be compensated by reimbursement of actual out-of-pocket disbursements plus fees at the annual rate of $30,000 (Canadian) with respect to the Wellington property and $10,000 (Canadian) with respect to the Cligga property, provided work on the property in respect of which the fee is being paid is continuing. In accordance with the foregoing terms, the Company received fees with respect to the Wellington property only through August 31, 1976.

(NOTE F) — Commitments and Contingencies:

[1] Prado retains an undivided 15% carried interest in any future earnings from mining rights for the Cligga property transferred by the Company to Limited (Note B).

[2] In connection with regional development grants received from the British Government (Note A[2]), the Company has agreed to hold Limited harmless and free of liability from any claim that might be made against it by reason of certain guarantees given to the British Government. The Company's contingent liability in this respect is limited to the amount of grant monies received by the Company.

[3] Pursuant to an agreement with International Mine Services Limited ("I.M.S."), an affiliated corporation, I.M.S. provides supervisory and administrative services to the Company for a monthly management and consulting fee of $1,500, plus costs and expenses. The agreement is terminable by either party upon 30 days' notice.

[4] An employment agreement between the Company and its president expiring on October 31, 1980 provides, among other things, that the latter shall receive as annual compensation an amount equal to 2% of the Company's earnings before taxes, but not less than $12,000 nor more than $36,000.

[5] The Company has an operating loss carryforward on a tax basis in the amount of $13,600 available to offset taxable income of future periods. The carryforward will expire August 31, 1979.

(NOTE G) — Change of Fiscal Year:

On October 1, 1974, the Company changed its fiscal year-end from September 30 to June 30; subsequently, however, the Company adopted a financial reporting period ending August 31 in order to allow sufficient time in future periods for inclusion in its operations of its equity in the profit or loss of Limited for the latter's fiscal years ending on May 31.

(NOTE H) — Event Subsequent to August 31, 1976:

As a result of increases in the projected cost of developing the Wellington property, Limited obtained an additional loan commitment in the amount of £700,000 from the bank referred to in Notes B[4] and [5]. The Company and its co-venturer, in November and October 1976, respectively, individually guaranteed repayment to the bank.

APPENDIX 6

OPERATING BUDGET

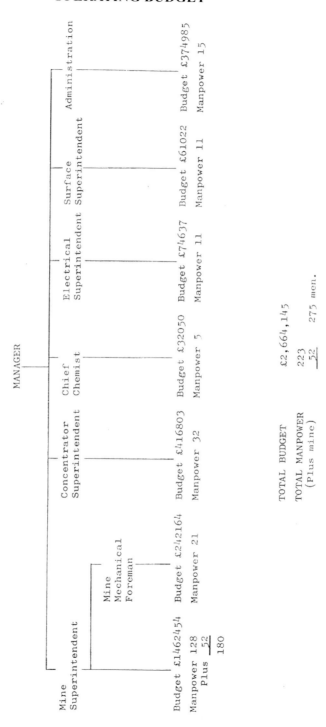

OPERATING BUDGET AND MANPOWER TOTALS for the period June 1st 1976 to May 31st 1977

MANAGER

Mine Superintendent
Budget £1462454
Manpower 128
Plus 52
180

Mine Mechanical Foreman
Budget £242164
Manpower 21

Concentrator Superintendent
Budget £416803
Manpower 32

Chief Chemist
Budget £32050
Manpower 5

Electrical Superintendent
Budget £74637
Manpower 11

Surface Superintendent
Budget £61022
Manpower 11

Administration
Budget £374985
Manpower 15

TOTAL BUDGET   £2,664,145

TOTAL MANPOWER   223
(Plus mine)   52
  275 men.

OPERATING BUDGET SUMMARY

Period June 1st 1976 to May 31st 1977

Period	Mine	Mine Mech	Conc	Assay	Elect	Surf	Admin	Total
1	69284	18628	21927	2465	5744	4694	28845	151587
2	81340	18628	26602	2465	5744	4694	28845	168318
3	95156	18628	24902	2465	5744	4694	28845	180434
4	99877	18628	27507	2465	5744	4694	28845	187760
5	104869	18628	30698	2465	5744	4694	28845	195943
6	115509	18628	31299	2465	5744	4694	28845	207184
7	117887	18628	33174	2465	5744	4694	28845	211447
8	123337	18628	36489	2465	5744	4694	28845	220202
9	125627	18628	37164	2465	5744	4694	28845	223167
10	124767	18628	39089	2465	5744	4694	28845	224232
11	129347	18628	36364	2465	5744	4694	28845	226087
12	134287	18628	36914	2465	5744	4694	28845	231577
13	141157	18628	34674	2465	5744	4694	28845	236207
Total	1462454	242164	416803	32045	74672	61022	374985	2664145

UNDERGROUND DEPARTMENT

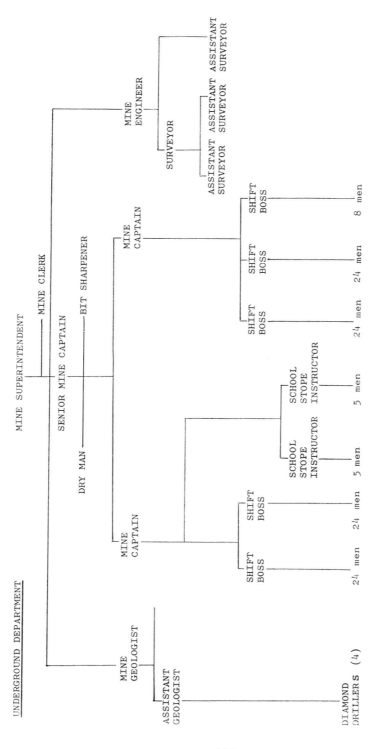

MINE SUPERINTENDENT

MINE CLERK

SENIOR MINE CAPTAIN

BIT SHARPENER

DRY MAN

MINE GEOLOGIST

ASSISTANT GEOLOGIST

DIAMOND DRILLERS (4)

MINE CAPTAIN

SHIFT BOSS — 24 men

SHIFT BOSS — 24 men

SCHOOL STOPE INSTRUCTOR — 5 men

SCHOOL STOPE INSTRUCTOR — 5 men

MINE CAPTAIN

SHIFT BOSS — 24 men

SHIFT BOSS — 24 men

SHIFT BOSS — 8 men

MINE ENGINEER

SURVEYOR

ASSISTANT SURVEYOR

ASSISTANT SURVEYOR

ASSISTANT SURVEYOR

ASSISTANT SURVEYOR

TOTAL: 139 — current

TOTAL: 180 — estimated 1.1.77.

109

MINE

BUDGET PERIOD: June 1st 1976 to May 31st 1977

Period	Drift	Raise	Room & Pillar Stope	Shrink-age Stope	Tramm-ing	Mine Direct Over-heads	Total
1							
Labour	3900	4680	4464	–	2460	25560	41064
Materials	4082	2640	3780	–	240	17478	28220
2							
Labour	5850	6240	5952	–	3280	26844	48166
Materials	6123	3520	5040	–	320	18171	33174
3							
Labour	7800	8580	7440	248	4100	28084	56252
Materials	8164	4840	6300	210	400	19030	38904
4							
Labour	7800	10140	8928	248	4920	27431	59467
Materials	8164	5720	7560	210	480	18276	40410
5							
Labour	7800	11700	10416	248	5740	26995	62899
Materials	8164	6600	8820	210	560	17616	41970
6							
Labour	7800	15000	11408	992	6560	27139	69499
Materials	8164	8800	9660	840	640	17906	46010
7							
Labour	7800	15600	11408	1240	6560	27139	69747
Materials	8164	8800	9660	1050	640	19836	48150
8							
Labour	7800	15600	11408	2480	6560	27139	70987
Materials	8164	8800	9660	2100	640	22986	52350
9							
Labour	7800	15600	11408	3720	6560	27139	72227
Materials	8164	8800	9660	3150	640	22986	53400
10							
Labour	7800	15600	11408	4960	6560	27139	73467
Materials	8164	8800	9660	4200	640	19886	51900
11							
Labour	7800	15600	11408	7440	6560	27139	75947
Materials	8164	8800	9660	6300	640	19836	53400
12							
Labour	7800	15600	11408	11160	6560	27139	79667
Materials	8164	8800	9660	9450	640	17906	54620
13							
Labour	7800	15600	11408	14880	6560	27139	83387
Materials	8164	8800	9660	12600	640	17906	57770

TOTAL MINE LABOUR   862776

         MATERIALS   599678   1462454

110

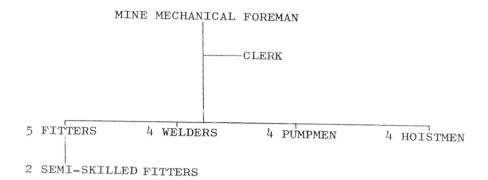

MINE MECHANICAL FOREMAN

CLERK

5 FITTERS   4 WELDERS   4 PUMPMEN   4 HOISTMEN

2 SEMI-SKILLED FITTERS

TOTAL: 21

MINE MECHANICAL MAINTENANCE

BUDGET PERIOD: June 1st 1976 to May 31st 1977

ACCOUNT	LABOUR	MATERIALS	TOTAL
Underground			
Mobile equipment	4,976	3,860	8,510
Locomotives	1,739	2,150	3,775
Ore cars	3,338	1,860	4,980
Loaders	8,046	4,650	12,170
Slushers	2,087	2,360	4,310
Rock drills	4,976	30,000	34,650
Diamond drills	417	5,000	5,390
Pumps	1,445	60,000	61,350
Compressors	1,445	1,860	3,210
Hoist, headgear, ropes	3,424	3,160	6,360
Mine ventilation	717	760	1,430
General underground	12,519	6,994	18,694
Fab. modification	5,457	3,490	8,590
Pumps operation	16,371		16,371
Hoist operation	18,190		18,190
Lubricating oils		4,400	4,400
Shop supplies		13,000	13,000
Supervision, holiday pay	13,478		13,478
TOTAL MINE MECHANICAL MAINTENANCE	98,625	143,544	242,169

CONCENTRATOR DEPARTMENT

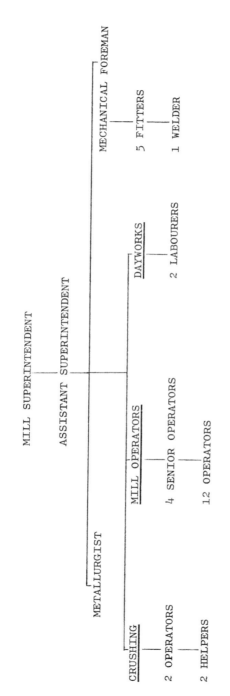

MILL SUPERINTENDENT

ASSISTANT SUPERINTENDENT

METALLURGIST

MECHANICAL FOREMAN

5 FITTERS

1 WELDER

DAYWORKS

2 LABOURERS

MILL OPERATORS

4 SENIOR OPERATORS

12 OPERATORS

CRUSHING

2 OPERATORS

2 HELPERS

TOTAL: 32

MILL OPERATING COSTS

BUDGET PERIOD: June 1st 1976 to May 31st 1977

	1	2	3	4	5	6	7	8	9	10	11	12	13	TOTAL
Labour														
Crusher operation	1050	1050	1130	1130	1130	1130	1130	1130	1130	1130	1130	1130	1130	14530
Mill operation	5300	6480	6480	6480	6480	6480	6480	6480	6480	6480	6480	6480	6480	83060
Holiday pay	670	670	670	670	670	670	670	670	670	670	670	670	670	8710
Supervision	1885	1885	1885	1885	1885	1885	1885	1885	1885	1885	1885	1885	1885	24505
Materials														
Power	3660	3660	4135	4485	4950	5235	7110	10425	11100	13025	10300	10850	8610	97545
Grinding media	2545	4460	3185	4460	5946	5946	5946	5946	5946	5946	5946	5946	5946	68164
Reagents (Ph)	620	1080	770	1080	1440	1440	1440	1440	1440	1440	1440	1440	1440	16510
Reagents (Flot)	1500	2620	1950	2620	3500	3500	3500	3500	3500	3500	3500	3500	3500	40190
Sub-total Operating	17230	21905	20205	22810	26001	26286	28161	31476	32151	34076	31351	31901	29661	353214

MILL MECHANICAL MAINTENANCE

		1	2	3	4	5	6	7	8	9	10	11	12	13	TOTAL
Crushing	Labour	325	325	325	325	325	388	388	388	388	388	388	388	388	4729
	Materials	450	450	450	450	450	450	450	450	450	450	450	450	450	5850
Grinding	Labour	439	439	439	439	439	524	524	524	524	524	524	524	524	6387
	Materials	895	895	895	895	895	895	895	895	895	895	895	895	895	11635
Flotation	Labour	244	244	244	244	244	291	291	291	291	291	291	291	291	3548
	Materials	410	410	410	410	410	410	410	410	410	410	410	410	410	5330
Gravity	Labour	325	325	325	325	325	388	388	388	388	388	388	388	388	4729
	Materials	600	600	600	600	600	600	600	600	600	600	600	600	600	7800
Thickening	Labour	163	163	163	163	163	195	195	195	195	195	195	195	195	2375
	Materials	130	130	130	130	130	130	130	130	130	130	130	130	130	1690
Reagents	Labour	82	82	82	82	82	98	98	98	98	98	98	98	98	1194
	Materials	15	15	15	15	15	15	15	15	15	15	15	15	15	195
Lubrication	Labour	49	49	49	49	49	59	59	59	59	59	59	59	59	717
	Materials	70	70	70	70	70	70	70	70	70	70	70	70	70	910
Shop supplies		500	500	500	500	500	500	500	500	500	500	500	500	500	6500
Sub-total Maintenance		4697	4697	4697	4697	4697	5013	5013	5013	5013	5013	5013	5013	5013	63589

	1	2	3	4	5	6	7	8	9	10	11	12	13	TOTAL
TOTAL MILL OPERATING COSTS AND MAINTENANCE	21927	26602	24902	27507	30698	31299	33174	36489	37164	39089	36364	36914	34674	416803

ASSAY DEPARTMENT

CHIEF CHEMIST

4 TECHNICIANS

TOTAL: 5

ASSAY DEPARTMENT

BUDGET PERIOD: June 1st 1976 to May 31st 1977

ACCOUNT	LABOUR	MATERIALS	TOTAL
Labour materials, salaries, holiday pay	23,406	4,650	28,056
Outside analysis			1,000
Equipment maintenance		3,000	3,000
TOTAL ASSAY DEPARTMENT	23,406	7,650	32,050

ELECTRICAL DEPARTMENT

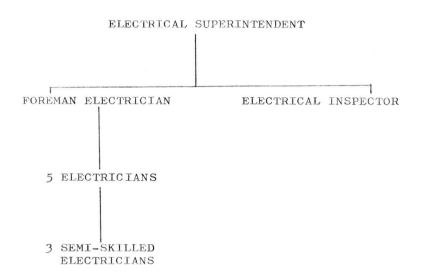

ELECTRICAL SUPERINTENDENT

FOREMAN ELECTRICIAN

ELECTRICAL INSPECTOR

5 ELECTRICIANS

3 SEMI-SKILLED
ELECTRICIANS

TOTAL : 11

ELECTRICAL DEPARTMENT

BUDGET PERIOD: June 1st 1976 to May 31st 1977

ACCOUNT	LABOUR	MATERIALS	TOTAL
Underground			
Locomotives	4,620	1,680	6,300
Shaft electrics	2,750	1,300	4,050
Generator	860	115	975
Loading pocket	860	560	1,420
Pumping	6,250	3,800	10,050
Cap lamps	2,230	560	2,790
Hoist	2,700	1,175	3,875
Compressors	1,360	430	1,790
Ventilation	660	210	870
Building maintenance	1,750	560	2,310
Sub-total (Underground)	24,040	10,390	34,430
Concentrator			
Crushing	1,560	460	2,020
Grinding	1,560	475	2,035
Flotation	1,250	400	1,650
Gravity	1,250	360	1,610
Thickening	960	250	1,210
Reagent	900	250	1,150
Building maintenance	1,250	380	1,630
Instrumentation	860	250	1,110
Process water	860	600	1,460
Sub-total (Concentrator)	10,450	3,425	13,875
General			
Miscellaneous surface	2,050	2,800	4,850
Yard lighting	860	185	1,045
Supervision	10,650		10,650
Workshop supplies		450	450
11 Kv network	2,050	680	2,730
Holiday pay	6,607		6,607
Sub-total (General)	19,060	4,115	23,175
TOTAL ELECTRICAL MAINTENANCE	56,707	17,930	74,637

SURFACE DEPARTMENT

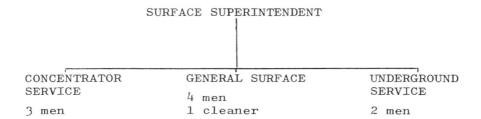

SURFACE SUPERINTENDENT

CONCENTRATOR SERVICE	GENERAL SURFACE	UNDERGROUND SERVICE
3 men	4 men / 1 cleaner	2 men

TOTAL: 11

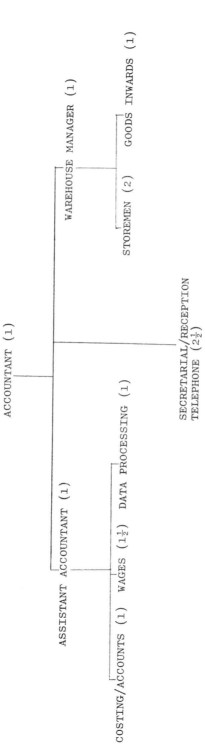

ADMINISTRATION DEPARTMENT

ACCOUNTANT (1)

ASSISTANT ACCOUNTANT (1)

COSTING/ACCOUNTS (1)   WAGES (1½)   DATA PROCESSING (1)

SECRETARIAL/RECEPTION
TELEPHONE (2½)

WAREHOUSE MANAGER (1)

STOREMEN (2)   GOODS INWARDS (1)

TOTAL: 13 Full-time
          2 Part-time

NOTE: Administration Budget also includes Manager, not shown above.

ADMINISTRATION AND GENERAL OVERHEADS

	Per Period - £			Total for Year - £		
	Labour	Materials	Total	Labour	Materials	Total
Management/Admin Salaries	3200		3200	41600		41600
Cleaning		80	80		1040	1040
NIGC		300	300		3900	3900
Security		1150	1150		14950	14950
Warehousing	1000	20	1020	13000	260	13260
Van Running Expenses		80	80		1040	1040
Personnel Recruitment		100	100		1300	1300
Insurances		8500	8500		110500	110500
Pensions		1000	1000		13000	13000
Stationery		500	500		6500	6500
Telephone/Telex		900	900		11700	11700
Postage		60	60		780	780
Carriage & Freight		300	300		3900	3900
Staff Car Expenses		100	100		1300	1300
Travel Expenses - H.O.		800	800		10400	10400
Travel Expenses - Internal		800	800		10400	10400
Mining Rentals		430	430		5590	5590
Legal Fees		200	200		2600	2600
Audit/Accountancy		250	250		3250	3250
Rates		6000	6000		78000	78000
Bank Charges		80	80		1040	1040
Computer Supplies/Maintenance		150	150		1950	1950
Management Fees		1400	1400		18200	18200
Housing Costs		100	100		1300	1300
Discounts		(100)	(100)		(1300)	(1300)
Miscellaneous		200	200		2600	2600
	4200	23400	27600	54600	304200	358800
Interest			28845			375000

Capital Expenditure:

New Van	1600
Misc.Off.Equip't	1000
Balance of Computer Programming Costs	2000
	4600

Chapter 9

Hanging On

A letter dated 31st of March 1978 from Steve Kay, the President of Cornwall Tin and Mining Corporation, was sent to the shareholders. In contrast to the previous year's report that had predicted a successful future for Mount Wellington, this letter briefly informed shareholders of the expected closure of the mine. The letter was as follows:

We have unfortunately unhappy news to present to you at this time.

During the year under review the mine in Cornwall continued to experience problems which prevented it from reaching its goal of 600 tons per day. The operating costs were around £3,200,000. Revenues from 330.6 tons of tin metal produced were only £1,427,183.

An extensive in-depth exploration program was initiated to establish ore reserves necessary to maintain a profitable operation. The program has now been completed and the results are such as to preclude a reasonable chance of bringing the operation to a profitable level. Considering the price of tin and all aspects of mining and milling this ore, it is anticipated that the property will be closed down shortly.

Steve Kay's letter was sent to shareholders four days before the next management meeting that was held at Wellington on the 4th of April. We attended the meeting to supposedly discuss the future of the mine, but looking back it would appear the future of the mine had already been decided. The meeting was chaired by the manager, Mike Davies, with Nigel Deacon, our accountant taking notes. Roy Morgan, Mill Manager; Rudi Reckhart, Mine Superintendent; and Chris Burton our Chief Geologist were all present. Mike Maynard asked me to join them. The mood was sombre and it was obvious that the agenda had previously been discussed and agreed by Mike Davies and Nigel. This exercise seemed to be about ensuring there were no loose ends that might embarrass the company. It was known for some time that Consolidated Goldfields wanted to pull out of Wheal Jane, but in doing so would take the responsibility for closing Wellington.

I was eventually able to inform Mike Davies that we had an agreement with SWEB (South Western Electricity Board) to maintain our power consumption over a five year period. This was to offset the cost of installing overhead lines, 11,000-volt switchgear and metering etcetera needed to bring electricity onto the site. There were also conditions attached to the planning approval granted by Cornwall County Council in 1972 for permission to develop the mine site. A bond of £250,000 was required by CCC to cover the costs to reinstate the land in the event of Wellington being abandoned. I got the impression that Nigel was aware of the planning conditions, but he was keeping quiet and only taking notes throughout the meeting.

The Department of Trade and Industry called the next meeting which was held at Wellington on Friday the 7th of April and once again, I was invited to attend. Unfortunately, if there was a written agenda, I did not have one and I can only refer to memory to give outline of the subject. It was clear that pressure was being applied by the government to keep the mines open. We were being sounded out, as no doubt were Consolidated Goldfield, to keep the mines working and to ensure that the pumps were not turned off. I think that the men from the DTI were desperate to get a positive result and assured us that funding would be made available to help support the project. Before the meeting closed, Mike Davies informed the DTI that he would continue these discussions the following week with his directors and would keep the pumps running.

Tom Huxley came over from Geneva on the 12th of April to be briefed before travelling to London for the meeting with the Department of Trade and Industry. He took Mike Davies, Nigel Deacon and Chris Burton with him. Meanwhile back at Wellington, we had no idea what was happening other than that Mike Davies would be meeting the DTI and then flying to Geneva to discuss the offers made to keep Wellington and Wheal Jane operating. When Mike Davies returned to Wellington on Friday the 21st of April he announced that the mine was to close and all but essential staff were to be given a weeks' notice. The mill was to be shut down following the ore bins being emptied, while underground equipment was to be brought to surface. We were under no illusions and considering the problems facing the mine, we had anticipated this latest development.

I was invited along with senior staff to attend a presentation by Cargill's PR/recruitment department that Tom Huxley had organised and sent over from the Tradex office in Geneva. We thought this was more about PR than finding jobs, although within this vast organisation they did offer some of us work. The work was within the electrical maintenance department of a salt mine, located not in Siberia, but on an island off the coast of Louisiana in the USA. We were shown a film of giant electric saws cutting blocks of salt to be loaded in barges and towed up the Mississippi to Canada for de-icing roads. I learned that the wages were good and housing was cheap, but there was no mention of alligators or hurricanes; and although the work sounded interesting, it was not something that I wanted to do.

Following the news that the mine was to close, I had the unhappy task of letting some of my electricians go. This was made easier by a few who volunteered to leave and the remainder, who had not been with us for many weeks, were already expecting to finish. I kept on Terry Bray, Geoff Bray, John Triniman, Peter Stewart and Mervyn Skinner for the short time until the responsibility of running the pumps was resolved. On Friday the 28th of April, I went out with the electricians to Carharrack Social Club for a farewell drink. By then, most of the workforce had left. The blow of losing their jobs was softened with a generous redundancy payment – Cargill valued their image of a family business and were determined to avoid any bad publicity.

I had been considering my future for some time and had come to the conclusion that I wanted to remain in a mining related activity. The conditions now seemed favourable to develop a number of ideas. The incidence of mining related subsidence was rising and the increasing number of shafts that needed securing presented an opportunity for a small specialist company to carry out consulting and contracting work. I discussed this with Derek James, our Mine Captain, who was most receptive to the idea. The recent exploration programme which he had led with Dave Kneebone had logged a considerable amount of interesting information. Although they had failed to find sufficient ore reserves to feed the Wellington Mill, there were strong indications that a number of tin deposits could be viable if worked with a minimum of overheads. There were a number of treatment plants that would buy the ore, and further savings could be made with little or no pumping costs. A surplus of skilled workers plus cheap material and equipment were all available. I felt that this opportunity was too good to miss, and started to target people who I thought would have similar ambitions and the right mix of skills, and who might be willing to join us in forming a company. Dave Kneebone had a wealth of local knowledge and mining experience and gradually came around to the idea. Finally, I invited Tim Warner, who was Chief Surveyor and a highly qualified Mine Engineer, to join us; but he was reluctant to give us an answer and wanted time to think about it. On the day it was announced Wellington was to close, we got together and after further discussion I pushed to go ahead with the idea and suggested we name the new company "Cornwall Mining Services."

After deciding to form Cornwall Mining Services, we met with Mike Davies to explain our intentions. He offered to help in any way he could and said he would pass our information on to Tom Huxley. The next day I went with Derek to meet Mr Beauchamp to discuss the possibility of opening one of the Wheal Squire shafts in Trevince Woods. Meanwhile, the seemingly frantic round of meetings with the Department of Trade and Industry continued and the order to stop the pumps was again postponed. Before leaving for London with Nigel Deacon and Mike Maynard for another meeting with the DTI, Mike Davies asked Derek if we would plug two shafts on United Downs. This was our first job, and it encouraged us to press on and get established as a business. We registered as a partnership with Smith and Girdlestone, our accountants, on the 1st May 1978, but later dissolved the partnership and started trading as a limited company on 1st August.

On the 3rd of May, miners from Mount Wellington and Wheal Jane organised a march from Paddington Station to Westminster. It was a proud moment to see the banners and flags waving along the three mile route to Westminster, where they were met by David Penhaligon, Liberal Democrat Member of Parliament for Truro. It was noted how well behaved the marchers were during the hour long walk, which I am sure helped the cause. Mr Penhaligon, a true champion of Cornwall, addressed the House of Commons on Thursday the 11th of May with Mr Williams, the Minister of State, Department of Industry, making an encouraging reply. The following is a transcript of the speech.

This is the story of two tin mines in my constituency and some 750 jobs. The background is that in 1971 the Consolidated Gold Fields Company opened a mine not many miles from the village where I live. In 1974 a company called the Cornwall Tin and Mining Company opened one no further than a mile from the first mine, called Mount Wellington. Between them they provided some 750 jobs. In our area they were good and well-paid jobs. They were welcome and represented the whole hope in an area where unemployment is nearly endemic. The last figures I saw gave the average unemployment for my County as 11 percent; for men it is over 14 per cent.

I have elicited that there is not a labour exchange within 40 miles of Chacewater, the village nearest these mines, which has today a male unemployment rate of less than 10 percent. In this area there simply are no other jobs. There is certainly not a single job on offer which pays anything like the national average wage.

My involvement with this matter started about a week or so before the first mine announced its closure when certain things I heard made me put down parliamentary Questions to find out what was happening and whether the Government knew what was happening at the Mount Wellington mine. Eventually there was a meeting in Zurich where the directors announced that the mine was to close.

No more than two or three days later the Consolidated Gold Fields company made a similar announcement that its mine also was to close. The reason given at the time by Consolidated Gold Fields was that the water which had undoubtedly been a substantial problem in Mount Wellington, pouring in at some 8 million gallons a day, would follow the laws of gravity and quickly invade its mine. The cost of pumping this water out was understood to be £500,000 a year.

I must admit that it was this more than anything else which raised by suspicions and made me decide to launch a major attack in this place to find out what was happening.

There is no doubt that Consolidated Gold could have applied for temporary employment subsidy, and, virtually at the drop of a hat, received some £420,000 – at an annual rate. It would have given those in the locality some time to judge the matter and negotiate matters instead of looking down a gun barrel, as we have been doing ever since this announcement was made.

Indeed, Consolidated Gold was recruiting labour up to two weeks before its closure and I have long suspected – we shall probably never know – that the truth is that the company has been running this mine for some seven years with considerable managerial difficulties. It has had four or five managers since I have been the Member for Truro.

It is difficult to know whether mining is likely to be profitable; one never knows exactly what one will get until the mineral is dug out. Besides that, the pound is oscillating. But, for all that, last year some £6.8 million worth of minerals were produced – 950 tons of tin, 3,300 tons of copper, 3,250 tons of zinc and just over 1.4 tons of silver. The value of this on the metal exchange was nearly £7 million. Besides that, it must be remembered that Mount Wellington was making its own contribution as well. These mines make a significant balance of payments contribution, especially bearing in mind the number of people involved.

They have some strategic significance, too, as Cornwall has Europe's only supply of tin.

The absolutely horrifying secondary effects hardly need quantifying. The companies used outside contractors for all the painting, surface digging and building operations. They bought some £1½ million worth of supplies locally. The men themselves had a purchasing power of £2 million to £3 million.

The local reaction was swift and strong. Some 600 miners and their families came to London. They announced that they were prepared to give up next year's increment in pay—a substantial offer in these days of inflation.

The Cornwall County Council, which is not famous for throwing away money, quickly offered some £20,000 to enable the pumps to be run for a more substantial period while the problem could be studied sensibly. No wonder: in my village, if these mines totally collapse, I shall have 40 percent male unemployment; in the villages of Threemilestone, Crofty and St. Day the situation will be little better. The issue has not been off the local radio and television screens since it was first announced.

Cornwall has become cynical about the treatment given by the Government to its problems. Large sums of money are going to the steel and car industries. We argue that our problems are no different. This is a basic industry providing basic employment.

We hope that our treatment will be different on this occasion. Certainly, I must admit that the Minister has kept me extremely well informed since this saga started. I believe that on this occasion the Government are prepared and willing to give help. I know that they are now negotiating with other parties. There are problems of confidence in disclosing exactly what is happening and during the period of negotiation it is an absolute impossibility to give a blow-by-blow account publicly.

I should like some assurances from the Minister making it clear to people in my part of the country that the local appearance that these mines are lost is not the case, and that there is real and genuine help on the way. One rescue plan mentioned is that the shafts that run from Wellington towards Wheal Jane should be plugged, and that some extra pumps should be installed in Wheal Jane to hold back the water that is bound still to leak. Obviously, there would be some ancillary piping and this would cost a capital sum of some £600,000, including a considerable contingency in case some of the estimates have gone wrong. The actual operating cost increase in Wheal Jane is estimated at £100,000.

Facts in this case have been difficult to elicit, but as I understand it – and I have been assured on this point by some of those who work for the company – in the quarter before this terrible thing happened to my county the company was making a positive cash flow. Basically the company has developed and was ready to take the ore from what is called the ninth level in that mine. It had been driving a shaft down to the fifteenth level and had in fact reached a depth of 1,300 ft.

There is now considerable anguish in the area, as the negotiations go on behind closed doors, about the company's action in dismantling some of the facilities underground. There is a suspicion that the rescue operation is getting more difficult by the hour. There is no doubt that some substantial sums of money will be required. The company, Consolidated Gold Fields, negotiated, in June 1976, a loan of £2.5 million I have never been clear why that loan was not taken up, but it was negotiated and has never been used.

Let me warn the Minister that the alternative will be the loss of 700 or even 1,500 jobs. The Department of Employment officials, in an interview, told me that if the mines closed, they might be prepared to use the area for a special temporary employment subsidy scheme. One can imagine the cost and the loss of income tax, rates and national insurance contributions.

Headgear extension to accommodate new 5 ton skips.

Cage arriving at the No.7 Level.

7 Level conveyor from the ore pass to the loading pocket in the shaft.

7 Level electrical sub-station: 3300 Volt DOL vacuum contactors for the 300hp pump motors.

No. 1 pump station, 7 Level.

No. 2 pump station, 7 Level.

The escape way provided a safe route to surface via stopes in the event the shaft was unable to be used. This was accepted by the Mines & Quarry Inspectorate to enable the mine to operate with only one shaft.

Last of the electricians to finish on 19th May: Geoff Bray, Terry Bray, Mervyn Skinner, Peter Stewart, John Triniman and the Author.

Above all, there is the fear of living in an area with 40 percent unemployment and of being defeated and demoralised. Because of Cornwall's history, mining is more important than the number of jobs involved. There is all the mythology of mining – "Poldark" and the other series of which people are aware – and these mines represented in my area, a feeling that there would be growth in employment. The mines were new and we welcomed the general upturn in the growth of the Cornish mineral industry.

If nothing is done about these mines, I believe that the hope of any outside investment in Cornwall is finished. There will be no hope of persuading any of the large mining corporations to come to my county. The Government, despite my opposition, have saved a considerable amount of money by scrapping regional development grants for the mining industry in development areas. Perhaps some of that money could be used to assist my County?

I wish to put a number of questions to the Minister. Where do we stand in regard to pumping arrangements? I take the view that we are still fighting this battle and stand a reasonable chance of winning so long as the pumps are kept running. Will the Minister let my constituents know precisely what are the future pumping arrangements? How hard are the Government trying to rescue the position? Will he give some idea of the progress of negotiations? I recognise the difficulties, but what progress has been made in real terms?

Will the Minister also say what will happen if the negotiations with interested parties break down? What will the Government's attitude be in that event? Will they keep the pumps going for a period while some other party may be interested in the operation? The important question to which my constituents would like an answer is, "When will a decision be known?"

It is not difficult to realise the tragedy that hits a family in such an area when relatively well-paid employment is lost. One can imagine a family's feelings when its income is cut off. In the village of Threemilestone, scores of workers who have taken on mortgages in the last 12 or 18 months are now wondering where they stand. They are looking to the Government because they realise that there is nobody else who can give the guidance and assistance required to rescue this mining operation. I look forward with great interest to hearing the Minister's reply.

The Minister of State, Department of Industry (Alan Williams)
I wish to congratulate the Hon. Member for Truro (Mr. Penhaligon) on the way in which he has represented his constituents' interests. I know that he more than any other Member has ensured that he has kept in touch with

developments and has put forward any suggestion which he felt contained a possibility of saving jobs.

I share his feelings about the plight of constituents and the difficulties that would be caused in an area such as his constituency if all these jobs were lost. He can be assured by a Welshman who has seen coal mines disappear in so many parts of my own country that we fully appreciate not just the traumatic shock of losing an occupation—which is often a family occupation, involving grandfathers, fathers and sons—but the effect on the community in which that particular industry is based.

Because I understand the feelings that must prevail in the Hon. Gentleman's area, I suppose that I have spent more time on this issue since the situation hit us than on any other—and the Hon. Gentleman is aware that my Department is not short of issues that demand Ministers' time. Everything has been accelerated by the decision of the Mount Wellington owners to close their operations. As the hon. Gentleman said, they are pumping out 7 million gallons of water a day. After a short while, when that water reaches the higher levels, it goes through old workings and begins to pour into the Wheal Jane mine, which is itself already pumping 4½ million gallons a day.

The Hon. Gentleman rightly indicated that what has happened to the world price of tin, but in particular what has happened in terms of the quality and quantity of tin that has been extracted from the Mount Wellington mine, dictated the decisions of that firm. Because of the link between the pumping operations, the decision of the one firm inevitably precipitated certain decisions for the Wheal Jane operation.

As soon as we were told that the two firms were contemplating closure we entered into discussions with them to try to establish any organisation which would give a chance of survival and viability for the two mines or for either mine. We were willing to support either of the firms or both, or one of the mines or both. There was virtually no option we were unwilling to look at, except the possibility of 100 percent Government funding.

I am sure that most hon. Members will accept that it is very difficult for the Department to accept an offer which suggests that the Government pick up all the bills and that should there eventually be any profit someone else takes it but retains the right to close the operation at any time suitable to him. This would not give security to the workers of Cornwall, because they would still have the threat hanging over their heads.

Therefore, far from the Government's refusing financial support, as reported in some newspapers, and even on the BBC this morning, we have made it clear that financial support is available. As the Hon. Gentleman pointed out,

£400,000 a year of temporary employment subsidy could be available in the case of one mine alone. There is assistance available under Section 7 of the Industry Act. But it is a requirement that in giving that assistance we give it for a project that eventually will become viable. One of our difficulties has been that the two companies currently operating have each reached the conclusion in relation to their own operation that it is non-viable in its present form.

This does not preclude – and this is what we are pursuing – the possibility of alternative methods of working. It does not preclude the possibility of its being saved by other owners. As the Hon. Gentleman rightly suggested, it is very important to Government to observe confidentiality. Indeed, we have had specific requests from the parties that we are negotiating with that we do not mention their names. I can understand that, and we must respect their wishes.

The negotiations are still continuing. The companies are having evaluation work done, assessing the prospects of the mine. I do not want to hold out false hopes at this stage, but the fact that we are all still working at the matter at least indicates that there is some hope, though I do not pretend that it is great hope.

It has been suggested that one could flood the old workings of the Mount Wellington mine, but it has been made clear that this is not a guaranteed solution. I believe that it is not unfair to say that Consolidated Gold, for example, is far from convinced that that would be a successful formula, if the flooding worked, there would be a £650,000 initial cost, as compared with a running cost of £500,000 a year for the pumping operations.

Up to now, we have not ruled out either solution. We have indicated that we are willing to finance the pumping operation in the Mount Wellington unit certainly for another week . I made an offer to finance it for a month. It is unfair to say that the offer was turned down, but Consolidated Gold felt that it would prefer to finance the first week. It was its decision, not ours. I have assured the parties to the negotiations that it is our intention to try to keep pumping operations going while there is a chance of negotiations being meaningful and successful.

I have therefore committed the Department to financing another week's pumping in the Mount Wellington unit, and the Cornwall County Council has generously indicated that it will finance the pumping operations for the Wheal Jane unit. So the flooding hazard at least will not precipitate the collapse of the negotiations.

There have been suggestions – the Hon. Gentleman has heard the rumours

– that certain items were being removed from the Wheal Jane mine which would make it virtually impossible for that mine to reopen, certainly in the short term. I pass on the assurance that we have received. We have been assured by Consolidated Gold that it has no intention of removing essential equipment from the mine while there is a possibility of a successful conclusion to the negotiations.

Indeed, only today, as a result of the hon. Gentleman's discussion with me, I sent my regional industrial director to the mine to see for himself rather than just rely on reports. He discussed the situation with the local management. We have had an assurance that nothing critical to the future of the mine will be removed and also that nothing critical to its future has been removed.

The Government remain willing to help. Government finance is available, but it has to be for realistic projects. It has to be on the basis of a project that offers the possibility of viability. I would not expect conclusions within a matter of days. I think that the type of negotiations going on will certainly take most of next week because a considerable amount of evaluation and financial negotiation and calculating has to be undertaken. But I will, as far as confidentiality permits me, keep the hon. Gentleman informed. As he knows, I am flying to America tomorrow, but I have left instructions that I am to be kept informed of all developments while I am away, and I will ensure that the hon. Gentleman has all the information that we can give him during the next week.

Mr Penhaligon

I thank the Minister of State for that reply. Can he say a few words about the guarantee of viability? There are so many moving ends in a tin mine that I suspect that one decides whether it will make a profit or loss before one does the accounts. One does not know what is round the corner. What does the right hon. Gentleman mean by "guarantee of viability"? Certainly, a viable situation ought to be credible. But what does "guarantee" mean in this rather unusual context?

Mr. Williams

That is a fair point. Obviously, in something like mining one can never have absolute guarantees, because one only needs to get one rift and one has lost one's chances of viability.

When a project is put to us, we assess it to see whether there is a reasonable prospect of viability being achieved, not necessarily in the first year. We usually look at about a three-year period to see whether viability could reasonably be attained on the basis of that project within about three years.

If it could, we would then feel that it met the criteria which Government apply.

The last of the electricians were laid off on the 19th of May 1978. I had come full circle from where I had started in October 1973 when we were waiting for finance to start the mine. It had been a roller-coaster ride, but now I was being asked to remain with the mine to fulfil statutory requirements and take responsibility of the electrical installation. There was still no news, but as long as the pumps were kept running, there was still hope that Wheal Jane would remain open.

FINAL SHAREHOLDERS' REPORT

CORNWALL TIN & MINING CORPORATION

President's Letter

March 31, 1978

To the Shareholders,
Cornwall Tin & Mining Corporation

We have unfortunately unhappy news to present to you at this time.

During the year under review the mine in Cornwall continued to experience problems which prevented it from reaching its goal of 600 tons per day. The grade of ore both mined and recovered was disappointing.

Operating costs were around £3,200,000. Revenues from 330.6 tons of tin metal produced were only £1,427,183.

An extensive in-depth exploration program was initiated to establish ore reserves necessary to maintain a profitable operation. This program has now been completed and the results are such as to preclude a reasonable chance of bringing the operation to a profitable level. Considering the price of tin and all aspects of mining and milling this ore, it is anticipated that the property will be closed down shortly.

However, there is some good news, in the last year the company has acquired an 8% working interest in a very promising uranium exploration program in Nova Scotia, Canada. Our interest extends over some 1000 square miles on which a number of encouraging uranium discoveries have been made. Assay values of up to 46 pounds U_3O_8 have been returned from leached outcrop. We are hoping to discover that there will be an improvement in grade with depth.

A program budgeted at $500,000 will be conducted this spring which will include diamond drilling to test for commercial concentrations of uranium.

The following pages contain the financial statements of the Company as of August 31st, 1977. These statements were prepared before the disappointing news regarding the mine was known.

Respectfully submitted
    On behalf of the Board of Directors

Stephen Kay
President

Chapter 10

A False Beginning

It was clear that Consolidated Goldfields were no longer prepared to continue with the losses incurred in operating Wheal Jane and, with no possibility of future profits, were determined to close the mine. It was said that the capital cost to bring Wheal Jane into production was over £6m, and they only made a profit for one out of seven years of operating. Numerous managers had come and gone attempting to improve efficiency, but generally had failed. It was now understood that Wheal Jane and Wellington could no longer be run as separate concerns. It would take a joint effort to keep the workings clear of the tremendous flows of water which threatened to flood the mines. It was a similar situation that faced Cargill-Tradex with their jointly financed Cornwall Tin and Mining Limited, the company that owned 51% of Mount Wellington. The remaining 49% was owned by Cornwall Tin and Mining Corporation, which was registered with the Securities and Exchange Commission, Washington DC and was a mix of company and private shareholders. Tradex did not include their junior partners in their talks with the Department of Trade and Industry, and wanted to close Wellington without incurring the bad publicity that would follow their actions. With over £4.2m spent in setting up Wellington and a further £3.2m in operating costs, the total investment would have been in the order of £7.5m. The income from the sale of tin would have been in the order of £2m, so with little or no immediate reserves of ore it would be impossible to continue without incurring huge losses. Any further thoughts that Tradex may have had to diversify into mining would now be abandoned.

By the end of May, the government was believed to have found the company to take over the task of operating Wheal Jane. It was said that it took considerable arm-twisting and financial inducement to persuade RTZ, an Anglo-Australian Conglomerate and the world's second largest mining company, to take over Wheal Jane. This came as a great relief to all the workforce plus local suppliers and businesses providing services to the mines. Consolidated Goldfields and Cornwall Tin and Mining Limited would also have been relieved, although for different reasons.

Now that RTZ would be taking over the responsibility of the pumping, Tom Huxley could focus on the disposal of the concentrator and associated infrastructure. Nigel Deacon continued to stay on top of the accounts and tying up loose ends. Roy Morgan was retained to keep the concentrator in good order in the event a buyer could be found. I was asked to stay to comply with the statutory requirement to maintain the electrical infrastructure and to apportion the meter reading between our power consumption and that of RTZ; of course, RTZ had the lion's share due to the pumping costs.

Wheal Jane was now preparing to take over the pumping duties and were sending its maintenance engineers to Wellington. Their field of responsibilities included underground pumping, the winder and the compressors. They also took over the pump-men, winder drivers, banksmen, landers and on-setters (in coal pit bottoms only). By now, my workload had shrunk to a daily routine of inspecting the electrical infrastructure around the site. I occupied the rest of my time promoting the interests of Cornwall Mining Services. I sent numerous letters to publicise the business and to offer our services. We discussed the possibilities of setting up and running a mine museum with underground guided tours. Although we considered this to have little chance of success, we proceeded with the next step towards developing the Mount Wellington Mine Museum. I applied to Carrick District Council for outline planning consent for change of use from Mine Office to Mine Museum. Next, I went to see Nigel Deacon to discuss our plans and get his reaction. The meeting was brief as Nigel said it was unlikely the company would agree to our proposal, as they wished to sell the site as a going concern. We now had no alternative but to withdraw the planning application.

It was rumoured that Steve Kay was threatening action as the original (but now minority) shareholders were unhappy with the disposal of the mine. They thought they were entitled to a percentage share of the proceeds from the sale of Mount Wellington. This did not sit well with Tradex as they had poured money into keeping the mine going virtually all the time it had operated. It seemed that Tom Huxley and Nigel Deacon were determined to keep Steve Kay from further involvement in any negotiations concerning Mount Wellington.

Many years later, I was surprised to read that the mine had gone into receivership and was then sold by the administrators of Cornwall Tin and Mining Limited to a Falmouth scrap dealer. I cannot believe that this happened and can only surmise that this was a ploy to throw Steve Kay off the scent that a major company was in discussion over the future of the mine. Tom Huxley would not want Steve Kay involved in any claims that would jeopardise talks with prospective buyers.

At the time, we were oblivious to any behind the scenes dispute and I was happy to bank my redundancy cheque and continue receiving a salary from Cornwall Tin and Mining Limited. Soon after Cornwall Mining Services withdrew proposals for a Mine Museum, we began to hear that Hydraulic Tin had been bought out. This was a small, privately owned tin processing plant located in the Carnon Valley below Wellington. It was managed by Neville Ebsworth who had previously been the General Manager at South Crofty. Despite a somewhat Heath-Robinson appearance, typical of Cornish innovation, this was a very efficient, well run enterprise – in part due to the previous manager, Richard Mozley. Richard left Hydraulic Tin to start his own business and spent most of his working life inventing and developing machinery and equipment for the recovery of very fine tin. His first machine, installed at Geevor, was known as the Mozley Table and was designed to replace the round frames and vanners which had previously been used in Cornish mines. The table was further developed by Bartles (Carn Brea) Ltd. and sold as the Bartles-Mozley Concentrator; they were used to great effect at South Crofty, Wheal Jane and Mount Wellington. Richard Mozley has been described as one of the greatest inventors of mineral processing equipment. His machines for the recovery of very fine minerals have been installed in concentrating plants all over the world.

Neville's right hand man was Owen Champion who ran the mill with a handful of key workers. Owen was old school and what he didn't know about tin was not worth knowing. I had the impression he could tell you the size of every nut and bolt in the mill, where it was located and who had fitted it. One of his many skills was the ancient method to evaluate tin ore, known as vanning.

For many years, Hydraulic Tin had been trucking in dump material and tailings from old mines to their treatment plant at Bissoe. It was very important to understand the overall costs of this activity as profit margins were tight. The traditional and sometimes the only method used to evaluate the tin found on dumps was by vanning, carried out by the assayer using a Cornish Vanning Shovel. The shovel was specialised and the most important tool the prospector or tin-streamer had. But it was the way it was used and subsequent evaluation which made the difference between profit and loss. Ultimately, the Transport Manager, Terry Nicholls, was responsible for the removal of dump or tailings back to Bissoe, leaving the site tidy. His estimated cost for this work would be used in the future negotiation to acquire the dump. I wondered if Billiton would understand all of this tradition in the weeks ahead when inevitable changes would be made.

The company that bought Hydraulic Tin was at that time the little-known Billiton Minerals. Billiton was founded in 1860 when its articles of association was approved by a meeting of shareholders in The Hague, Netherlands. The company then acquired the mineral rights of Billiton and Bangka, two islands off the eastern coast of Sumatra. Billiton initially set up tin and lead smelting in the Netherlands and then followed up with bauxite mining in Indonesia and Surinam in South America. In 1970, Royal Dutch Shell acquired Billiton and it became their mining and exploration division until it was demerged in 1994. In 2007, Billiton made an attempt to take over RTZ but the offer was rejected on the grounds the share deal undervalued the company. Billiton abandoned further attempts to take over RTZ due to global recession. Billiton, having evolved after many acquisitions and mergers, is now known as BHP and is the largest mining company in the world.

We knew that Billiton were in talks with Tradex towards the end of 1978, but I was puzzled about their intentions regarding Mount Wellington. After failing to find an ore reserve to sustain a 600 ton per day mill, how would Billiton be able to achieve this? I was to learn a bit more when I met with Steve Braithwaite, a mining engineer sent by Billiton to ensure there was a smooth transition for the takeover of the mill and majority of the surface infrastructure. Steve had contacted me during the first week of the new year 1979 to set up a meeting with SWEB to discuss electrical supply. I arranged the meeting for Thursday 11th January with Barry Parker, Steve Braithwaite and myself in attendance. The meeting was a general interest discussion to give Steve an idea of available services. Steve was a very likeable, down to earth character who confessed he much preferred underground hard rock mining to reclaiming surface mineral deposits – it was a sentiment I shared. A brief statement of the 1st of February announced delays to the project and purchase of Mount Wellington Mine. On the 18th of February, I met two mechanical engineers who were sent over from The Hague to carry out inspections and survey the mill equipment.

Neville Ebsworth contacted me on the 2nd of March and I was surprised when he offered me a job with Billiton. He wanted my personal details so accounts could include me on the payroll. My starting date was planned for the 12th of March. It was noticeable that a few of the recently appointed staff members were beginning to arrive at Wellington to take up their duties. I spent three days with Vim Kuh, Billiton's Chief Electrical Engineer, who came over from The Hague to inspect the electrical installation. We included a visit to Hydraulic Tin and I introduced him to Neville and to Owen Champion, who gave us a conducted tour of the plant. Vim was a keen photographer and was delighted to have the contrast of Wellington and Bissoe Mills as subjects. He wanted something of interest to show back at Head Office. We found out later that Vim's camera skills were in demand as his photos were often used in Billiton's monthly magazine. His photos of Wellington and Bissoe looked very professional.

A number of portacabins had been set up at Bissoe to provide office accommodation for the extra staff that had been hired in preparation to start the new project. Steve Braithwaite was now using Bissoe as his base and he worked from one of the portacabins. I arranged to meet Terry and Steve and hoped Steve would explain the overall idea behind the project. Billiton had been developing their expertise in the recovery of very fine low grade tin and the first phase of their project was to treat the Wheal Maid Tailings. It was now necessary to plan for the most economical method to transport the tailings from Wheal Maid to Mount Wellington. I would prepare costing to provide electrical power for a slurry pump and agitator. Steve thought to use dumper trucks, but Terry could see too many problems and the idea was dropped. It was important to ensure the distribution of tin was kept at a fairly even value; to help achieve this, the tailings would be taken from various locations in the dam. It would then be dug out and taken to a holding tank and passed over a screen that removed rock, stones and undesirable material likely to block the pump.

Steve thought the best method would be a dragline. He had used them in the past and was familiar with the Ruston Bucyrus. A dragline was eventually bought despite costing over £70,000. I thought this was extravagant, particularly as we had to virtually account for every penny that was spent over the past few years. I soon found I would have to get used to the idea of big spending. I was now able to plan for the tailings project. The Wellington site was fortunately the nearest source of power which was located approximately one mile to the west of Wheal Maid. The supply to Wheal Maid would be by underground cable fed from our 11kV ring main system and therefore would not require to be separately metered. I rounded up enough men and with the help of South Western Electricity Board's equipment, rollers etc. we managed to get the cable installed. I used SWEB for the 11kV cable joints to connect to the 11kV switch gear and a 11kV–415V transformer located at the slurrifier site. This gave us the simple and most cost-effective method to provide power for the agitator and slurry pump, etcetera.

By May, most of the staff members were recruited and were taking up their duties. The most notable was Conrad Edwards, whose job title was Managing Director. His family business was a small specialist lead smelting works located in the Midlands, which had been taken over by Billiton Minerals. His reputation of being a skilled negotiator was now going to be put to good use by Billiton. The Technical Manager was Dick Rabelink, who had been employed for his experience as a Metallurgical Engineer. He brought with him Frans Maas, a less experienced mechanical engineer who had previously worked at a bauxite mine in Surinam, South America. The other senior staff to join us made the short journey across the Carnon Valley from Wheal Jane and were Simon Camm and Eric Crowther. Simon was appointed as our Chief Geologist and Eric was our Chief Chemist. Simon later studied Cornish gold deposits and was the author of *Geology and Landscape of Cornwall and Isles of Scilly*, plus *Gold in the Counties of Devon and Cornwall*.

To welcome the new management, Roy Morgan and his wife laid on a sumptuous buffet. I had not realised the number of staff that were now employed and it was difficult for all of us to squeeze into the office. After Roy made his welcome speech, Conrad Edwards took over to introduce the senior staff. Then it was left to Dick Rabelink to explain Billiton's presence in Cornwall and their involvement with Bissoe and Wellington. Dick said that he and Billiton had been working on the recovery of low-grade tin deposits and the re-treatment of tailings. When the mill at Wellington became available it was an ideal situation to test and run through the practicalities of the process. I wondered where they would find sufficient ore reserves to supply a 600 tonne per day mill. That thought was soon answered when Dick continued explaining the project. The plan was to feed the Wellington Mill with tailings from Wheal Maid. The exercise was to get the mill up and running ready for the next phase of the project, which was to recover tin from Restronguet Creek. The Carnon River had from time immemorial carried the debris and waste from the mining parish of Gwennap that flowed into Restronguet and silted up the creek. Using modern methods and technology, Billiton believed that the millions of tons of mud that filled the creek contained a viable reserve of recoverable tin.

Soon after Dick Rabelink started at Wellington, he introduced weekly technical meetings. This gave me an opportunity to declare a possible conflict of interest, which Neville Ebsworth was aware of as he had recently asked Cornwall Mining Services to carry out a number of jobs for Hydraulic Tin. However, I wanted Dick to know first-hand that I was a director of Cornwall Mining Services and did not wish to influence matters that might cause problems. He did not think this would be an issue and I, for my part, could not see it would interfere with my work at Billiton.

Before I joined Billiton, Cornwall Mining Services had been awarded a contract to reopen the small Ladyswell Mine on the outskirts of Cloniklity, located approximately one hours' drive south west of Cork in Ireland. The mine had produced barite and was jointly owned by a local consortium and Milchen Incorporation, an American company. The Irish manager had contacted us after reading our advert in the *Mining Journal*. Tim Warner and myself flew to Cork from Plymouth to meet the Irish manager and an American mining engineer, who was in charge of the project. They wanted us to supply men to help them get the mine into production and to refurbish and install a small electric hoist, compressor and pumps. Returning to Cornwall, Tim priced for the miners and I submitted my estimate for an electrician and mechanical fitter plus my fees for a week out there to finish off and commission the hoist. We found the compressor motor needed rewinding and was sent to Bandon for a complete overhaul. I managed to employ Terry Bray as site electrician There was an excellent service available on weekends and I was able to get a flight on a Friday leaving Plymouth around 6.00pm, arriving in Cork two hours later. I would be met at the airport and driven to the Emmet Hotel on the outskirts of Cloniklity. After supper, I had enough time to catch up on the news and sample some fine Irish beers. Derek James was running the project and was ably assisted by two former Wellington shift bosses, Tiny Marsh and Peter Thomas. I then had a full day to complete my work, leaving Cloniklity the next day at 10.30am to get home Sunday evening around 5.30pm. This was all done before being offered a job with Billiton. The Irish contract came to an end in July 1980 and provided us with a perfect start to the business. At its peak, we had 26 men working in Ireland and the contract was worth approximately £292,000 which helped us establish the business.

At Wellington there were modifications to the mill that included the installation of extra flotation cells, and alterations to the electrical supply for process pumping from County Adit and for SWEB to change the metering to separate the Wheal

Jane power supply. A shower block was built at Bissoe and manpower steadily increased throughout all departments, as new positions were created to manage the diversification of jobs. One interesting appointment was that of Dave the boatman, who was responsible for a Zodiac inflatable with outboard motor that he used for taking out samplers and our environmental people to recover water quality, etcetera. I was fortunate to be added to Dave's long list for an afternoon's boat trip around the creek. There were also way-leave officers to identify owners of property along the foreshore of the Creek. That proved the easy part compared with the difficulties establishing mineral rights and ownership. A young engineer, Chandra Derve, was an expert on tailing dam design and construction and was responsible for tailings disposal.

The engineering department also expanded, with Frans Maas employing key workers to take charge of the mechanical maintenance. These included Terry Carter, a well-known member of the Troon sporting family, one of the few players who gained county honours playing both cricket and rugby for Cornwall. His supervisory and engineering skills were gained working at Holman's. Conrad Bell, who had worked as a draughtsman at Bartles (Carn Brea) Ltd, was taken on and being a perfectionist brought his own drawing board with him. Frans also employed Brian Brokenshire as his maintenance clerk. Meanwhile, I brought Geoff Bray back to continue with his old job as a foreman electrician. Even I was given another job when Conrad Edwards called me up to his office to tell me that managing directors in charge of Billiton companies were being advised to appoint Energy Managers, but the most amusing and the briefest appointment made the front page of the Billiton Magazine. The ground workers that laid the pipeline from Wellington to Wheal Maid Tailings Dam were finding it difficult to get the pipes through a tricky section. The rough, uneven terrain ruled out the use of motorised vehicles, so one of the crew suggested using a shire horse. A few days later, a shire horse arrived on site ready for work. This was too good a photo shoot to miss, so pictures of "Dobbin" dragging lengths of pipe through thick undergrowth were sent to Head Quarters in The Hague.

We still experienced problems in the mill and expenditure must have been rising at an alarming rate. We seemed to want for nothing, even to the extent of being provided with several four-wheel-drive Daihatsus to make it easier to visit the outlying sites at Wheal Maid, Restronguet, etcetera. These proved very popular, so much so that when you really needed one, they had all been booked out. Senior staff were given company cars. Roy Morgan had an unfortunate incident with his week-old Ford Escort during a very stormy night. He had parked in his usual spot next to his concrete block boundary wall and next morning he discovered the wall had collapsed on the car during the night. He managed to eventually get into work with the passenger side caved in, so from then it was known as Roy's banana car.

We were all treated to various courses, and those who had access to the ve-

Office Staff prepared to march on London to petition the Government: L – R Roger Scoley, Sue, Mary, John, Maddy, Margaret and Joanne.

hicle pool were obliged to have four-wheel-drive training. This instructor was Colin Dennis, whose electronics skills were employed working on process controls and instrumentation at Hydraulic Tin. His previous work in the motor trade was thought to be sufficient to organise the training. Conrad Edwards suggested it would be a good idea if I were to attend a two-day Energy Management course, which was being held at Shell Transport and Trading Centre. My thoughts were shared with many of the participants, who agreed that energy management should be a natural consideration for mechanical and electrical engineers in which to design, install and operate equipment as efficiently as possible. I noticed that South Crofty were advertising in the local press for an Energy Manager at this time, but I'm not sure if the vacancy was filled.

At the start of 1981, Matthew Hall Ortech were brought in for talks to improve tin recovery and to prepare the mill to treat the Restronguet Creek material. Dick

Dick Evans, last shift. Cornwall Tin and Mining Ltd cease working on Friday 28th April 1978.

Mining equipment brought to surface: battery locos and loading shovels.

Rabelink briefly mentioned he was considering an electric powered dredge with trailing cables to connect at various substations along the foreshore. This idea was to reduce sound levels. I was asked to prepare costs for trailing cables. BICC could supply a Type 321 95mm2 pliable armoured cable, which for a 500 metre length cost a staggering £39,000 and weighed approximately 7 tonnes – that thought was put on the back-burner.

With the arrival of new management at Wheal Jane, a major project was started to renovate the County Adit. This work would allow the free drainage of water into the Carnon River rather than overflowing into the deep mine working, where it had to be pumped out at considerable cost. Included in this major undertaking was the construction of a new portal and tunnel to bypass the old twin portals of the County Adit. Directing this work was Mike Shipp, the very experienced Chief Surveyor at Wheal Jane. The water that flowed from the County Adit was pumped up to the mill, and any disruption to this supply would shut the mill down. Mike was aware of how important it was to maintain the supply and did his utmost to prevent any unnecessary stoppages.

Discussions between Dick Rabelink and Harry Barlow from Matthew Hall Ortech continued throughout February, March and April, but we had little or no feedback. This was so different to the approach of Kilborn Engineering when they had designed and constructed the mill six years previously. Then at least we had known what was going on. It was decided that a new office block was needed and Conrad Edwards called in Ted Price to discuss design and specifications – G. Thomas were to be subcontractors.

I was preparing the monthly energy report when Conrad Edwards asked to see me in his office. He said that there was an oversight in planning certain budgets for the Restronguet Creek project. He wanted me to supply him with the running costs to pump 25 tonnes of slurry per hour the 5km from Restronguet to Wellington. This seemed an odd request as I thought that this would have been one of the first items to be costed. I said I would have it ready in a few days. Before I returned to my office, I went to see Terry Nicholls who had surprisingly received a similar request, but using trucks. We decided to meet and discuss the situation before submitting our findings to Conrad, and both came to similar conclusions. I needed to recheck the calculations and went to see Conrad to give him the bad news. The cost of pumping the slurry was more than the tin was worth. This reminded me of the time I was growing up in Tuckingmill when my mate's uncle would tell us mining tales. When he worked as a shaft sinker at Roskear Shaft New Dolcoath, his favourite saying was, "Not enough tin to make an earring for a mouse".

A management meeting was held at 10am on Tuesday the 12th of May. After a brief discussion it was decided to close Wellington and Hydraulic Tin by Friday the 15th of May and keep a small maintenance team. The Restronguet Creek project was to continue as a study until August.

Being part of the maintenance team would offer no challenge and there would be no future with Billiton so it was time for me to move on. Jack Symons and Nick Worrall offered me a job as Consultant Engineer at Wheal Concord which would have been interesting. However, I had set up Cornwall Mining Services on May 1st 1978 to provide a future income and to help create new opportunities that could be developed by the Company. I gave Billiton my notice to leave on Friday the 29th of May and started with Cornwall Mining Services on Monday 1st of June 1981. This marked the end of my involvement with Mount Wellington Mine.

Chapter 11

The Geology of Mount Wellington Mine

The mine is located within slates and siltstones of the Mylor Formation of the Late Devonian Epoch. These rocks have been thermally metamorphosed by the granite, which can be seen outcropping to the west and south-west. The rocks, known locally as "killas," were also cut by a number of elvan dykes. These sheets of intrusive igneous rocks are chemically similar to the granites but post-date them by up to 15 million years. An extensive diamond drilling programme in 1964 intersected the No. 1 Lode beneath an elvan sheet in 46 of the 69 holes drilled. The lode and elvan are south-westerly extensions of the B-lode and B-elvan at Wheal Jane. Five other lodes are in the mine: Nos. 2 and 3 (the main lodes), Wheal

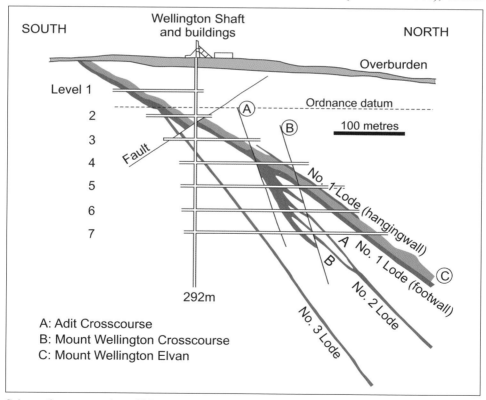

Schematic cross-section of Mount Wellington Mine showing the realtionships of the different geological structures to the shaft and levels.

Redrawn from Kettanaha, Y. A. and Badham, J. P. N., 1978. Mineralization and Paragenesis at the Mount Wellington Mine, Cornwall. *Economic Geology* Vol. 73, pp486-495.

Andrew Lode, Trenares Lode, and the Hot Lode. The Trenares Lode is within the Mount Wellington sett but not worked. The Hot Lode however was formerly worked to a depth of 230 fathoms at the United Mines; at Mount Wellington it was found in the adit but not worked. Where it was worked at depth in the United Mines the mining conditions were appalling, with air temperatures around 51°C and water temperatures up to 49°C. At the present time it is of interest for the lithium minerals in the hot waters.

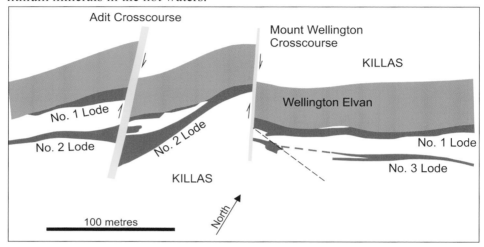

Geological plan of Mount Wellington Mine at the No. 4 Level showing the relationship between the No.1 and No.2 lodes.
Redrawn from Kettanaha and Badham 1978.

The No. 1 Lode lies in the footwall of the elvan which has sharp contacts and is in places sheared, mineralised, and brecciated. The resultant breccia of killas and bits of chilled elvan and vein quartz were replaced by the lode. There is a thin, intermittent development of a similar lode in the hanging wall of the elvan, but this was not economically recoverable. The lode has a strike length of over 1.5km in the Mount Wellington leases and a further 5km through the Wheal Jane property to the north-east. Its thickness varies between 1m and 19m, with an average of 3.6m. It has been recognized in drill core at 300m depth, but the full extent down dip is unknown.

The Nos. 2 and 3 Lodes are effectively identical to each other and similar to the No. 1 Lode. The No. 2 Lode was developed below the No. 1 Lode and is cut by two crosscourses (see below). To the east it is terminated at its intersection with No. 1 Lode; this may mean that it is a branch of No. 1. No. 2 Lode is developed over a strike length of 200 m, thickness of 2m and down dip extent of at least 450m. No. 3 Lode was only developed to the east of the Mount Wellington Crosscourse. It strikes parallel to the No. 1 Lode, but dips more steeply, at 50° to the north. These lodes are thinner than the number 1 lode, being on average 2.4m and 1.8m respectively. The lack of crosscutting relations between the numbers 1, 2, and 3 lodes, along with similarities in their mineralisation and paragenesis suggest that the lodes were formed at the same time.

Most production came from the No. 1 Lode east of the Mount Wellington Crosscourse and half from the No. 2 Lode west of this fault. These lodes contained iron, zinc, tin, arsenic, copper, titanium, and smaller amounts of lead, silver, gold, tungsten, bismuth and antimony. The lodes are similar to the lodes in Wheal Jane, and both mines produced tin, copper, and zinc concentrates. The Hot lode, rich in copper at the United Mines, was not economic at Mount Wellington. Similarly the Wheal Andrew lode was not economic where it was exposed in the workings. The caunter lodes and crosscourses were weakly mineralised, mostly with sulphides, and not of any economic significance.

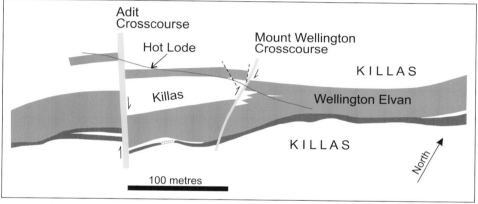

Geological plan of Mount Wellington Mine at the No. 1 Level in the Hot Lode area. Redrawn from Kettanaha and Badham 1978.

Crosscourses are a type of fault which trend northwest-southeast. They cross the trend of most Cornish lodes and elvans and offset them slightly vertically and a significant amount horizontally. There are two important crosscourses which fault the lodes and elvans; they are also weakly mineralised, but not in any significant amounts. The Adit Crosscourse is up to 4m thick and usually consists of banded quartz (chalcedony) veins. It is poorly mineralized, predominantly with marcasite, a variety of iron sulphide. It can be traced for over 800m, mostly to the north of the mine. In the upper levels the Adit Crosscourse is a single structure but splits into two at depth. The Wellington Crosscourse contains sulphides, chlorite, and quartz and varies between 15cm and 3m in thickness; it has a strike length in excess of 500m.

Mineralisation at Mount Wellington is described as 'complex' and in the past this type of mineralisation was difficult, often impossible, to process with the techniques available. Not only were the minerals often so intermixed as to be difficult to separate, but the suite included many minerals which, at the time were

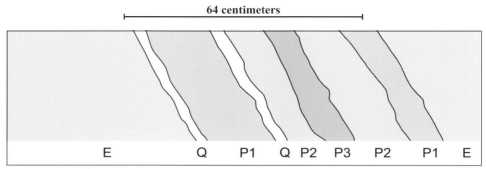

64 centimeters

E   Q   P1   Q P2   P3   P2   P1   E

E: grey elvan with specks and veinlets of pyrite; Q: white quartz veins; P1: hard grey compact veinstone with some pyrite; P2: soft greenish earthy peach; P3: soft blue earthy peach.

**Section through "The Wellington Lode", probably the No. 1 Lode, at adit level.
Redrawn from Dines, H. G., 1956. *The Metalliferous Mining Region of South West England*, Vol. 1 p427. HMSO, London.**

impossible to deal with because they were chemically complex. The mineralisation occurred in at least four different phases, the first being responsible for the presence of cassiterite and the second for the bulk of the sulphides, including pyrrhotite, arsenopyrite, and chalcopyrite. Small grains of gold, a little galena and large amounts of pyrite are associated with this phase.

Phases A and B constitute the bulk of the mineralisation in all three lodes. More sulphides are associated with phase C, predominantly arsenopyrite and pyrite, with lesser amounts of sphalerite, chalcopyrite, and pyrrhotite. Small amounts of cassiterite and wolframite were also formed. There are also tiny amounts of silver, gold, galena, bismuth and complex bismuth-lead, silver, iron, arsenic sulphosalts. Sulphosalts are minerals which contain a metal (*e.g.* copper, lead, silver), a semi-metal (*e.g.* arsenic, antimony, bismuth), and sulphur. Phase D was responsible for introducing more sulphides and minor amounts of cassiterite. Once again many of the sulphides were complex types, with a small amount of gold and silver.

Chapter 12

Mount Wellington: Early History

The early history of what is now known as Mount Wellington Mine is part of the great tale of copper mining in Gwennap. At various times it has featured as Wheal Friendship, Wheal Andrew, Nangiles and Wheal Magpie. It was part of the United Mines and then Clifford Amalgamated from 1865.

The mine's recent history begins in the 1920s when the three Wellington bothers began work there on tribute in the Wheal Andrew section of United Mines, previously known as Wheal Andrew.

1926

Captain Josiah Paull reported that the Wellingtons were working a lode 30′ wide and assaying 38 to 58 lbs of tin per ton, producing 6.75 tons of concentrate the previous year. He reckoned that a profitable mine could be worked if an adit were driven from the County Adit entrance 300′ into the hillside at a cost of £3-5,000. Prospecting continued in a small way over the next few years, mainly by Argus Concessions but only with a handful of men.

1935

Mount Wellington Mining, backed by the British Non-Ferrous Mining Corporation Ltd. Acquired the rights on United and Consolidated Mines, Wheal Clifford and Wheal Andrew.

2nd February: In an article on the new company Josiah Paull's report said: "This lode . . . is purely tin bearing and my attention was drawn to it some 12 years ago when 3 brothers named Wellington, from whom the lode evidently derives its name, were mining it in a small way and taking their ore to a little 5 head Cornish stamps down the valley and there treating it for its tin content. The adit at that time was choked and the brothers were using a small shaft up the hillside and stoping away the lode at a depth of perhaps 40 to 50 feet below surface, hoisting it with a horse and carting it away to their little stream works. I understood from the Wellingtons at the time of my visit that the ore they were breaking was yielding an average of 30 lb per ton and from smelters' statements of tin purchases from them, which they showed me, I have no reason to doubt their statement regarding the yield. The workings around the shaft they were working in crushed at a later date, Putting the shaft out of action, and, as the adit was choked, they had no means of access to their work, and being only ordinary Cornish miners had not the money

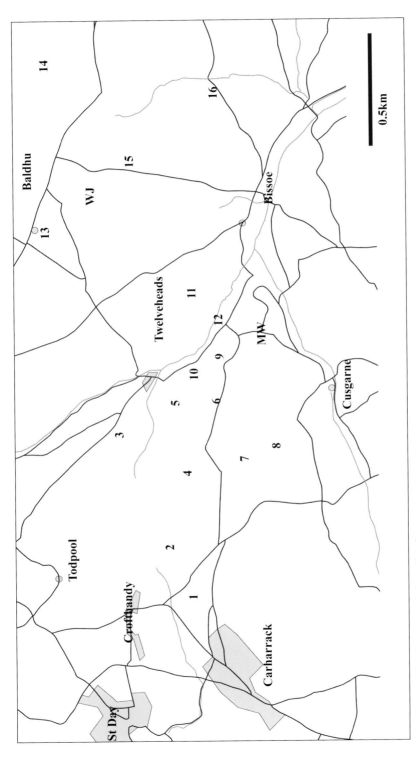

The Mount Wellington mining district.

MW: Mount Wellington Mine; WJ: Wheal Jane

1. Wheal Virgin; 2. Wheal Maid; 3. Wheal Henry; 4. Wheal Lovelace; 5. Wheal Fortune; 6. Wheal Union; 7. Wheal Girl; 8. East Ale & Cakes Mine; 9. Wheal Andrew; 10 Cusvey Mine; 11. Nangiles Mine; 12. County Adit portal; 13. Wheal Falmouth & Sperries; 14. (Old) Wheal Jane; 15. West Wheal Jane; 16. Wheal Le Despencer

to either open up the adit or put down another shaft".

Since acquiring the option on the sett they had cleared the adit for several hundred feet from its outlet and done some development work on the lode at adit level.

Mr Paull took samples of the ore and he reported that the samples taken from the drive gave ore assaying 30 lbs and from the rise 16 lb per ton. "When I again went underground on September 12th the rise had been extended through the lode and was holed into the crushed workings where the Wellington brothers originally worked. As the ore from the continuation of the rise was mixed up with the ore sampled on my earlier inspection, I supervised the breaking of two samples of ore from the sides of the rise itself, each representing approx. 5 ft. in width, and beyond the point where my samples of July 16th came from. These two samples, each of quite 30 lb, assayed by vanning 46 and 76 lb black tin to the ton over a total width of lode of at least 25 ft.. The contour of the country on strike admits of a very large tonnage of ore being quickly developed with no pumping and next to no pumping charges, and there is ample water available from the County adit for all crushing and concentrating processes, and there are excellent facilities on the slope of the hill for laying out a site for a mill and concentration plant, apportion at least of such a site could be on waste land of small value".

The Chairman is Mr Cyril F. Entwistle and in addition to Mr Paull there are two other directors – Mr Frederick E. de Paula, a director of Temoh Tin Dredging Ltd and Mr R. C. N. Robinson who is Chairman of Agnes [Angus?] Concessions Ltd. The directors estimate that, with tin at £200 the profit will be £41,300 . . . The purchase consideration has been fixed at £45,000 payable as £5,000 in cash and £40,000 by the allotment of 400,000 shares fully paid. The working capital will be £46,000.

5th February: Shares in Mount Wellington Mine Ltd advertised for sale

23rd March: Since start last February the power plant consisting of a 1,500 cubic feet per minute compressor has been delivered. Cornwall Electric Power Co. Ltd., is in the process of putting in a short power line from their adjacent grid system. The mine buildings are nearing completion; various working points are being prepared ready for intensive development when the power plant is completed.

May 4th: Two working shafts, Robinson's and Wellington have been completed to adit and driving is proceeding east and west. The 2 shafts are 400 ft apart; driving from the east (Robinson's) has advanced 20 ft. in values averaging 32 lb. over 6 ft. and driving west from Wellington Shaft 24 ft. in values averaging 40 lb also over 6 ft. When the 1,500 cubic feet per minute Bellis and Morcom air compressor is running progress will be more rapid.

May 11th: Follow up remarks from 4th May above. The erection of the necessary mine buildings have been completed, including a steel-framed corrugated-iron engine and general machinery house 100 ft. by 40 ft., assay office, mine office, carpenter's shop, transformer and switch house.

June 29th: Second progress report. Surface equipment complete including the compressor. This is driven by a 300hp motor controlled from a five-panel switchboard, capable of distributing power for all future mining and milling requirements up to 1,000hp. While this work was in progress, mine development proceeded under subsidiary power, and approx 1,000 ft of development work was done. A portion of this footage consisted of enlarging existing shafts, particularly one that for some years to come will serve as the main shaft. This has been equipped with suitable headframe and electric hoist. In addition, some 2,000 ft. of adit has been cleared and retimbered where necessary. The development so far as it has proceeded indicates that at least 150,000 tons of payable ore are now available for milling. The directors have decided to install a treatment plant and a mill capable of treating from 120 to 150 tons per day has been purchased and preparations are advanced for erecting it on a site now being laid out. It is expected that the installation will be complete in about 9 months and that during such time sufficient ore will be developed to justify working to a much larger milling capacity in the future.

October 26th: Ore has been found beyond the fault.

December 14th: Report from February 6th to 30th September. Total proceeds of shares was £63,787 after payment of preliminary expenses there remains about £20,000 for further expenditure. Almost all of the mill equipment has been delivered.

December 21st: First Ordinary General Meeting. Details of expenditure.

1936

March 21st: Progress report No. 4. Up to date the main lode has been driven on at adit level for a total distance of 1,300ft measured from the adit mouth to the extreme west end. Of this about 70% is payable. A crosscut has been put through from Friendship Shaft 70ft. below adit and the values on the short distance driven are slightly superior to those on the corresponding adit level. Under these circumstances the board has decided to complete the necessary arrangements for the erection of the first section of the 200 tons per day mill which will have a crushing capacity of 40-50 tons daily. The work of erecting the plant started on Mar 2nd and should be in operation on or before July next.

April: First section of the mill has been erected and expected to be in operation by July. A crosscut from the Friendship Shaft has, it is stated, opened up 80,000 tons of probable ore, in addition to the 100,000 tons available above adit.

May 9th: Good progress with mill. The bulk of the heavy concrete work was completed, and the steel framed building is well advanced. The board decided to extend the time for exercising the options to subscribe for 150,000 shares at 2s. 6d. each, which expired 30th June 1936 till 30th June 1937.

November 11th: 4 stamps running, 12 tables, pulveriser and 2 flotation cells. Workings about 200ft deep. Wide orebody 20-25lbs. Friendship Shaft very old with a ladder shaft alongside.

December 17th: November production - 968 tons 23.1lb/ton, 60% recovery.

1937

Mount Wellington Mine acquired the rights on Nangiles and West Wheal Jane. Their object was to work for tin, initially above adit, in the Consolidated and Wheal Jane lode system which extends some 3 miles.

January: For the year to September 30th the report stated that a further 100,000 tons of ore has been developed bringing the total up to 200,000t. The first section of the mill is in operation with a daily capacity of 40 to 50 tons per day. A large amount of work has been done towards the erection of the two further units, which will bring the capacity up to 150 tons per day.

March 20th: 120 employed

July: Robinson's Shaft has been enlarged to 3 compartments to the required depth and that production from three units of the mill will commence about the end of the month.

September: The new headframe and winding engine have been installed at Robinson's shaft.

December: In the report to September 30th it was stated that arrangements had been made with the British (Non Ferrous) Mining Corporation to furnish the capital necessary for future development, and to increase milling capacity to 1,000 to 2,000 tons per day should such a course be justified. The Corporation is to take up 250,000 2/- shares at par with the right to acquire a further 1,250,000 up to June 1940.

1938

January 15th: Production 20 tons, 4 days lost due to Christmas. Preparations for implementing the intensive development program well in hand. Arrangements being made to carry out various experiments in connection with endeavour to improve normal tin dressing. In future, usual milling programme will be subordinated to these experiments.

January: Report of third Ordinary General Meeting. In summary capital to be increased to £300,000 and rights as noted in Dec. Board are Sir Cyril Entwistle

(C), F. E. de Paula, Josiah Paull, R. C. N. Robinson and J. C. Allen

March 12th: Production January & February was 24.5 tons of black tin. Mill only ran part time owing to breakdown of the crusher station and experiments on milling improvements. New development programme proceeding normally both laterally at adit level and in connection with shaft sinking to next level.

June: Production since January 10th last was 40.5t of tin concentrate. Milling suspended due to low prices. Coactively clearing the Wheal Jane adit as it was part of the same area held by the Company.

June 28th: Report for period December 21st 1938-May 1939. During the period under review work has consisted almost solely in dealing with the metallurgical problems of the ore above adit, but owing to difficulties inherent in the ore it has not been found possible to increase the yield to a point that would show a satisfactory profit at conservative metal prices on the greater part of the ore available above adit. Diamond drilling to test the Wheal Sperries Wheal Jane lodes below the deepest workings is now proposed.

July 2nd: The board has decided to extend until 30th June 1939 the time for exercising options to subscribe 150,000 shares at 2/6.

October 8th: Report for 30th May to 31st August. Operations continued both with improvements in ore treatment and investigating ore reserves. Licence acquired over Nangiles-Wheal Jane extension of the lode east. Work started on July 4th. A total length of 5,140 ft. remaining available to be sampled gave 20.88 lb over 11 ft. – the total width not being accessible. Some 60% of the lode above adit has not been stoped.

November 5th: Clearing Wheal Jane adit - 30 employed.

November 26th: Mr A. T. C. Hawkins - manager. Mine has sold 182 tons of concentrate and in addition will be a big producer of pyrite. Aim to reach 1,000 to 2,000 tons per day.

December 10th: Consulting engineers are Messrs. R. C. N. Robinson & Co. A plan of the property with photos enriches the annual report. For the period 1st September 1937 to 3rd April 1938 milled 15,038 tons value 0.705% tin for 114.59 tons of 41.4% concentrate. The consulting engineers lament the closing of the mill. In Mount Wellington 15,000 tons at 26 lbs is blocked out for stoping. Large potential reserves in Wheal Jane.

1939

June 3rd: Report for period 21st December-19th May. During the period under review work has consisted almost solely in dealing with the metallurgical problems of the ore above adit. Much investigation has been done on the laboratory scale on the samples from the various setts. Owing to the difficulties inherent in the ore it has not been found possible, in the present state of metallurgical knowledge, to increase the yield to a point which would show a profit at conservative metal prices on the greater part of the ore above adit. Therefore the directors are compelled to utilise the remaining restricted resources now available to the company to obtain indications of ore below adit that may be of a grade that will be profitable under existing conditions. With this object in view they propose diamond drilling to test the Wheal Sperries-Wheal Jane lodes below the deepest workings.

August 26th: Major Raymond Claude Neale Robinson died Truro on 13th August. Was consulting engineer to Mount Wellington.

December 16th: Work stopped due to lack of finance. Mr. John C. Allen has written a report on the ores on behalf of the British (Non-Ferrous) Mining Corp. Ltd.

1940s
November 1940: Recommenced prospecting at Wheal Jane.

Chapter 13

Mount Wellington: Later History

The later history of Mount Wellington is complicated by numerous changes in ownership; this started in 1982 when Carnon Consolidated, a subsidiary of RTZ, purchased the freehold interest in Mount Wellington, Wheal Maid and Hydraulic Tin. In 1982 Crofty had been acquired by Charter Consolidated from St Piran Ltd, a subsidiary of the Siamese Tin Syndicate Ltd. RTZ then acquired 40% of Charter's holdings; in 1984 RTZ acquired the remaining 60% and South Crofty became part of Carnon Consolidated Ltd. Following this South Crofty, Mount Wellington and Wheal Jane operated as a single unit; Wheal Pendarves, to the southwest of Camborne, sent its ores to Crofty for processing. In 1984 operations produced an estimated 35,000 tons of ore, or 230 tons of tin metal.

Unfortunately, in 1985 the price of tin collapsed. Wheal Pendarves closed in 1988 and, with reduced ore going through the mill at Crofty, this was also closed and Crofty ore was trucked to Wheal Jane until the mine's closure later in the year. In this year RTZ sold Carnon Consolidated to a management consortium. In order to benefit the employees, who received twenty percent of the equity, a trust was established. Carnon Holdings Limited was incorporated at this time and remained owed by RTZ. The end for mining was in sight however and in 1990 Wheal Jane, along with Mount Wellington, the Wheal Maid decline and the Wheal Maid tailings lagoons, were closed.

Plans to develop, or redevelop, the Mount Wellington site commenced in 2003. Previous "un-neighbourly" schemes had been opposed but the idea to turn the site into a science and technology park were acceptable. This would have kept some of the buildings, most of which had already been vandalised, as a tribute to Cornish miners. A wildlife habitat was also to be included, though the priority was well-paid, permanent, jobs for locals. On 5th August 2003 planning permission was granted to Paul Isherwood, though existing buildings were to be retained, altered and refurbished. This did not go ahead; a review of the site took place in April 2004 with no result except the demolition of the top of the headframe in 2005.

On 15th January 2007 Mount Wellington was acquired by Richard Freeborn of Mount Wellington Mine Ltd (and owner of Kensa Engineering Ltd, manufacturer of heat pumps) and the mine was officially re-opened by Tim Smit from The Eden Project on 22 January. Since May that year a number of companies have moved to the site. In May the old engineering building was refurbished but, unfortunately the Wheal Jane mill was demolished in August. In 2010 redundant concrete structures at Mount Wellington were also demolished. The remains of the headframe were demolished in November and metalwork from the lime silo and conveyor belt was scrapped.

On Saturday 5th March 2016, St Piran's Day, the Cornish Radio Amateur Club made a special one-time-only broadcast at Mount Wellington Mine. The club obtained a Special Events Station Licence to activate the use of the Cornish mine as an amateur radio station and used the letter K as a locator in the station's call-sign.

Chapter 14

A Glossary of Terms Used in Mineral Dressing

ACIDS
Acids are very reactive chemical substances. They are highly corrosive, particularly in their concentrated forms. Every precaution must be taken not to allow skin contact with them. NEVER add one acid to another and never add water to sulphuric acid.

ACTIVATOR
A reagent added to a flotation process to increase the activity of a compound or to speed up chemical reaction, e.g. by accelerating the attraction to a specific mineral surface of desired collector, e.g. copper sulphate activates sphalerite for flotation with xanthates.

ALKALIS
Alkalis are also very corrosive reagents and are opposite in action to acids, *i.e.* an alkali will neutralise an acid. Common examples of alkalis are soda ash (sodium carbonate), lime and caustic soda (sodium hydroxide).

AERATION
This is the term applied to the dispersion of air into the pulp in a flotation cell.

AGITATION
Agitation is the stirring of the pulp in an agitator, conditioner or flotation cell to prevent settling out of the solids.

ARSENOPYRITE
Arsenopyrite is a sulphide mineral containing arsenic (46.0%), iron (34.4%) and sulphur (19.6%). This is floated off in the bulk sulphide flotation circuit.

ASSAYING
This is the "measuring" of the amount of certain specified elements contained in a mineral. The element mostly measured at Billiton Minerals is tin.

ATTRITION
Attrition is the process of wearing away of a surface by repeated hammerings. In grinding, this process helps to break up the ore particles by chipping tiny fragments of lumps off ore.

BALL MILL
This is a grinding machine on a large scale. It is a steel drum usually lined with rubber and a little over a third full of steel balls. The mill is rotated on its long

axis and the tumbling action of the steel balls achieves the required reduction of particle size.

BLOWER
A blower is a large fan used to distribute large volumes of low pressure air to the flotation cells.

BLENDING
Blending is a mixing process commonly used in milling operations where batches of ore have different characteristics. The various batches are mixed – or blended – so that the characteristics are evenly maintained.

CASSITERITE
The main tin bearing mineral containing 79% tin and 21% oxygen.

CHALCOPYRITE
Chalcopyrite is a copper bearing sulphide mineral containing iron (30.4%), copper (34.6%) and sulphur (35.0%).

CIRCULATING LOAD
Whenever material is returned from part of a circuit to the head of that circuit a circulating load is produced. In many operations this is done deliberately to improve performance. However, circulating loads must be carefully controlled so that the whole operation is kept in balance.

CLASSIFIER
A classifier is a device which separates fine particles from coarse, or light particles from heavy in the same operation. Examples of classifiers are the cyclone, the hydrosizer, the screen and the rake classifier.

CLEANING
In flotation a rougher concentrate is upgraded by cleaning. This involves the elimination of unwanted gangue mineral which has flotated in the rougher stage but is undesirable in the final concentrate.

COLLECTOR
This is an organic compound which attaches to a specific mineral to render it water repellent and thereby float it, *e.g.* xanthate collects sulphides, CA540 collects cassiterite, as does PH-PEP.

CONCENTRATE
Usually when ore is separated into its valuable and worthless constituents the valuable part is called the concentrate.

CONCENTRATION
Concentration is the process of upgrading an ore by removing large amounts of worthless materials.

CONDITIONING

The preparation of pulp for treatment (usually flotation). During conditioning, the various chemical reagents have time to react with the minerals.

DENSE MEDIA SEPARATION (DMS)

This is frequently referred to as Heavy Media Separation (HMS). It is the process by which two or more minerals of different specific gravities are separated in a fluid medium which has a specific gravity high enough to float one mineral and allow the other to sink.

DENSITY (PULP DENSITY – P.D.)

The pulp density is usually expressed as the weight, in grammes, of one litre of pulp. The measurement is normally made on a MARCY scale, when a container holding exactly one litre of pulp is suspended from the scale. The reading is directly in grammes per litre.

N.B. Sometimes metallurgists refer to the pulp density in percent solids, but care must be taken with this as the conversion of one form of expression to the other depends entirely on the specific gravity of the solids.

DEPRESSANT

A reagent used in flotation processes to render specific minerals non-floatable, usually by preventing collector action, *e.g.* DA811 depresses tourmaline.

DESLIMING

This is the classification process of separating very fine material from the coarser fraction.

DILUTION

This refers to the amount of water added to a pulp. Hence a dilute pulp is one which contains very little solid material.

DISPERSANT

A chemical used to promote the removal of slime from particle surfaces, e.g. sodium silicate disperses quartz slimes.

DISTRIBUTOR

A distributor is a device for dividing a stream into two or more fractions.

FEED

This is the untreated material entering a process.

FEEDERS

Machines or devices used to control the rate at which materials are delivered to a machine or process. They can be used to control feed rates in the process itself, or of reagents used in the process.

FILTRATION

The separation of a liquid (usually water) from a pulp containing solids and liquid. In a filter the liquid passes through the filter material and the solids are left behind. Filtering rates may be increased by the application of a vacuum or compressed air.

FLOATS

This is the term used to describe the material which floats in dense media separation.

FLOCCULANT

A flocculant is a chemical used to increase the settling rate of fine solids suspended in water. It acts by causing numbers of fine particles to join together to form a much larger particle, called a floc. The floc settles faster than the individual finer particles.

FLOTATION

This is a process of separating valuable minerals from the worthless constituents of the ore. The process depends on the ability of the desired mineral to attach itself to an air bubble and rise to the surface of the pulp in the flotation machine.

FLOW SHEET

A flow sheet is a descriptive diagram which traces the paths of the various products of the process.

FROTHER

Chemical agent added to pulp before or during flotation to promote transient froth in the cells, *e.g.* pine oil in sulphide flotation and M.I.B.C. in tin flotation.

FUEL OIL

This is a light fuel oil (say diesel) which is sometimes added to a flotation process in small quantities to modify the froth condition. Care must be taken with this as too much will kill the froth.

GALENA

This is a sulphide mineral of lead containing 86.6% lead and 13.4% sulphur. It is blue-grey in colour and metallic in appearance and is much heavier than most other minerals in the ore. It occurs only in small quantities in this area.

GANGUE

This is the term applied to the worthless material such as killas, quartz, tourmaline, fluorspar etcetera, from which the valuable material (in our case cassiterite) is to be separated.

GRADE

The grade of an ore, concentrate or tailing usually refers to the content of the valuable mineral it contains.

GRINDABILITY

This is a measure off the amount of work necessary to grind a material to a certain degree of fineness. Hard material requires more energy than softer material. Thus the grindability of hard rock is higher than that of soft rock.

GRINDING

The process of breaking down ore particles to very fine sizes. It is usually carried out in ball mills or rod mills, although there are other types of grinding machines in use.

IMPELLOR

This is the moving part inside a pump chamber, and its rotation causes the pumping action. The rotating part of a flotation machine is also frequently referred to as the impellor: in this instance it is actually acting as an air pump.

INTERLOCKS

These are electrical safety devices built into the circuits to prevent incorrect starting of machinery and to prevent damage.

LAUNDERS

Gutters which convey material from one place to another by gravity. The wide channels which collect the froth coming off flotation cells; also the channels which collect the various products round a shaking table.

LIBERATION

In ore dressing, liberation refers to the freeing of one type of mineral from another. This may be the freeing of a valuable mineral from the gangue or one valuable mineral from another. The object of grinding ore is to liberate valuable minerals from worthless ones. Once liberation has been achieved, a separation process such as tabling or flotation can be applied to recover the valuable mineral.

LIME

A reagent used to controlling pH, making the slurry more alkaline. It is possible to raise the pH of a slurry to about 12 by using this reagent.

LINERS

These are wearing plates, usually made of rubber or hard steel, introduced to cut down erosion of the main structure. Examples are Ball Mill Liners, Pump Liners and Chute Liners.

MAGNETIC SEPARATION

The process of separating magnetic minerals from non-magnetic materials. In simple terms, cassiterite is non-magnetic, tourmaline is weakly magnetic and iron is strongly magnetic.

Low density magnetic separation refers to the separation of strongly magnetic and non-magnetic materials. A machine of this type is the "Rapid" magnetic separator.

High density magnetic separation refers to the separation of weakly magnetic and non-magnetic materials. A machine of this type is the "Jones" magnetic separator.

MESH
The mesh number is the number of openings in a wire screen per linear inch. This system has now been replaced by describing the opening size in microns.

MICRON (abbreviation µm)
One millionth of a metre. Alternatively, one thousandth of a millimetre. This system is used to describe the size of fine particles, e.g. 10µm, 45µm etcetera. (One thousandth of an inch is 25.4 microns).

MIDDLINGS
A middling particle is usually a composite particle consisting of heavy valuable mineral closely and finely associated with much lighter gangue material. This association imparts a specific gravity to the particle between that of the heavy mineral and the gangue. On a shaking table, the middling's band appears between the concentrate and tailings and is recirculated for retreatment, usually after re-grinding.

MILLING
Milling is the process of separating valuable minerals from worthless ones. Grinding, classification, gravity and flotation are all parts of the overall milling process.

MINERAL
A mineral is a naturally occurring combination of elements. It usually has a definite composition, appearance and other particular properties. Metals occur, combined with other elements, in the form of minerals, for example cassiterite, the most common tin mineral, is tin combined with oxygen in the ratio 78.6% to 21.4%.

MODIFIER
A reagent occasionally added to a flotation circuit to modify the texture of a froth. For example fuel oil makes the froth less brittle.

NUCLEAR DENSITY GAUGE
A device built into a pulp stream on a section of the pipework. It has a radioactive source which emits gamma rays. These rays are passed through the pulp onto a detector which measures the intensity of the rays. The amount of radiation absorbed is proportional to the pulp density and the result is displayed on a meter.

ORE
Any rock which contains a valuable constituent which can be removed and sold at a profit is known as ore. If the mineral which is valuable cannot be economically extracted then the rock is not an ore.

OVERFLOW

This is the material discharging from the top of a device, *e.g.* cyclone overflow, thickener overflow, classifier overflow.

OVERSIZE

This is used in screening to indicate the material too large to pass through the screen.

OXIDE

A chemical compound in which ore or more metallic elements are combined with oxygen. It can usually be processed to remove the oxygen, thereby liberating the metal. An example of this is cassiterite, from which the oxygen is removed in the smelting process to liberate tin metal.

pH

This is a measure of the acidity of alkalinity of a solution. pH range is from 0 to 14. pH 7 is neutral, less than 7 is acid and more than 7 is alkaline. The further away from 7, the more acid or alkaline a solution becomes.

PANNING (VANNING)

This is the technique of separating heavy mineral grains from light ones, e.g. gold from gravel or cassiterite from quartz. It is used for a rapid check on table or flotation products and is carried out on a vanning plaque or specially shaped vanning shovel.

PARTICLE

A particle is a discrete, or separate, piece of material and can refer to a large lump of rock or a piece with a very small diameter (say 1- 2 microns).

PREFERENTIAL GRINDING

When an ore contains a number of minerals of varying hardness then the softer minerals are ground finer than the harder during the grinding process. Also, in a grinding circuit where classifiers (say cyclones) are used, although a heavy mineral may be ground sufficiently fine for subsequent treatment, its weight may cause it to discharge from the classifier underflow. This, of course, returns the particle to the grinding mill with the result that such particles are ground much finer than the rest of the ore.

PYRITE

This is a mineral composed of 46.5% iron and 53.5% sulphur. In the locality of Mount Wellington it is not regarded as a valuable mineral and is therefore discharged as a tailing.

PULP

A mixture of ground ore and water. Sometimes referred to as slurry.

PULP DENSITY (P.D.): See DENSITY.

REAGENT

This is a chemical used in the milling process (usually, though not exclusively flotation) to achieve separation of the valuable mineral from the gangue.

RECLEANING

This refers to stages of cleaning after the first stage, e.g. at Mount Wellington there is one stage of cleaning followed by four of recleaning.

RECOVERY

This is the amount of an element in the concentrate compared with the original amount in the feed. It is usually expressed as a percentage.

RETREATMENT

This is a section of a circuit, gravity, flotation or classification, where a part of the ore is given separate further treatment when it does not produce satisfactory results in the first treatment.

RIFFLE

This is a device for splitting a sample into halves. (Sometimes called a splitter).

ROTOR

The part of a machine which rotates or spins in fixed bearings, e.g. the impellor of a flotation machine, a pump impellor (particularly a MONO pump), the armature of an electric motor.

ROUGHING

The first stage of any separation process. In this stage as much as possible of the valuable mineral is recovered along with some gangue. The concentrate from this stage is sent to the cleaning process.

SAMPLING

The collection of a small part, or sample, or a large batch of material such as that the small part truly represents the overall composition of the material.

SAMPLE SPLITTER

A device or machine for splitting large samples into smaller samples which are representative of the original sample.

SAND RELIEF GATE

The is a small, variable gate or valve sometimes found at the tail end of flotation cells which allows coarse material, which has sunk to the bottom of the cell, to be exhausted from the system.

SCAVENGER

This is a stage in flotation, usually treating the rougher tail, where the slower float-ing valuable mineral is recovered. The scavenger concentrate is normally returned to the head of the roughing stage. There are occasions when a cleaner tail is also scavenged and the concentrate returned to an earlier stage of the process for re-treatment.

SCREENING

This is the process of separating fine particles from coarse by passing the material over a screen. A screen can be a woven wire mesh; a steel plate punched with circular, square or rectangular holes; a thick rubber sheet punched with holes; a sheet of polyurethane punched with holes or steel "wire" with a wedge-shaped cross section and the "holes" as elongated slots. The holes, or apertures, can vary from several inches down to about 40 microns (remember that 50 microns is about two thousandths of an inch).

SIEVES

These are small screens used in the laboratory for determining the particle sizes present in a sample.

SILICA

Silica is one of the main gangue minerals in more ores. It is the oxide of the element Silicon. Although it is regarded as valueless in the mill, it is useful in smelting operations as a flux for removing impurities in the form of a slag. Quartz is a form of silica.

SINKS

This is the heavy mineral which sinks in heavy media separation.

SIZING

This is usually used to describe the laboratory operation of sieving a sample into a number of particle size fractions. It is also used sometimes to refer to the proportion of material coarser or finer than a certain size, e.g. 89% - 300μm, 12% - 45μm.

SKIRTING BOARDS

These are guides, usually rubber trimmed steel or wood, used to direct feed onto a conveyor belt so that the belt is evenly loaded, or to stop spillage over the sides of the belt at the feed point.

SLIMES

These are the very fine particles, usually less than about 10 microns, present in a pulp. An exception to this is the material treated in the gravity circuit on the so-called "slimes tables". This material is often as coarse as 70 microns.

SMELTING

This is the process in which the valuable metal is extracted from the concentrates. It is carried out through chemical reactions which take place at very high temperatures and involves the melting of the products.

SODA ASH

This is the common name for Sodium Carbonate. Its solution (usually 10%) is added to a pulp to increase the pH.

SOLUBILITY

This is the ability of a solid to dissolve in a liquid.

SPECIFIC GRAVITY (S.G.)

This is the weight of an object compared with an equal volume of water (S.G. = 1). Some familiar Specific Gravities are: Water, 1; Quartz, 2.65; Tourmaline, 3.0 - 3.2; Cassiterite, 7.0.

The units used are usually grams per cubic centimetre (g/cc, or g/cm3) or kilograms per cubic metre (kg/m3).

For instance, if 1 cubic centimetre of water weighs 1 gram then 1 cubic centimetre of cassiterite weighs 7 grams. The density of pulp is often expressed in this way.

STAGE ADDITION

This refers to the addition of a reagent at several successive points in a circuit rather than all at once at the head of the circuit. It is done to achieve better control over the flotation of certain minerals.

STATOR

This is the opposite of a rotor. It has a fixed position in a machine relative to some associated rotating part. For example the stator of a flotation cell surrounds the spinning rotor; the stator of a MONO pump is the rubber surrounding the spinning rotor.

SULPHIDE

This is a chemical compound or mineral which contains sulphur combined with metals but not with oxygen. Examples are Pyrite, Chalcopyrite, Sphalerite and Galena.

SULPHURIC ACID

This is a very strong acid and is used in flotation to lower the pH of a pulp. Hand with great care at all times.

TABLING

The process of separating heavy minerals from light minerals by passing the pulp over a shaking table.

TAILINGS (TAILS)

The residue, or waste material left after the valuable mineral has been extracted from an ore.

THICKENING

The removal of some of the water from a pulp by allowing the solids to settle and the water to overflow from the top of the thickener. It enables a smaller volume of material to be handled at a higher pulp density.

TIN DRESSING
This usually refers to the removal of sulphides from table concentrates by flotation.

UNDERFLOW
This is the material leaving the underflow cone of a thickener or the apex (spigot) of a cyclone.

UNDERSIZE
Used in screening to indicate the material which has passed through a screen.

VISCOSITY
The viscosity of a solution or pulp is its resistance to flow. A substance with high viscosity will flow much more slowly than one with low viscosity. A flotation pulp with high density will have a higher viscosity than a dilute pulp.

XANTHATE
Xanthates are organic compounds, some of which are widely used as collectors in the flotation of sulphides.